THE JAM AND MARMALADE BIBLE

Jan Hedh

Photography by Klas Andersson

The Jam and Marmalade Bible

Translation by Stine Skarpnes Osttveit

SKYHORSE PUBLISHING

A large thank you to Magne Haugen for his eminent help with the photos.

Copyright © 2012 by Jan Hedh
Photographs copyright © 2012 by Klas Andersson
English translation copyright © 2012 by Skyhorse Publishing, Inc.
First published by Prisma, Sweden, in 2006, as *Sylt Och Marmelad* by Jan Hedh and Klas Andersson. Published by agreement with Norstedts Agency.

Skyhorse Publishing books may be purchased in bulk at special discounts for sales promotion, corporate gifts, fund-raising, or educational purposes. Special editions can also be created to specifications. For details, contact the Special Sales Department, Skyhorse Publishing, 307 West 36th Street, 11th Floor, New York, NY 10018 or info@skyhorsepublishing.com.

Skyhorse® and Skyhorse Publishing® are registered trademarks of Skyhorse Publishing, Inc.®, a Delaware corporation.

Visit our website at www.skyhorsepublishing.com.

10 9 8 7 6 5 4 3

Library of Congress Cataloging-in-Publication Data is available on file.

Cover design by Jane Sheppard
Cover photo credit: Klas Andersson

Print ISBN: 978-1-5107-1762-6
Ebook ISBN: 978-1-62087-494-3

Printed in China

Foreword

The basements at both my grandmother and mother's houses were always fully stocked with jars of jam, pickled beets, onions, and cucumbers of every kind—Asian cucumber, salt cucumber, and my mother's specialty, mustard cucumber with yellow mustard seeds that we preferably ate instantly. The jars were beautifully stacked on the shelves with handwritten labels and the date it was made. Their kitchens always had an aroma of juice and jam and they would make "left-over juice" with the berries that had been used for blackcurrant jelly—a ready-to-drink juice for everyday use—so that not a single raw material was wasted. In the kitchen, juice would be slowly draining and the strong scent of vinegar from the pickled green tomatoes and onions pinched the nose.

As a child during the '50s I would always accompany my mother and grandmother to the market in Tomelilla and the Möllevångsmarket in Malmö. They would inspect the raw materials and I would help carry them home to our kitchen. My mother would always make "drottningssylt," a jam made out of raspberries and blueberries, for the rice pudding on Christmas eve, and my father needed blueberry jam for his thin and crispy pancakes. My mother's blackcurrant jelly would be served with the Sunday roast and roasted chicken. My father would go buy the meat and would loudly and clearly request which exact piece of meat he wanted.

Green tomato marmalade with ginger and cinnamon was served with a fresh pot of tea and my mother's tasty graham crackers. My mother was

very talented in the kitchen and had been taught in a rectory as a young girl, which she often mentioned while she was baking or cooking in the kitchen. When we were really pulling out all the stops we would serve calf with a creamy sauce and marble potatoes and pickles with fresh parsley and jelly.

We would most often serve lingonberry jam with potato puffs, meatballs, and crispy spareribs. Small, beautiful beets would be served with the homemade Christmas pressed brawn and calf headcheese, that they would call "bigat." A bottle of vinegar would always be placed on the table with these kinds of foods. You rarely see the bottle of vinegar on any dinner table these days, but in my parent's home it would often be brought out, especially when we ate things like beans, eel, or catfish with horseradish sauce.

We would often eat lingonberry jam with cold milk as an everyday dessert, and on Saturdays and Sundays lingonberry pears and ginger pears would be served with whipped cream. Jam and whipped cream was a natural side to waffles and pancakes. French toast with applesauce, and pancakes with bacon with stirred cranberry jam made the mouth water. Lingonberry jam would also be served with stuffed cabbage rolls and cabbage pudding. When I think back on my childhood the scent of cooked foods in the kitchen is prevalent, and I also remember my parents discussing the quality of the ingredients available. They wanted the best-quality meats for the beef stew and good ground pork for meatballs and so on.

When I first began working at the Savoy in Malmö, they would serve small pickled beets with the stuffed cabbage rolls, instead of cranberry jam, which is a combination I also very much enjoy. The Hotel Savoy in Malmö had regulars such as Sten Broman, Fritiof Nilsson Piraten ("the Pirate") and Bank Director Lindskog. These men loved traditional home-cooked foods, which were prepared perfectly under the supervision of the main chef Einar Petterson. Now and then we would serve Småländsk cheesecake with redcurrant jam and lightly whipped cream, which tasted amazing. The cheesecake was delivered by train from a specialist in Småland to Malmö central station. After the split-pea soup on Thursdays, we would serve pancakes with raspberry, cloudberry, or strawberry jam and lightly whipped cream for dessert.

When I first started out as a pastry chef apprentice I was fortunate enough to work in multiple places where many of these traditions were still in place. We would pickle and preserve orange peels and green, yellow, and red pears for the decoration of tarts and as an ingredient in frozen pudding that would be served with cotton candy. Pineapple slices would be worked into pralines and apricots were soaked in water and then boiled into jam, marmalade, or jelly. Applesauce and apple jelly, raspberry jam, strawberry jam, gooseberry jam, prune jam, and banana jam were often prepared and made use of in bakeries back then. Generous amounts of jam would be used for roll tarts, puffed pastries, biscuits, and thumb print cookies. A variety of compotes, like apple compote, prune compote, apricot compote, and plum compote would be served with pastries.

However, it was not until I travelled outside of Sweden that I would learn how to properly boil jam and marmalade the traditional way. In Switzerland and France the traditions were strong and the fruit and berries of high quality.

When we first started boiling jam and marmalade the traditional way at Olof Viktors bakery in Glemminge, Sweden, we experienced an instant success. Today, we boil about 400 jars daily in our jam boilery. Plum tomato marmalade with Tahiti vanilla and macaroon almonds is the most popular jam variety to eat with cheese, which it seems is what jam is most used for these days. At Hedh & Escalante Chocolatier in Malmö they also boil many different kinds of chocolate marmalades and South American varieties.

Three years ago project manager Hans Naess and I met in Flen, where we decided to start an educational program for jam makers. We visited the queen of jam and marmalade, Cristine Ferber, in Alsace, France, to have a look at, as well as taste, her products. Our goal was to boil jams of similar superior quality without the help of processed pectin and other unnatural preservatives. We also visited Britain in order to study their preserve traditions as well. We have now founded Svenska Syltsällskapet (The Swedish Preserve Organization). In order to join the organization you have to pass an exam: you have to boil small batches of jam in copper kettles without processed pectin or preservatives.

I dedicated the summer and fall of 2005 to boiling preserves and writing texts on that exact subject. With me I had the pastry chef apprentice Jan-Erik Lilja, who also helped me with my previous book, *Chocolate*. He was a great help in the creation of this book. There have been early mornings at the market "Möllevångstorget" in Malmö where fresh fruit and berries were bought followed by long days in the kitchen with hot copper commodities and hundreds of sterilized jars. Jan-Erik once pleaded to not have us begin at 6 a.m. every single morning, to no avail. The hunt for certain fruits or berries could be quite enthralling, and we would not let anything get in the way of getting precisely the raw materials we wanted. Jan-Erik has, just like myself, a great passion for the art of sweets and I wish him the very best of luck with his future career as a pastry chef, a career which has given me so much.

Lastly, I would like to dedicate this book to my dear mother that we photographed at our cordial and cake party at my sister Gunilla's house. It was my mother's genuine interest in food, coupled with my years of study at the Savoy Hotel in Malmö, that formed the basis of my development as a pastry chef.

Malmö, March 2006
Jan Hedh

Jan Hedh's partner from Chocolatier AB, Maria Escalante, with his daughter, Cecilia.

Jan's mother, Kerstin Hedh, surrounded by young relatives and friends.

INTROD

UCTION

The History of Sugar and Preserves

Honey is the oldest sweetener in the world. Old cave paintings illustrate how they would gather honey from wild bees, at least ten thousand years ago. In Egypt there's been discoveries of five-thousand-year-old tomb paintings that show people producing honey by squeezing honeycombs.

Researchers have found that honey was used for baking and conservation. As time passed humans learned more about the bee and the combs, and many authors in antiquity describe the methods of beekeeping. During the Middle Ages honey had a very important function as a sweetener for food, pastries, and wine. The very first preserves were most likely based on honey.

Berry and fruit preserves from the bakery Henri Auer in Nice.

Honey is produced by bees that collect nectar from flowers, which is then converted into honey in the hive. The water-retaining nectar contains cane sugar, which breaks down into fructose and glucose with the help of bee enzymes. The nectar contains about 40 percent sugar, while the finished honey contains 75 to 80 percent sugar.

The first plant used for the production of sugar on a large scale was the sugarcane. In India, people learned to squeeze the juice from sugarcane as early as the year 300 BC. Eventually, people learned that it was possible to evaporate the water in the sugarcane juice through boiling and thereby obtain sugar in solid form. Sugarcane plantations spread eastward to China and west to Persia, and through the spread of Islam during the 600s the Arabs finally brought sugar to the Mediterranean region.

During the Middle Ages, Venice was Europe's main place of import for sugar. Refineries were also built there, and the sugar was then exported to the rest of Europe from Venice. However, it was still a luxury that few had access to. The first we know that sugar was mentioned in Sweden was in a document from 1327 in connection with the funeral of St. Bridget's father.

The Spanish and Portuguese colonizers brought the sugarcane with them to West India and Brazil, and before long the plant had spread throughout most of the New World, including the Philippines and Australia. Sugar was still considered a luxury at the beginning of the 1700s,

but with time the production increased and sugar was made available for most people. By the middle of the 1800s the yearly consumption of sugar in Sweden had reached around 9 lbs (4 kg) per person.

As time passed sugar rapidly became a necessity for the peoples of Europe. A new source of sugar was now grown, in the form of a sugar beet. This plant contained the same amount of sugar as sugarcane, about 17 percent. Nordic beet sugar production began in 1837, when the first sugar manufacturer was built in Malmö.

Preserving fruit and making jam became popular during the Middle Ages in the Near East, where they had access to sugarcane. It is said that it was the Knights Templar who brought the process of producing jam and marmalade with them when they returned to Europe.

The first book on the art of boiling jam and preserving fruits was published in 1541 in Venedig and Lyon in France with the title *Le Bastiment de recettes*. Multiple books explaining "the sweet art" soon followed. The French also perfected caramel production and no country compares to France when it comes to their selection of tasty and beautiful caramels. In 1801 a very important work was published in France: *L'art de confiseur* (*The Art of Confectionary*).

The confectionary Henri Auer, Patissier, Confiseur, 7 rue Saint-Francois-de-Paule in Nice, is the most established specialist of preserved and candied fruits in France. The amazing boutique has roots back to the 1820s.

In Sweden, Carl J. Grafström's book *Konditorn, handbok i konsten att tillverka sockerbageir- och konditorvaror* (*The Pastry Chef: A Guide to the Art of Creating Sweets and Pastries*) was published in 1892. In this book Grafström writes about the preservation of berries, pickled fruits, and syrups without preservatives.

The Swedish name for jam, "sylt," stems from the word "salt," as salt would be used in the process of preparing pickled fruits or vegetables. When sugar became more easily available and we started using sugar instead, the name carried over, even for "sugar preserving." The practice of making jams, marmalades, and jelly was far from common until the 1900s, when the price of sugar had decreased enough that it could be used for more general purposes.

The inside of the confectionary Henri Auer, with heritage from the 1820s.

Approximate sugar content in percentage of the edible portion of common fruits and berries			
Apples	7.9	Oranges	8.9
Apricots	8.3	Papayas	8
Bananas	13.5	Passion Fruit	8
Blackberries	5.7	Peaches	6.4
Blackcurrants	10.3	Pears	9.2
Blueberries	6.4	Persimmons	14
Cactus Pears	11	Pineapples	11.2
Cantaloupe	8	Plums	8.2
Cherimoya	14	Pomegranates	12
Cherries	11.3	Raisins	59.5
Clementines	8.2	Raspberries	4.1
Cranberries	4	Red Currants	7.5
Currants	15.1	Strawberries	7.4
Dates, Dried	69.3	Watermelon	9
Figs, Dried	59.9		
Figs, Fresh	12	*Vegetables*	
Gooseberries	5.4	Beet	6.8
Grapefruit	6.5	Cabbage	3.4
Guavas	7	Carrots	6.1
Honey Melon	10	Celeriac	4.4
Kiwi	5	Corn	3
Lemons	2	Onions	4.8
Limes	1	Parsnips	3.9
Lychee	17	Peppers, Red	4.5
Mangos	14	Red Cabbage	3.5
Musk-Melon	5	Squash	1.9
		Tomato	3.3
		Turnips	3.9

Fruits and Berries

Fruits and berries contain a high amount of water and delicate aromas and therefore need to be treated with care. The high percentage of water, among other things, means that the cell walls are filled with fluids. There you can find pectin, a group of carbohydrates that is important because of the ability of the cells to form jelly. When the fruit ripens, the cells and their pectin levels change. The cell system softens and the ripe fruit has a good balance of aroma, acids, and juiciness. Before the fruits ripen they contain solely tannic acid, also called tannin. This helps create a defense against bacteria and mold. In other words, a high tannin percentage will act as a preservative.

Today, fruits and berries are mostly stored frozen or as a preserve. You may freeze berries and fruits you intend to preserve or use for juice or cordial. Some of the pectin percentage will be damaged during freezing, but this will not have a large effect on your final result.

Sugar Content

In order to determine how much sugar you should add during the preparation of jam it is vital to have an idea of the sugar content of some berries, fruits, and vegetables. (Sugar content is always dependent on where the fruits or berries are grown—climate and quality of dirt—and may therefore vary, but not significantly.)

Sugar

It is common to use a larger amount of sugar for marmalade than for jam, as the sugar makes the marmalade firmer. In English, only marmalade made out of citrus fruits is called "marmalade." Everything else is called "jam," translated as "sylt" in Swedish. Today, with the rising popularity of using jam with cheese as opposed to the traditional use of marmalade, very few even know the difference between the two. In this book, however, I will not be limiting the term "marmalade" to only recipes made with citrus fruits.

It is most common to use granulated sugar for jam, marmalade, and jelly. Chemically speaking, whether sugar or sucrose comes from sugarcane or sugar beets, it is exactly the same. (The larger percentage of sugar production in the world comes from sugarcane.)

Different varieties ranging from unrefined to slightly refined raw sugars from sugarcane may create many interesting taste effects, just like coconut sugar and palm sugar. Brown sugar is created through mixing granulated sugar with dark syrup. There are also special jam sugars that contain pectin, which will help the solidifying of the jam.

Despite all this, granulated sugar is the most common variety used. It provides a clean flavor without any aftertaste; it gives volume, works as a flavor enhancer, and helps provide the right consistency. Sugar is also a preservative. If the sugar content surpasses 65° Brix (see beneath *refractometer* in the diagram "If you want to work like a pro," p. 29), no microorganisms will normally be able to grow in the cordial or preserve. When you boil with lower amounts of sugar, for instance, 1 lb (500 g) per 2 lbs (1 kg) of berries, the jam has to be stored in the fridge, or else it will grow mold. The professional will always use a refractometer in order to accurately measure this (see picture, p. 28).

If the amount of sugar is not sufficient, it will not be adequately implanted in the berries or fruit. The sugar content should be 67° Brix with a refractometer or 220°F (105°C) with a sugar thermometer. If the sugar content is too low, the jam, marmalade, or jelly will grow mold. If you use less sugar you will need to add preservatives or store the jam, marmalade, or jelly in the fridge.

Boiling Sugar

Supplies for Boiling Sugar

A copper pot without a tin coating is ideal for this purpose. It distributes heat well and prevents easy burning. But a regular stainless saucepan will also work just fine.

You need a brush to keep the walls of the pot clear of any sugar crystals while boiling. If you don't brush the sugar crystals down, the sugar can "die" and crystallize.

A sugar thermometer is needed in order to measure the temperature correctly. If not, you may use cold water and do a so-called hand-test (see below).

Important Temperatures

Use a sugar thermometer to measure temperatures or do a sugar test, also called a hand test.

Fine thread test at 220°F (105°C): Fill a bowl with cold water and dip your fingers in the water. Then quickly pinch a piece of jam between your thumb and index finger and then place your finger back in the water. Pull your thumb and index finger apart, about 2 cm/ 1 inch. The jam or jelly should then form a fine thread that quickly breaks and leaves a small pearl of sugar.

Strong thread test at 222–224°F (106–107°C): The same as above, but the thread should not break as easily.

When I first started out as a pastry chef we didn't use a thermometer when boiling jam; rather we used a jelly test combined with a thread test to determine when the jam was done. In Switzerland they used to say that a pastry chef had the thermometer in his fingers. However, it goes without saying that a thermometer is both easier and more precise, especially if you are not used to doing hand tests.

A very important temperature when preserving is 234–240°F (112–114°C); at this temperature the sugar test is called a "strong flight test" or "light marble test" with old pastry diction. The French call this test for the "grand soufflé" at the border of "petit boule." The test is performed in the following way: Dip a perforated skimmer with large holes in the pot, lift it up, and blow vigorously; the bubbles should then fly out in the air.

Use a thermometer and make sure the walls of the pot are clear of sugar crystals.

Strong flight test and light marble test at 234–240°F (112–114°C). You dip a perforated skimmer with large holes in the pot, lift it up, and blow hard. The bubbles should then fly in the air as pictured.

Boiling Caramel Out of Sugar

You boil sugar when you want to create a concentrated sugar mixture. When you boil caramel out of sugar, it is important to have a sufficient amount of water so that the sugar can dissolve. Assume 2 cups (500 g) water for 2 lbs (1,000 g) sugar at most. Most common is 1 ½–1 ¾ cups (350–400 g) of water per pound of sugar.

2 lbs (1,000 g) sugar
1 ²⁄₃ cups (400 g) water
1 cup (300 g) glucose

Glucose, starch syrup, is a clear and thick sugar mixture. It is made up of starch extracted from corn, wheat, and potatoes. Adding starch syrup will help prevent the crystallization of the sugar and increases the hygroscopicity, which is the ability to absorb moisture, and viscosity, which is an indication of how thick the syrup is. The glucose prevents the sugar from crystallizing both while boiling and stewing.

If you wish to make stewed caramel you should add ½ tsp (3 g) tartar to make the caramel extra smooth. When acid is added to sugar, the sugar is divided into two simple sugar varieties that are not as exposed to crystallizing, or "die," as a pastry chef would say.

Basic Sugar Syrup

For sorbet, ice cream, pastries, desserts, chocolate mousse, fruit salads, and more, the hydrometer should show 32° Baumé. See p. 29.

4 cups (1,000 g) water
3 lbs (1,350 g) sugar
1 ¼ cup (250 g) glucose or honey

1. Pour the water into a large saucepan and add the sugar. Mix well with a whisk.
2. Place the saucepan on the stove and let it come to a boil. Occasionally brush the inside of the saucepan with a brush that's dipped in water to avoid sugar crystals in the completed syrup.
3. Remove any foam.
4. Add the glucose or honey and bring to a boil once more. Clear any foam if necessary.
5. Boil to 220°F (105°C).
6. Pour through a strainer into a jar with a lid.
7. Cover with the lid immediately to avoid the formation of a sugar crust on the syrup.

Store in the fridge.

Tip!
For sorbet and fruit ice cream:
When I was young they would always mix 2 lbs (1,000 g) fruit purée or fruit juice and 4 ½ cups (1,000 g) basic sugar syrup with a whisk. Then, they would add 4 cups (1,000 g) water and measure it all with the sugar meter. Water would be added until the sugar meter showed 17–18° Baumé. At that degree the sorbet would have the right sugar content and was ready to be frozen.

The ice cream would contain the ideal 26 percent sugar and needed a fridge at 55°F (13°C). If the meter showed a low percentage, additional sugar syrup would be added. If the percentage was too high, they would add water till they reached the right sugar content and also some lemon if needed.

Pectin

A variety of types of pectin may be found in the cell walls of fruits and berries. When you boil jam you release the pectin and the acids. This results in a firm and gluey texture, and the jam will maintain its color as well as its vitamin C content. Both jam and marmalade are kinds of jelly, a gel, which is a result of the fruit's pectin, gel substance, plus sugar and water. In order for it all to work properly there has to be a sufficient amount of acid; in other words the pH levels should be low, preferably between 2.6 and 3.4.

The pectin in apples, quinces, currants, gooseberries, and citrus fruits will ultimately produce the best jelly. The results will also be better with unripe fruits, as opposed to overly ripened fruits. This is because the unripe fruits are more acidic and will have lower pH values.

The main purpose of the boiling is to loosen the pectin and the acids, as well as force release of air, so that the berries won't float to the top. In addition, the boiling process will dissolve the sugar and evaporate the water. The temperature of the finished jam should be between 217–230°F (103–110°C). Commonly, we never boil to a degree higher than 230°F (110°C), because the jam will then end up with a taste of caramel.

The pectin is released while boiling and it is therefore crucial that the boiling happens as quickly as possible. Accordingly, you shouldn't boil larger quantities than 3 ½ lbs (3 kg) fruits or berries to obtain a gel. If the quantities are too large and it is cooked for too long, you will often end up with gluey jam and marmalade, and sugar crystals may form after a while. Instead of turning into a jelly, it will become gluey as a result of slow boiling and the large quantity.

The Fruits Containing the Most Pectin
All citrus fruits, quinces, cranberries, all currants, gooseberries, and apples.

Fruits and Berries That Have Medium Pectin Content
Apricots, bananas, raspberries, plums, blackberries, blueberries, and green tomatoes.

Fruits and Berries with the Least Pectin Content
Pineapple, cherries, chestnuts, figs, strawberries, kiwis, passion fruit, lychees, mangos, papayas, melons, peaches, nectarines, pears, red tomatoes. You will sometimes need to add apple juice or apple jelly, gooseberries, or red currants in order to help these stiffen and develop into jelly.

Lemon and Lemon Juice
Lemon juice adds a fresh taste and helps the pectin in the fruit react and form gel. The fruit acid helps bind the water. Adding lemon in the marinade prevents the fruit from oxidizing and facilitates the mixture of fruit and sugar so that the sugar may more easily penetrate the berries. It also gives the jam a more appealing color and helps prevent bacteria and mold, which ultimately means that the jam is better preserved.

The lemon juice will also help prevent the jam from crystallizing, which may be a common problem if the jam does not contain enough acid or has cooked too slowly or too long. Lemon acid may also be used as a substitute, but it is not as natural as lemon, which gives a more rounded aroma.

Jam should have a pH level of about 3. You may control this with a special pH meter, which can be bought in drug stores.

The Pectin Test

If you work like a professional and have access to 96 percent liquor, you can do a pectin test in order to assess if unknown berries or fruits contain sufficient pectin percentages or if you may need to add apple juice or apple jelly. In that case, do the following:

Crush a tablespoon of fruit or berries with a fork so that the juice seeps out. Scoop one tablespoon of the juice and mix it with a tablespoon of 96 percent liquor. If a gel appears within one minute this proves that the fruit or berry contains enough pectin to form jelly.

Adding Supplementary Pectin or Additives

Industrially manufactured pectin is usually divided in two categories, citrus pectin and apple pectin.

Pectin that quickly stiffens is most often used for jam and jelly. Yellow pectin, with added sodium polyphosphates, is used for fruit paste. Pectin is typically added at the beginning of the boiling process or as the manufacturer otherwise instructs on the package. When the boiling is complete it is common to add some lemon acid to help the thickening process.

Other ways to obtain the ideal thickness are to add carrageenan, which is an extract from seaweed, or locust bean gum, which is extracted from locust beans.

Preservatives

Benzoic acid
Atamon, a mixture of benzoic acid and sodium benzoate
Sorbic acid
Potassium sorbate

Out of the preservatives listed above, the benzoic acid is the most common. If you wish to use any of these, make sure to read the package carefully. Since I personally do not enjoy adding industrially manufactured pectin, very few recipes in this book will include these preservatives.

Making Pectin

Pectin is the key to obtaining a jelly-like texture. By making your own pectin you achieve a much more concentrated taste and aroma in the jam, compared to the results when you use the industrially manufactured pectin that bind a lot more water and therefore create lighter and milder jams, marmalades, and jellies.

Apple jelly may be used as a base for jams and jellies with berries that have lower pectin content. This base jelly tastes wonderful and is great to keep in the fridge for when you boil jam with berries and fruits that do not contain enough pectin to obtain the right texture on their own. It helps the other berries and fruits form jelly. Apple juice may also be used. You should add about 8–12 oz (250–350 g) apple jelly or 1 ½–1 ²/₃ cups (350–400 g) apple juice per 2 lbs (1 kg) of fruit. You can use gooseberries or red currants for this purpose as well.

For red berries, such as cherries, strawberries, wild strawberries, and raspberries, you may use red currant jelly and red currant juice instead of apple jelly or apple juice. Generally this will taste better with red berries.

Use red currant juice and red currant jelly the same way as you would the apple jelly and juice. See recipe p. 79.

As exemplified in Carl J. Grafström's book *Konditorn* from 1892, pastry chefs used white currants for this purpose in the past as well. He describes how it is vital for any pastry chef to stock white currant jelly as pectin for preserving, which he had learned in France. Back then, they would always use apple jelly for renettes.

Apple Jelly as a Base Jelly

Add 9–12 oz (250–350 g) apple jelly per 2 lbs (1 kg) of fruits or berries that do not contain a sufficient amount of pectin. You may also replace the apples with white or red currants, or even gooseberries if available.

6 ½ lbs (3,000 g) green apples
9 cups (2,000 g) water
2 lemons, juice
4 ½ lbs (2,000 g) sugar

1. Rinse the apples and cut them in quarters. Bring the apples (with the cores), water, and lemon juice to a boil. Cover with a lid and then let simmer so that they soften and fall apart, about 30 minutes.
2. Drain in a strainer. Press all of the juice out with a large spoon.
3. Pour the juice and the fruit into a strainer lined with cheesecloth and let it drain on its own till the fruit mass feels dry. This usually takes about 60 minutes.
4. Add the sugar and empty it all into a pot. Bring it to a boil and remove foam now and then so that the jelly becomes clear and beautiful. Brush the inside of the pot with cold water so that the sugar does not crystallize.
5. Boil to 220°F (105°C) or 67° Brix. Test to make sure that the jelly has fully formed on a plate as well.
6. Pour the jelly into sterilized jars. Screw the lids on immediately. Preserve them in the oven at 175°F (80°C) in a water bath, for 20–30 minutes. Store the base jelly in the fridge.

Make sure to always use good-quality fruits and berries and to rinse them thoroughly. Remove all the foam that may contain yeast bacteria and carefully brush down the sugar crystals. This way the products will keep. Never consume jam, marmalade, or compote that's moldy. Even if it is only visible on the surface, the yeast and molding process will have spread throughout the entire jar. However, if you are meticulous and do everything as instructed the jam or marmalade will keep for at least a year.

There is usually no need to add additional water when you boil jam since the purpose is most often to boil the water away. However, there are certain exceptions, for instance, lingonberries or currants, which have tough skins and need to be softened before you add the sugar. Sometimes, syrup will be boiled to a certain sugar level in order to shorten the boiling time of the jam. Ideally, you should not boil quantities larger than 3 ½ lbs (3 kg) fruits or berries.

Boiling Jam in One Step

With this method you will obtain jam that is easier to spread since the berries are more crushed than they are using other methods.

1. Mix berries or fruit with lemon juice and sugar using a wooden spoon. Blend thoroughly, until the fruit or berries start to release juice.

2. Empty everything into a pot and let it come to a boil. Make sure to remove foam carefully. Occasionally dip a brush in cold water and brush away any sugar crystals, so that they do not end up in the finished jam.

Apple Juice

You may use this juice or cordial as pectin when you boil jam, marmalade, jelly, or fruit paste. It is common to add 1 ½–1 ⅔ cups (350–400 g) juice per 2 lbs (1 kg) of berries or fruit. You may replace the apples with red or white currants, or gooseberries.

6 ½ lbs (3,000 g) green apples
9 cups (2,000 g) water
2 lemons, juice
(det ger ca 2 000 g saft)

1. Bring the water, rinsed and chopped apples, and lemon juice to a boil. Let it simmer until the apples are soft and falling apart, about 30 minutes.
2. Empty into a strainer. With a large wooden spoon, work to squeeze out as much of the juice as possible.
3. Pour into a large strainer lined with cheesecloth and let it drain on its own till the fruit mass feels dry, about 60 minutes.
4. Measure the wanted quantity into small jars and freeze the clear apple jelly for future use.

Boiling Jam

Since I prefer not to use manufactured pectin in my products many recipes like this appear in my book. My old-fashioned methods give the finished product a more natural aroma and a different character.

3. Boil to about 220°F (105°C) or 67° Brix, depending on the kind of fruit or berries and how ripe they are. Make sure that the jelly has stiffened. There are a few indicating factors you could look for to make sure that the jam is finished. The berries or fruit will begin to turn transparent and the surface of the jam will look wrinkled when you lightly shake the pot. Small drops and a coat will form on the wooden spoon when the jam is completely done.

4. Make sure that it is finished by performing a jam test on a cold plate (see p. 20), which should confirm that the jam has formed jelly, which it usually does at 220°F (105°C) or 67° Brix.
5. Pour the jam into sterilized jars and immediately screw the lids on tight. Turn the jars upside down a couple of times (see pictures).

Boiling Jam in Two Steps with Marinating Overnight

This method is preferable when you want to make jam in which the berries or fruit maintain more of their shape. The fruit or berries absorb the sugar while it is marinating and the aroma turns out significantly stronger.

DAY 1

1. Blend berries or fruit, sugar, and lemon juice in a bowl. Mix well so that the blend starts to release juice.
2. Empty everything into a pot and let it come to a boil while stirring.
3. Pour into a bowl and let it cool. Place it in the fridge overnight.

DAY 2

1. Pour the entire mixture into a pot and let it come to a boil. Carefully remove the foam. Brush the inside of the pot with a brush dipped in cold water. Continue brushing during boiling to make sure that the sugar crystals don't end up in the finished jam or marmalade.

2. When the outside is free from foam, and the fruit and berries are turning transparent, the jam is close to ready. By then it should also be forming jelly and the surface will wrinkle. Make sure that you have the right temperature with a thermometer. Perform a jam test on a cold plate as well, to make sure that the preserve has formed jelly, which it usually does at 220°F (105°C) or 67° Brix.

3. Scoop the jam or marmalade into jars just as described on p.18 in Boiling Jam in One Step.

Boiling Jam in Two Steps with Marinating and Boiling of the Drained Syrup

This method is preferable for when you would like to shorten the boiling time, in order to preserve the aroma and color. The berries and fruit will also maintain their shape better.

DAY 1

Marinate the fruit or berries in sugar and lemon juice. Mix well with a spoon. Cover with plastic wrap and let the mixture sit overnight or for a couple of hours in order to enhance the natural fruit flavor.

DAY 1 OR 2, DEPENDING ON RECIPE

1. Pour the berry or fruit blend through a strainer so that the syrup can drain out.

2. Empty the syrup into a pot. Let it come to a boil and remove foam. Brush the inside of the pot with a brush dipped in cold water to make sure that the sugar crystals don't end up in the finished jam or marmalade.

3. Place a thermometer in the blend and let it boil till it shows 234–240°F (112–114°C), or you can do the "strong flight test." Dip a creamer with holes in the blend, remove it, and blow hard. When you see bubbles form, the temperature is at 234–240°F (112–114°C). See picture on p. 14.

4. Add the berry or fruit blend and boil while stirring. Remove the foam carefully. Brush the inside of the pot continuously so that the jam becomes beautifully clear.

5. When the fruit or berries turn transparent, the preserve is close to done. The mixture should then have formed jelly and its surface should turn wrinkly if you shake the pot. Control the temperature. It should be at 220°F (105°C) or 67° Brix, unless the specific recipe instructs otherwise. (In certain instances the boiling process may be different because of the kind of berry or fruit used, their ripeness, sugar content, and water content).

6. Always perform a jam test on a cold plate even if you have a thermometer, or only do the jam test.

It is most difficult to determine solidification with a thermometer when boiling citrus marmalades. They can form a beautiful jelly even though the mixture itself may not look finished.

The Method with Boiling Syrup

This method is mostly used in order to shorten the boiling time when preparing larger batches.

1. Boil syrup out of sugar and water depending on the recipe, to about 234–240°F (112–114°C). Make sure that the texture is right by doing a strong flight test, see p. 14.

2. During boiling, occasionally brush the inside of the pot with a brush dipped in cold water to keep sugar crystals from ending up in the finished jam or marmalade. (This is a general rule for every time you boil preserves.)

3. Add the fruit or berries and boil to about 220°F (105°C) or 67° Brix, depending on what kind of fruit or recipe you are following. Perform a jam test on a cold plate as well, or, if you do not have a thermometer, do only the jam test. Do the test when the fruit is turning transparent and the jam or marmalade is starting to combine and form jelly.

How to Boil Jelly

Use fruits or berries that have high pectin content. They should not be too ripe, as the pectin levels decrease as the fruits or berries ripen. You don't need to add lemon when you intend to make jelly from berries with a black color, which most every other jelly will need. If you, for instance, intend to make jelly with strawberries, raspberries, cherries, or blueberries, you will have to add about 25 percent of another fruit that has high pectin content, like red currants or gooseberries, to make sure that jelly forms.

Another option is to add apple jelly or apple juice to help fruit and berries with lower pectin content to form jelly.

If you wish to flavor the jelly with herbs, spices, liquor, or wine, this should be added during boiling.

Two Classic Methods

The most common of the two is method 1. Both of the methods give the same results, but method 2 tastes a little fresher and is especially suitable for black currants or blackberries. My mother would always use method 2 when she made black currant jelly. Her jelly would sometime keep for years.

Gooseberry Jelly with Method 1
2 ½ lbs (1,100 g) gooseberries, green and unripe
(2 lbs [1,000 g] net weight)
1 cup (250 g) water
Juice of 1 lemon
Quantity of sugar equal to the weight of the drained juice

1. Rinse the berries and place them in a pot with water and lemon juice. Bring it to a boil and cover with a lid. Let it simmer for about 15 minutes.
2. Pour into a strainer and carefully squeeze out all of the juice with the help of a spoon.
3. Empty the mass into a strainer lined with cheesecloth.
4. Let it drain till the fruit mass is completely dry and all the juice is drained. It takes about an hour.
5. Weigh the drained juice and add the equal weight of sugar.
6. Empty into a pot and boil while foaming so that the jelly becomes beautifully clear.
7. Brush the inside of the pot with a brush dipped in cold water as soon as you detect deposits on the inside—this is to prevent sugar crystals from forming in the completed jelly.
8. Boil to 220°F (105°C), or 67° Brix. At this temperature most jellies will be ready.
9. *Make sure that the jelly is done by scooping a little onto a cold plate and seeing if it stiffens. Drag your finger through the jelly—it should not merge back together (see photo on p. 21). You will often be able to tell whether the jelly is done or not by observing the spoon. When drops and a coat form on the spoon, you should measure the temperature of the jelly.
10. Scoop into sterilized jelly jars. Screw the lids on immediately and turn the jars upside down a couple of times. If you prefer you may place the jars in a water bath in a 175°F (80°C) oven for about 20 minutes. This way the jelly will keep better.

Previously, people would pour melted paraffin on top of the solidified jelly to make sure that no air could enter. Afterwards they would screw the lids on tight. This method also works perfectly.

Jam/jelly test

Black Currant Jelly with Method 2
2 lbs (1,000 g) black currants
1 cup (250 g) water
Quantity of sugar equal to the weight of the drained juice

1. Rinse the berries and drain.
2. Boil the berries and water for 15 minutes. Pour the mixture into a strainer and squeeze all of the juice out with the help of a spoon.
3. Empty the mass into a strainer lined with cheesecloth. Let it drain for about 1 hour or until the drained fruit mass is completely dry.
4. Set the oven to 210°F (100°C).
5. Measure and weigh the drained juice. Measure an equal amount of sugar.
6. Warm the sugar on a baking sheet with elevated edges or in a baking pan in the oven for about 10 minutes.
7. Bring the drained juice to a boil. Make sure to remove all the foam and other impurities.
8. Remove the pot from the heat. Add the sugar and stir vigorously till it is completely dissolved and the surface starts to wrinkle.
9. Scoop into sterilized jars. Screw the lids on and turn upside down a couple of times. (You need to do this quickly because the jelly stiffens rapidly)

NOTE! If the jelly boils for too long it becomes rubbery. If the jelly ends up rubbery and doesn't set properly, the berries do not contain enough pectin, or they are too ripe. This kind of jelly will also be filled with sugar crystals after a while.

If the jelly doesn't boil for long enough it won't stiffen, but rather turn out watery. Sometimes it may take a couple of days until the jelly stiffens completely in the jars, depending on the kind of berries or fruit used.

Cold-Pressed, Cold-Stirred Jelly

This jelly is especially good and luxurious if you make it with sea buckthorn—but you can use any high-pectin berry or fruit you wish.

2 lbs (1,000 g) fruit or berries rich in pectin
Juice of 1 lemon
Quantity of sugar equal to the weight of the drained juice

1. Squeeze the juice from the fruit or berries in a juicer. Add the lemon juice.
2. Set the oven to 210°F (100°C).

3. Warm the sugar in a baking pan with edges for about 10 minutes.
4. Measure and weigh the juice. Add an amount of sugar equal to the weight of the juice.
5. Mix with an electric whisk for about 30 minutes. Remove foam carefully.
6. Pour directly into sterilized jars. Screw on the lids.

Store in the refrigerator.

Preserving Fruits and Berries

The practice of preserving fruits or making candied fruits, *fruit confits*, is based on a technique that the French learned from the Italians, who in turn had been taught by the Arabs. However, it was the French who developed the practice into an art form, and you will find the highest number of practitioners in Provence in France. Preserved fruits are often glazed so that they will keep for years, or candied to stop them from drying up. Today, many French cooks pickle greens and vegetables the way they would preserve fruits. Green, fresh almonds and walnuts are preserved as well, just like the famous chestnuts, *marrons glaces*.

The most important element of making preserved fruits and berries is the art of preserving the color, aroma, and shape. The fruits have to be blanched in lightly simmering water so that they soften completely and easily absorb the syrup. Cool the fruit quickly in cold running water so that the boiling process halts. Place the fruit in jars and pour the syrup on top so that the fruit doesn't shrink. Repeat this process for 5 days, till the fruit

is completely preserved, see Preserved Citrus Peels on p. 107. Sometimes it may take up to 6 days (to 36° Baumé).

The preserved fruit will keep for at least a year after finishing this process; this is because the water in the fruit is now replaced with sugar. It is important to begin with a light syrup and then slowly add more sugar each day until the fruit is transparent and completely preserved, which is when the last layer of syrup shows 36° Baumé on the aerometer.

In certain instances alum may be added with salt in order to open the fruit during the blanching. This way it is easier for the fruit to absorb the syrup. Between 1–2 tsp (5–10 g) salt is usually added to a batch. In France, they will sometimes soak fruits with high water content, like melons, in saltwater for three days before they are boiled so that the amount of water decreases. This way the shape of the fruit is more likely to keep during the blanching.

Every fruit that has been preserved may easily be candied. Let the fruit dry on a rack for two days. Candy it the exact same way that you would candy flowers (see p. 208). It will keep at room temperature for several years. An alternative is to glaze them, see below.

Glazing Fruit

You may glaze every kind of preserved fruit. Dry the preserved fruit on a rack for 24 hours.

2 lbs (1,000 g) sugar
1 2/3 cups (400 g) water
1/3 tsp white wine vinegar

1. Boil sugar, water, and vinegar in a saucepan. Brush the inside of the saucepan with a brush dipped in cold water in order to prevent sugar crystals from forming. Boil till a thermometer shows 234–240°F (112–114°C), or do a strong flight test with a creamer, see p.14.
2. Set the oven to 210°F (100°C).
3. Pour a third of the sugar mixture out on the table and work it with a spatula back and forth, just like a fondant, till the sugar mixture starts to whiten.
4. Place it back in the saucepan with the rest of the sugar mixture. Stir attentively so that the glaze achieves a milk-like texture and starts to stiffen along the edges.
5. Dip the fruit in the glaze with the help of a fork, and let the surplus run off on a rack. Place the rack with the fruit in the oven for about 5 minutes. Keep the oven door open, and keep the fruit in the oven till the glaze feels hard. Let the fruit cool and store at room temperature.

Caramelized Fruit

Fruits with a dry surface, for instance the cherries in the photo below, may be dipped in the cooled caramel till a thread is formed. The thread should be cut off and the berry is served as a petit four or as a garnish for a dessert or tart. You may also dip physalis the same way, or you can dip dates filled with marzipan in the caramel. (Boiling Caramel Out of Sugar, p. 15)

Boiling Fruit Paste

Today, pectin named Ruban Vert is most commonly used in making fruit paste. But the traditional method without pectin is still the best and most labor-intensive.

Old-Fashioned Fruit Paste

Making fruit paste involves concentrating fruit flesh and sugar through boiling. It needs to be boiled for a lengthy period of time, with constant stirring with a large ladle. When the mass becomes really concentrated, it will splash easily.

For fruits and berries with low pectin content, which is most, you need to add apple juice for it to stiffen properly. The apple juice helps the fruit form jelly. It binds the fruit mass and provides the right structure. Here you may alternate between a multitude of fruits and berries. Never add glucose to this fruit paste, as glucose will make it gluey and it will never fully stiffen.

Basic Recipe
Fruit purée and apple juice
Quantity of sugar equal to the weight of the purée and apple juice combined

1. Pass the boiled fruit through a food mill.

2. Add the apple juice, which will shorten the boiling time. Weigh the mixture, and add as much sugar as the fruit paste and juice weighs.
3. Empty the mixture into a pot.
4. Boil while stirring. When the mass is beginning to pull away from the sides of the pot along the edges, it is close to ready. Now and then brush the inside of the pot with a brush dipped in cold water to prevent sugar crystallization.
5. Line a baking pan with parchment paper and add the fruit mass. (If you're really professional, pour the fruit mass into a frame made out of metal rods that are about ½ inch [10 mm] thick, which lies on cheesecloth.)
6. Let it stiffen for 24 hours. Turn the mass over and let it rest for an additional 24 hours. Cut into small squares and roll them in sugar.

This old method gives a more concentrated fruit paste than you will get if you add pectin. It is difficult to use a thermometer here since the mass is so thick. Still, the temperature should be at about 224°F (107°C) or 75° Brix (see p. 28) when the paste is ready.

Fruit Paste with Pectin

This method is not as time-consuming and the fruit paste is not as concentrated as the previous. It is very important to use the right kind of pectin, otherwise it won't work correctly.

The lemon acid activates the pectin and makes the paste stiffen. Make sure that you are ready before you add the acid; you will need to pour the paste out immediately, or else it will harden in the pot.

Boiling Chutney

My first meeting with this kind of preserve was, as it is for most, through mango chutney. You can prepare chutney based on any berry, fruit, or vegetable imaginable. Chutney should be sweet and sour, while also spicy. The balance between sweet and sour is very important. Make

sure that you use good-quality vinegar. Ginger is a great ingredient in most recipes. Chilies are best suited when you want the outcome to be hot.

Chutney needs to be boiled for a significant amount of time in order to obtain the right texture, between 30 and 60 minutes. Store chutney in the refrigerator; it will keep for a very long time.

The leftover berry mixture from drained jelly and juice is great for boiling chutney (you may also bake bread with this mixture).

Classic Spices and Added Flavors for Jam and Marmalade

Dried Spices

Vanilla: Both Bourbon vanilla, which is produced in Madagascar, the Comoros, and Réunion, and Tahiti vanilla from Tahiti are great to add for flavor when you are boiling jam or jelly. Bourbon vanilla has the most classic vanilla taste. Tahiti vanilla is larger, fruitier, and sweeter—perhaps the finest of the vanilla beans. You can also find Mexican vanilla in certain stores. Mexican vanilla is thinner with a hint of pepper in its taste.

Cinnamon: Real cinnamon, which stems from Ceylon and India, is grown, among other places, in Kenya, Tanzania, and Sri Lanka. It is significantly lighter than other kinds of cinnamon and has a round and refined aroma. You can buy real cinnamon in spice specialty shops. Regular household cinnamon is multiple shades darker and much thicker. Its taste is also notably stronger.

Tonka Bean: Sometimes referred to as fake vanilla, it creates a good taste and round tone.

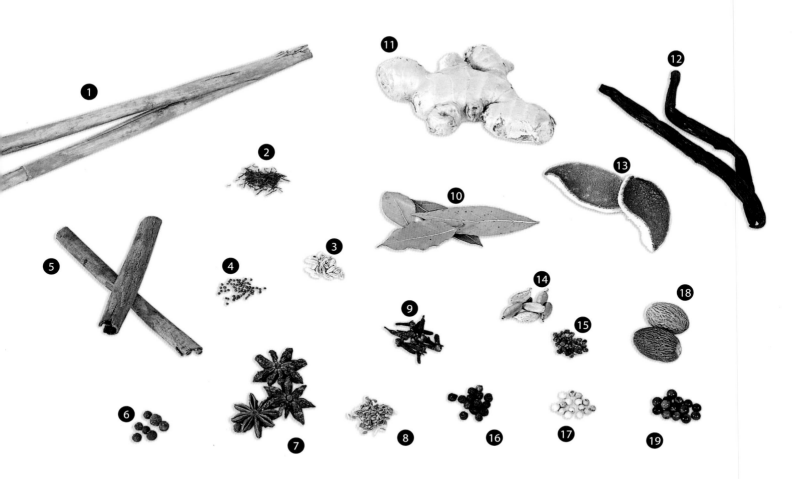

1 Cinnamon 2 Saffron 3 Fennel 4 Mustard seed 5 Kassia 6 Pepper 7 Star anise 8 Aniseed 9 Cloves 10 Bay leaves 11 Ginger
12 Vanilla 13 Seville orange peels 14 Cardamom pods 15 Cardamom 16 Black pepper 17 White pepper 18 Nutmeg 19 Green pepper

Other Suitable Spices: Star anise, coriander, aniseed, fennel seeds, licorice, cardamom, cloves, whole or ground coriander seeds, dried and ground ginger, saffron, mustard seeds (for chutney), nutmeg, and various kinds of pepper (white, black, and green pepper, mixed pepper, Sichuan pepper, different kinds of dried and smoked chilies, long pepper, Korean red pepper), sea salt, bay leaves, and dried orange peels (to add a taste of bitterness for marmalades).

Fresh Spices
For instance, fresh grated ginger, galangal, gari, lemongrass, lime leaves, and grated lemon zest.

Fresh Herbs
Basil, various kinds: for raspberry or peach, and more
Fresh coriander: for tropical fruits
Lemon balm: for citrus fruits
Mint, various kinds: good for jelly, jam, and pickled preserved fruit
Rosemary: for citrus fruits, plums, blackberries, raspberries, and more

Various chilies.

Many herbs taste great with almost everything, including: lemongrass, fruit sage and pineapple sage, thyme, lemon, oregano, and others.

1 Basil mint
2 Chocolate mint
3 Moroccan mint
4 Orange-mint
5 Raripila-mint
6 Ginger mint
7 Gussum mint
8 Green (sweet) mint
9 Apple mint

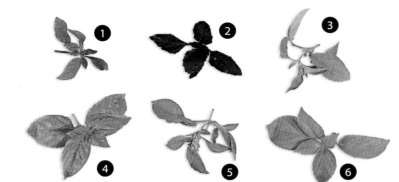

1 Thai basil
2 Red rubin basil
3 Lime basil
4 Cinnamon basil
5 Lemon basil
6 Mrs. Burns lemon basil

1 Small sorrel
2 Chicory
3 Large bistort
4 Mustard greens
5 Leaf mustard
6 Angelica
7 Pine shoots
8 Pepperweed
9 Masterwort
10 Violet
11 Spignel

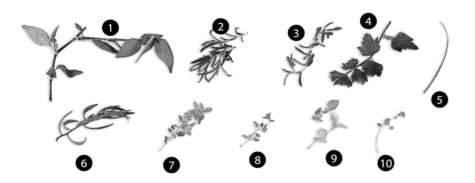
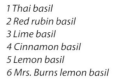

1 Vietnamese coriander
2 Rosemary
3 Winter savory
4 Celery
5 Chinese chives
6 French tarragon
7 Lemon thyme
8 Thyme
9 Vanilla oregano
10 Marjoram

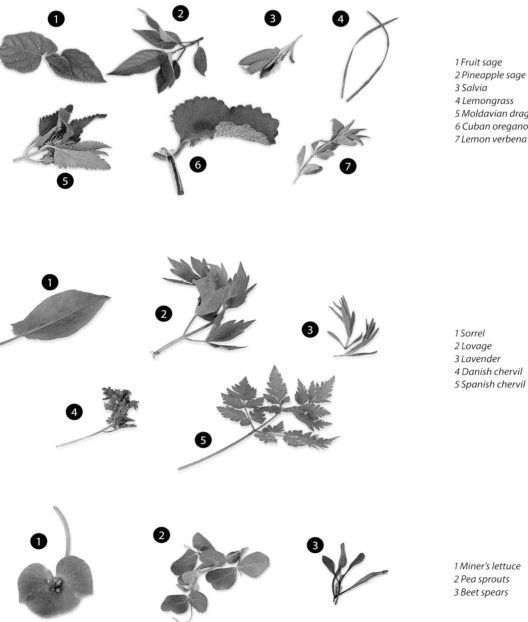

1 Fruit sage
2 Pineapple sage
3 Salvia
4 Lemongrass
5 Moldavian dragonhead
6 Cuban oregano
7 Lemon verbena

1 Sorrel
2 Lovage
3 Lavender
4 Danish chervil
5 Spanish chervil

1 Miner's lettuce
2 Pea sprouts
3 Beet spears

First and foremost, all kinds of herbs need to be blanched so that the chlorophyll, which you find in every green leaf, maintains its color. Dip the herbs in boiling water, and then quickly rinse them in cold water. Finely chop them and add them at the end of the boiling time.

Flowers

Dried lavender flowers, violets, orange flowers, elder flowers, acacia—but use this seasoning carefully. Apricot jam or plum jam with lavender is a classic. Flower marmalades are often based on a fruit jelly, to which fresh or dried flowers are added. But use caution when you add the flowers so that the marmalade doesn't end up with a perfume taste.

Honey

Honey is produced from the nectar of blossoms by honeybees. The plant affects the flavor. One may also caramelize honey, which gives it a milder taste: 5 tbsp (100 g) of honey equals 7 tbsp (100 g) of sugar. Never use more than 1 ¼ cups (500 g) of honey per 2 lbs (1 kg) fruit, because the preserve may become chewy during boiling if there is too much sugar.

1 Walnuts
2 Macadamia nuts
3 Pecans
4 Hazelnuts
5 Marcona almonds

Vinegar, Spirits and Wine

You may use a variety of vinegars for chutney or even jam. Traditional balsamic vinegar in a raspberry jam, for instance, is very tasty.
Spirits: Whiskey, Calvados, Cognac, Armanac, Kirschwasser, Tequila, Pernod, and more.
Wine: Different kinds of wine can be great for added flavor.

Chocolate

Multiple kinds of dark chocolate with a high percentage of cocoa: Valrhona Grand Cru Guanaja, Valrhona Grand Cru Manjari, Valrhona Grand Cru pur Caraïbe or a high-quality cocoa like Valrhona's (22–24% cocoa butter).
White chocolate: For a lemon curd
Milk chocolate: For instance, for milk marmalade

Almonds

You may use almonds just as they are, as long as they're shelled, or you may lightly roast them. Preferably, you should choose Spanish "Marcona" almonds or Italian almonds from Bari.

Nuts

Hazelnuts: preferably from Piedmont in Italy or from Spain. First, roast them and then shell them by rubbing them against each other in a kitchen towel.
Walnuts: preferably French from Grenoble
Pecans: Spanish, if possible
Macadamia nuts
Pine nuts

Other Flavors

Dried fruit: You may soak or boil apricots, date, figs, and plums, and add them to jam in tasty bites.
Coffee: Preferably Arabica, whole roasted beans
Tea: A variety of brewed quality teas
Coconut: Preferably from the Philippines
Raisins
Pickled fruit
Pickled orange or lemon zest

Equipment for Preserving

Copper Pot. When you are boiling jam it is a great advantage to have a copper pot. Since the copper conducts heat perfectly, the jam boils more quickly and forms jelly. Always clean the pot with salt and vinegar to remove the coating from the preserve. Rinse with cold water before you use it. If you use a copper pot with bent edges, as pictured on p. 28, the boiling will take less time and the fruit and berries will better maintain their color because they do not boil as long. If you do not wish to invest in a copper pot you should use a stainless-steel pot with a thick bottom instead.

Remember to never keep something in a copper pot for long periods of time, because the copper taste may transfer. For instance, you should never marinate fruit in a copper pot.

Spoons
  Make sure that you have a couple of long spoons made out of wood.
Digital scale
  Get a reliable digital scale for weighing the ingredients.
Citrus press
Cherry/olive pitter
Citrus zest grater
Grater
Sieves
Cheesecloth
Jam fillers
Measuring cup
Scissors and knives
Creamer
Skimmer

Juicer
Mixer/food processor
Food mill
  (for fruit purée)
Ladle for scooping

Jars
  Buy them quite small, about ½–1 lb (250–375 g), so that the jam won't go bad quickly after the jar has been opened.
Labels for pasting on the jars.
Sugar thermometer
  A sugar thermometer that measures up to 390°F (200°C). Always store it hanging, and not laying in a box, so that it will last longer.

A hydrometer (sugar thermometer): You should always take measurements with the hydrometer at eye level, to ensure accuracy. The syrup should be kept at room temperature. The exception is when you measure syrup for liqueur pralines and syrup for candying.

The hydrometer is especially important when you need to measure with great precision. Stick it in the syrup and let it sink down. If the measured sugar content is too low then you need to boil the syrup to evaporate more water. If it is too high, add water until the right level is met.

The refractometer is a meter that provides fast and accurate information. It is used to measure the amount of sugar or glucose in a liquid. Clean water will show 0° Brix, while 10 percent sugar solution will show 10° Brix.

When you measure the sugar content, remember that the jam or syrup should be at room temperature, about 68°F (20°C), if the refractometer is to measure correctly. First, place a jam sample on a plate and let it cool for 1 minute. Raise the cover of the refractometer and place a drop of jam or syrup on top. Cover with the cap. Raise it up to your eyes to read the values..

If You Want to Work Like a Professional

Hydrometer, sugar thermometer: If you want to candy or preserve fruits you should get a hydrometer, which measures Baumé. This will measure the sugar content. See picture on p. 28.

Refractometer: A professional instrument for measuring sugar in liquids. The measuring scale is called Brix, which provides a measurement of the density of a liquid. The scale is calibrated against a sugar solution with a known concentration.

pH-measurer: You may find these as single sticks in drug stores.

Sterilizing Jars and Lids

Set the oven to 210°F (100°C) and place the newly rinsed jars with the lids in the oven for 10 minutes. If possible, scoop the jam into the jars while they are still warm with the help of a spoon or measuring cup. To avoid a mess you can use a funnel, which makes it easier to keep the jars clean.

Pour the jam, marmalade, or jelly to the rim of the jar. Screw the lid on entirely and tighten as much as possible. Turn the jars upside down a few times and let them sit and stiffen overnight. Wash the outside of the jars. Write labels and add to the jars right away.

If you use paraffin, first let the jam, marmalade, or jelly stiffen and cool in the jars. Then melt the paraffin in a small saucepan and pour over the preserve. Let it stiffen. Repeat the process once more, so that the content is completely without air pockets. Screw the lid on. This method works perfectly well; however, it is rarely done today.

Preservation

Would you like to process your preserves so as to lengthen their shelf life? Set the oven to 175°F (80°C) and place the jars in a hot water bath. Let them sit in the oven for 20 minutes. The sugar increases the osmotic pressure and lowers the water activity, which means that fruits in syrup, cordial, or jam maintain their flavor and taste for a long time. Furthermore, the process prevents the growth of yeast, mold, and other microorganisms.

This method and time works for fruit, cordial, and jelly, but not for other preserves like, for instance, meats.

The World of Microorganisms

– Bacteria are tiny, one-cell organisms. They multiply by dividing. In the beginning there might be few, but after just 6 hours they will have multiplied to a quarter of a million.

– Yeast and mold growths are 10 to 1,000 times larger than bacteria. They are most comfortable in temperatures between 75–115°F (25–45°C) and pH-values between 3–5.

– Certain mold species can form toxic substances, such as mycotoxins.

– Never eat jam, sauce, or marmalade that is infected with yeast or mold. Even if the mold is only visible on the surface, it will have spread throughout the preserve.

– If you are meticulous and follow the instructions correctly, jam or marmalade will keep for at least a year.

– Always use a clean spoon when you open a new jar of preserves. Store the **opened jar** in the fridge and the contents will keep just fine.

Troubleshooting

There's a liquid layer on the surface of the jam, marmalade, or jelly
– This may be a result of short cooking time or insufficient pectin content in the berries. Boil the jam for a while longer.
– Make sure that the berries and fruit are not overly ripe. Add apple pectin or apple jelly.

The jam or jelly will not stiffen
– You haven't performed the jelly or jam test, or you have not used a thermometer. Boil the jam to a higher temperature and perform a jelly or jam test.
– The berries or fruit were too ripe.
– You forgot to add the lemon juice.
– You haven't added apple pectin or apple juice for berries or fruits with low pectin content.

The jam or jelly crystallizes
– You have not brushed the inside of the pot to avoid sugar crystals.
– You have boiled the jam or jelly for too long: when the preserve becomes harder than it should, sugar crystals develop because of the low water content.

The jam or jelly is gluey and sticky
– You may have boiled too much at once. When this happens, the sugar inverts and it becomes gluey during long periods of boiling. The shorter the boiling time, the nicer the gel.
– You may also have boiled the preserve for too long. In that case, the preserve hardens.

The jam or jelly is not clear
– You haven't removed enough of the foam from the surface.
– You have boiled at a temperature that is too low.

The jam or jelly is starting to yeast and mold
– The jars and lids were not properly sterilized.
– You did not pour the preserve into the jars right away.
– You forgot to turn the jars.
– You stored the jars in a too-warm environment.
– The berries and fruits were not sufficiently fresh when boiled.

Apple

Malus domestica

The cultivated apple tree stems from multiple growth species, most likely including the crabapple. Europe was cultivating a large variety of apples as early as the Middle Ages. Out of the more than 1,000 kinds of apples that exist today, Sweden is growing about 20 of them. Most of the apple cultivators in Sweden can be found in the eastern part of Skåne. The oldest apple variety we know in the Nordic countries is the Gravenstein apple.

Apples may be divided into so-called dessert apples, which are sweet and aromatic when raw, and apples for cooking, which have a sharper taste and high tannin content. Some varieties are excellent for eating raw, while others are very sour and are therefore better suited for purées or poaching. The types that remain hard and retain water during heating are perfect for pies and tarts, whereas kinds that easily soften are great for making baked apples or jam. Whether the apple is hard, soft, sweet, or sour does not only depend on the kind of apple, but also the season.

The color of ripe apples may vary from green and yellow to a deep red. The most popular variety in Sweden is Ingrid Marie, which is sweet enough to eat raw. Granny Smith is the most popular apple variety worldwide, together with Golden Delicious. Belle de Boskoop, Alice, and Cox Pomona are other examples of apples for cooking. Renettes are a group of cooking apples, which are both firm and aromatic. Examples of Renettes are Cox Orange and Ribston.

The dessert apple will most often have a pH-value of 3.4 and contain 15 percent sugar, while a green apple has a pH-value of about 3 and 12 percent sugar.

American apple pie, Austrian apple strudel, German Käsekuchen (cheesecake) with apple, French apple tart, and apple cake from Skåne are just a few of the tasty creations based on apples.

Added Flavor

Spices: Cinnamon, cassava, nutmeg, ginger, cloves, tonka bean, vanilla and cardamom.
Herbs: All kinds of basil and multiple varieties of sage.
Citrus fruits: Every kind of citrus, lemon to enhance a sour taste or to help stiffen the texture when making jam.
Sugars: All kinds of sugars, including honey, but make sure you don't add more than 4 tbsp (3.5 oz) honey per 2 lbs (1 kg) of apples or the sugar will invert during boiling and the jam will turn out oily.
Wine and liquor: Rum, cognac, whiskey, cider, and white and red wine.
Fruit combinations: Lingonberries, cranberries, red currants, gooseberries, pears, and any other sort of fruit or berry that will complement the apple.

Caramelized Apple Jam with Butter

Try this delicious apple jam with chilled vanilla sauce for dessert.

4 ½ lbs (2,000 g) apples, Gravenstein
(4 lbs [1,500 g] net weight)
1 vanilla bean
1 ¼ cups (300 g) water
1 ½ lbs (700 g) sugar
Juice of 1 lemon
½ cup (100 g) butter

1. Rinse, peel and core the apples and slice them in small wedges.
2. Slice open the vanilla bean; remove the seeds, and add on top of the apples.
3. Pour water, sugar, and lemon juice into a saucepan and boil. Brush the inside of the pot continuously, by using a brush dipped in cold water.
4. Add the apple wedges and vanilla. Stir while boiling. Boil to 220°F (105°C), or do a jam test, see p. 20.
5. Take the saucepan off the stove and add the butter.
6. Pour the jam into sterile jars and screw the lids on right away. Turn the jars upside down a couple of times.

Makes about 4 ½ lbs (2,000 g) jam.

Seedless Apple Jam

This jam is firmer and well-suited for pastries where the jam should be stiff and kept in one place. I recommend using Transparante Blanche, which is great for any kind of mash.
During my time in the restaurant business, we would often boil massive amounts of apple jam for Skånsk Apple Cake. After every third round of boiling, we would save the water and make jelly.

4 ½ lbs (2,000 g) sour apples for cooking, such as Transparante Blanche
4 cups (1,000 grams) water
Juice of 1 lemon
1 lb (500 g) sugar per 2 lbs (1 kg) apple purée

1. Rinse the apples and slice them open. Place them in a saucepan with the water and lemon juice and let it come to a boil.
2. Let it boil under a lid till the apples soften completely, about 20–30 minutes.
3. Remove the apples and run them through a strainer.
4. Weigh the purée and add the correct amount of sugar. Boil the purée and sugar in a saucepan. Seedless jam burns easily, so make sure you stir often while it boils.
5. The sauce is done at 220°F (105°C), or you can do a jam test with a cold plate, see p. 20.
6. Pour the jam into sterile jars and screw the lids on right away. Turn the jars upside down a couple of times.

Makes about 3 ¾ lbs (1,500 g) jam.

Apple Jam for Meals

Follow the exact same instructions as the Seedless Apple Jam, except only add ½ lb (200 g) of sugar and let it boil to 215–218°F (102–103°C).

Apple Jam with Cinnamon and Calvados

4 ½ lbs (2,000 g) sour apples for cooking
(4 lbs [1,500 g] net weight)
2 ½ lbs (1,050 g) brown muscovado sugar
⅓ inch (1 cm) real cinnamon stick
2 lemons, juice
¾ cup (150 g) calvados
1 ¼ cup (300 g/3 dl) apple cider

1. Rinse, peel, and core the apples and slice them in small wedges.
2. Put all the ingredients into a saucepan and stir while boiling. Remove foam so that the jam is clear. Brush the inside of the pot with a brush dipped in cold water.
3. Control the temperature as the apples become transparent and the mixture thickens.
4. The sauce is done at 220°F (105°C), or do a jam test, p. 20.
5. Pour the jam into sterile jars and screw the lids on right away. Turn the jars upside down a couple of times.

Makes about 4 lbs (2,000 g) jam.

Apple Jam with Lingonberries, Cinnamon, and Genever

Follow the instructions above, except replace the muscovado sugar with white sugar. Substitute half of the apples with lingonberries and use Dutch gin instead of calvados.

Apple Compote

This is a great filling for pies and apple cakes. Use cocoa butter instead of unsalted butter if you are going to conserve the compote.

2 ½ lbs (1,200 g) apples, preferably Cox Orange
(2 lbs [1,000 g] net weight)
1 vanilla bean
Juice of 1 lemon
¾ cup (200 g/2 dl) apple cider
7 oz (200 g) sugar
¼ cup (60 g) unsalted butter (or cocoa butter)

1. Peel and core the apples, and slice them in wedges.
2. Slice open the vanilla bean and remove the seeds with a sharp knife.
3. Bring the apples, lemon juice, apple cider, and sugar to a boil in a saucepan. Place a lid over the pot and let it boil for 30 minutes, till the apples fall apart.
4. Remove the vanilla bean and boil at a high temperature till the compote thickens.

5. Put the compote into a food processor and blend into a chunky purée. Whisk in the butter.
6. The apple compote may also be conserved, so that it will keep longer. However, if you are planning on conserving the compote, don't add the butter.

Apple Jelly

Keep this jelly in your cupboard and add to jams made with berries that are low in pectin, as it will help the jam stiffen.

If you want you may add spices for flavor, such as vanilla, cinnamon, green cardamom, rosemary, or thyme. You can make this with paradise apples—a jelly my grandmother would always serve with pot-roasted chicken and cream sauce.

Jelly Base
3 ⅓ lbs (1,500 g) green apples for cooking, such as Renettes
6 cups (1,500 g) water
Juice of 1 lemon
2 lbs (1,000 g) sugar

1. Rinse the apples in cold water and cut them into 4 pieces. Place them in boiling water with lemon juice.
2. Let them boil slowly under a lid for 30 minutes till the apples start falling apart.
3. Drain and lightly crush with the back of a spoon.
4. Pour the apple mixture into a strainer lined with cheesecloth and let it drain on its own for about 60 minutes or until the fruit mass is dry.
5. Measure the remaining juice; it should be about 4 ½ cups (1 liter). Add the juice and sugar to the saucepan and boil on the highest temperature. Brush the inside of the pot with a brush dipped in cold water.
6. When the mass reaches 220°F (105°C), the jelly is ready. Make sure that it's stiff enough by doing the jelly test on a cold plate, p. 20. (If it's still not stiff enough, let it boil a while longer.)
7. Pour the jelly in sterile jars and screw the lids on right away. Turn the jars upside down a couple of times.

Makes about 2 lbs (1,000 g) jelly.

Calvado Jelly
Follow the recipe above and add ½ lb (250 g) calvados during boiling. This is great with game.

Mint Jelly
Add 2 oz (60 g) blanched real peppermint leaves during boiling.

Apple Curd
See the recipe for lemon curd on p. 106, but replace the lime juice with freshly squeezed green apple juice. Add calvados, if desired.

Quince

Cydonia oblonga

The quince is originally from Central Asia, but it has been cultivated in Europe for thousands of years, both as a decorative plant and for its fruit. The quince that is grown in Sweden is shaped like a tall bush or a small tree. Its leaves are oval and somewhat shiny, and the flowers are pink or white. The fruits are yellow and similar to apples, and they ripen in the fall. Quince fruits are hard, and can't be eaten raw; however, they do contain lots of pectin.

The flowering quince (*Chaenomeles*) is an ornamental shrub with thorns. It blooms in the spring and its flowers are pink or white. The fruit is similar to the apple and high in pectin.

Quince contains a high amount of pectin and is great for stronger-tasting jellies, fruit jellies that are cut, sorbets, and marmalades. It has higher vitamin C content than both the orange and grapefruit.

Quince Jelly

Similar to the apple jelly, this is very useful as a pectin base.

4 ½ lbs (2,000 g) quince
4 cups (1,000 g/1 liter) water
Juice of 1 lemon
1 lb (500 g) sugar

1. Rinse and peel the fruit, and place it in water with lemon juice to keep it from browning.
2. Cut into wedges, while not removing the seeds. Put the fruit in a saucepan. Add water and lemon juice.
3. Let it boil under a lid till the fruit has gone soft and is falling apart.
4. Empty the fruit into a strainer and squeeze the juice out by pressing down with the back of a large spoon.
5. Pour fruit into a strainer lined with cheesecloth and let it drain on its own for about 60 minutes or until the fruit mass is dry.
6. Pour the juice into a saucepan and add the sugar. Let it boil till it reaches 220°F (105°C). Make sure that it's ready by doing a jelly test on a cold plate.
7. Pour the jelly into sterile jars and screw the lids on right away. Turn the jars upside down a couple of times.

Makes about 2 lbs (1,000 g) jelly.

Quince Jelly with White Wine

2 lbs (1,000 g) quince
Juice of 1 lemon
4 cups (1,000 g/1 liter) water
¾ cup (1 ¼ dl) white wine
1 lb (400 g) sugar
1 oz (40 g) lemon juice

1. Peel the fruit and slice them thinly. Place them in water with lemon to keep from browning.
2. Empty into a strainer and drain the lemon water.
3. Bring the water to a boil, add the fruit, and let it simmer under a lid for about 2 hours.
4. Place the fruit in a strainer and squeeze the juice out by pressing down with the back of a large spoon.
5. Pour into a strainer lined with cheesecloth and let it drain on its own for about 60 minutes or until the fruit mass is dry. This should make about 2 cups (500 g) of quince juice.
6. Blend the wine and sugar in a saucepan and let it boil till it's a gold-yellow caramel (350° F [180°C] if you use a thermometer).
7. Add the fruit juice and lemon juice and let it come to a boil. Brush the inside of the saucepan with a brush dipped in cold water. Remove the foam so that the jelly ends up completely clear.
8. At 220°F (105°C) do a jelly test on a cold plate, see p. 20. If the jelly is not stiff enough, let it boil for a few minutes longer.
9. Pour the jam into sterile jars and screw the lids on right away. Turn the jars upside down a couple of times.

Makes about 1 ¾ lbs (750 g) jelly.

Sliced Quince Marmalade

This marmalade is great with cheese.

4 lbs (2,000 g) quince
Juice of 2 lemons
4 cups (1,000 g/1 liter) water
The same weight of sugar as the weight of the purée

1. Rinse and cut each quince into 4 pieces.
2. Boil the fruit on low heat, in water with lemon juice, for about 2 hours under a lid.
3. Purée in a food processor and strain the mass with the help of a big spoon.
4. Measure as much sugar as the weight of the purée and add it to a clean saucepan.
5. Boil while stirring for 20–30 minutes, till it's a thick mash. Use a spoon with a long handle as the mass will spatter as it thickens.
6. Set the oven to 210°F (100°C).
7. Spread the mash thinly in a baking pan lined with parchment paper.
8. Place the pan in the oven and keep the oven door slightly ajar. Close the door after 3 hours and turn off the oven. Let the pan sit overnight.
9. In the morning, slice the marmalade into pieces and roll them in sugar. This will make it keep longer.

Makes about 3 ⅓ lbs (1,500 g) sliced marmalade.

Quince Jam

Follow the instructions for Apple Jam, p. 33.

Pear

Pyrus communis

The pear has been cultivated for thousands of years. Originally the fruit comes from China. Pears existed in Greece as early as 1,000 years BCE, and they travelled north with the Romans. The pear was especially popular in France. Pears were cultivated in Sweden during the Middle Ages, and during the 1700s there were multiple varieties of the pear already in existence. Today there are over 1,000 different pear varieties, which provide a huge selection, depending on season, taste, or aroma.

Some of the more common pear varieties are Williams, Greve Moltke, Clapps, Packham, Anjou, Herzogin Elsa, Passacrassana, Winter Nelis, and Alexandre Lucas. The varieties we would call *pears for cooking* include Anjou, Alexandre Lucas, Conference, Butterpear, and Williams. Superior dessert pears will most often have "beurre" in their names, which means "buttered." This describes their sweet and tender flesh. Dessert pears are usually tasty when eaten raw. The Williams pear is my favorite, both for eating raw when ripe and for cooking.

When I first started out as a pastry apprentice, at 15 years old, the recipe book was important. We pickled green pears every fall. This is how it would go: Fasta Greve Molke, Clara Frijs, or Esperens Herre were peeled and soaked in lemon water, with 2 tsp (10 g) salt and a pinch of alum per 4 cups (1 liter) of water, to keep the pears from browning. The stem was scraped, but not removed. Then we would boil the fruit in water that was kept right under the boiling point, with green food coloring. We allowed them to simmer till they felt completely soft. After the boiling, the fruit would be held under cold water. They were emptied into jars and pickled the same way as the lemon zest, p. 107, while the syrup was colored.

These were important at the bakery. We would carve them into green leaves for marzipan roses and create patterns to decorate frosted cakes. They would also be used chopped in frozen pudding, a specialty at many bakeries, which would be decorated with cotton candy.

Pear Jam with Fig, Cardamom, Cinnamon and Armagnac

½ lb (250 g) dried figs
¾ cup (150 g/1 ½ dl) Armagnac
2 ¾ lbs (1,250 g) pears, ripe but still firm
(2 lbs [1,000] net weight)
1 ¾ lbs (800 g) light muscovado sugar
4 cups (1 liter) water
Juice of 1 lemon
2 tsp (10 g) ground cardamom
⅓ inch (1 cm) real cinnamon stick
½ lb (250 g) apple jelly or 1 ½ cups (350 g) apple juice, p. 16–17

Pear Marmalade and Ligon Pear Jam.

DAY 1

Finely chop the figs and soak them in Armagnac overnight.

DAY 2

1. Rinse and peel the pears. Remove the cores.
2. Pour sugar, water, and lemon juice into a saucepan, with cardamom and the cinnamon stick.
3. Let it all boil and remove from the heat.
4. Slice the pears into small wedges and place them in the sugar mixture immediately to keep from browning.
5. Add apple jelly or apple juice and let it boil for about 25 minutes. Brush the inside of the pot with a brush dipped in cold water.
6. Add the figs and the liquor.
7. Boil to 220–222°F (105–106°C) or till the pear wedges are clear. Do a jam test on a cold plate, p. 20.
8. Remove the cinnamon stick. Pour the jam into sterile jars and screw the lids on right away. Turn the jars upside down a couple of times.

Makes about 3 ¾ lbs (1,700 g) jam.

Pear Jam with Chocolate

This is a classic blend in France, where it is named Belle Helene.

Half-Pickled Pears

2 cups (500 g/5 dl) water
Juice of 1 lemon
1 lb (500 g) sugar
1 ½ lbs (650 g) pear
(1 lb [500 g] net weight)

Pear Jam

1 cup (250 g/2 ½ dl) water
Juice of 1 lemon
2 ¾ lbs (1,250 g) pear
(2 lbs [1,000 g] net weight)
1 ¾ lbs (800 g) sugar
1 vanilla bean
12 oz (350 g) dark chocolate

DAY 1

Make a demi-confit of the pears (half-pickle).

1. Pour the water and lemon juice into a saucepan and bring it to a boil with ½ cup (125 g) sugar.
2. Rinse and peel the pears and dice them. Add them to the saucepan and let it simmer for 15 minutes. Add another ½ cup (125 g) of sugar and let it simmer for 15 minutes more.
3. Repeat the procedure two more times. The pears are now half-pickled.
4. Empty into a bowl and let it cool down. Keep it at room temperature overnight.

DAY 2

1. Place the half-pickled pears in a strainer and let them drain.
2. Pour the water and lemon juice into a saucepan and let it come to a boil. Remove from the stove.
3. Rinse, peel, and core the pears, and cut them into wedges. Add them to the water to keep from browning. Boil under lid on low heat till they fall apart completely. Purée them in a food processor or blender.
4. Pour the purée back into the saucepan and add sugar and the scraped vanilla bean. Boil on low heat while stirring often. Brush the inside of the pot with a brush dipped in cold water.
5. Boil to 220°F (105°C), or perform a jam test on a cold plate, p. 20.
6. Add the diced pear and let it come to a boil again.
7. Add finely chopped chocolate and remove the vanilla bean.
8. Pour the jam into sterile jars and screw the lids on right away. Turn the jars upside down a couple of times.

Makes about 4 ½ lbs (2,000 g) jam.

Ginger Pears

Feel free to use butter pears or Conference. Serve with some good-quality ice cream.

Since the sugar is added in small batches, the pears don't shrink like they would if all the sugar was added at once, which is the more common practice in most recipes.

2 lbs (1,000 g) sugar
4 cups (1,000 g/1 liter) water
½ cup (1 dl) lemon juice
4 ½ lbs (2,000 g) firm, ripe pears
2 tsp (20 g) dried ginger

1. Boil syrup made up of ½ lb (250 g) sugar, water, lemon juice, and dried ginger, in a saucepan.
2. Remove from the stove.
3. Peel and core the pears. Add them to the syrup and let it simmer for 15 minutes.
4. Add another ½ lb (250 g) of sugar and let it simmer an additional 15 minutes.
5 Repeat the procedure twice more, till the syrup contains the entire 2 lbs (1,000 g) of sugar.
6. Pour the jam into sterilized jars and screw the lids on right away.
7. Set the oven to 175°F (180°C). Place the jars in a water bath in the oven for 20 minutes. This will allow the pears to keep longer.

Glögg-Simmered Pears

Follow the recipe for ginger pears, but withhold the ginger and boil in glögg instead of water. Serve with vanilla ice cream.

Boiled Pears with Vanilla

The syrup may be flavored in many different ways with herbs or spices. Saffron pears are a Christmas classic. To make, just add ½ tsp (3 g) saffron to the liquids.

4 cups (1,000 g/1 liter) water
1 ¼ lbs (550 g) sugar
1 lemon, juiced
1 vanilla bean
5 ½ lbs (2,500 g) ripe, firm pears

1. Pour water, sugar, and lemon juice into a saucepan. Split open the vanilla bean, scrape out the seeds, and add it to the pot. Let it come to a boil.
2. Rinse and peel the pears and rub them with half a lemon to avoid browning.
3. Remove the cores with a spoon and place the pears in the syrup.
4. Poach them on low heat till they feel soft if you poke them with a fork.
5. Carefully scoop the pears into jars and pour the syrup over them.
6. Place the jars in a water bath in the oven. Let them heat up for 20 minutes at 350°F (180°C).

Caramel Pears

This is a specialty of Georg Maushagen Bakery in Düsseldorf.

Use the recipe above as a basis, but boil the sugar and 1 ½ cup (300 g) water into a brown caramel (350°F [180°C]). Add the remaining water and boil the syrup. Add the pears and poach them as described above.

Plum

Prunus domestica

The plum has been cultivated for at least 2,000 years. It is assumed that the plant was originally a combination of the cherry tree and the blackthorn. Today, we know of around 2,000 plum varieties. The fruits differ in size, shape, and color. In Sweden, we grow plums from August till October. The rest of the year we import plums from other parts of Europe, South America, and South Africa. Common Swedish plum varieties are Victoria, Opal, and Herman.

Reine Claude plums, which are green yellow with sweet and soft flesh, belong to the round plum family. This variety is great both for eating raw and for poaching. They are fantastic for jam and marmalades. Another variety, Mirabelles, are small and often perfectly round. They are sweet and have a great scent, and they may be yellow or red. They are commonly used for jams, marmalades, purées, preserves, and more. They are often pickled and kept in liquor, just like the Reine Claude plums.

Prune plums, see p. 48, are a blue or blue-violet variety of plum. They are small and oval with a pointed top. Certain kinds are dried into prunes.

If you combine half red Mirabelles and half green apples, you will end up with a beautiful jelly. The plum has, like most stone fruits, very low pectin content and will often need help from apple juice or apple jelly in order to form a gel.

Added Flavor

Spices: only vanilla
Herbs: lemon thyme, lemon verbena, lemon basil, orange thyme, and more
Wine and spirits: sweet dessert wines and cognac
Lemon and other citrus fruits

Reine Claude Plums in Armagnac

At the Confeiserie Zoo in Basel, Julius Perlia reigned. He was also the principal at the famous Coba school. The Reine Claude plum in Armagnac was their specialty. They were nicely wrapped and sold around Christmas. Here is the original recipe I wrote down in 1972:

Choose even and firm fruits without spots or stains. Work with small quantities; do not exceed 6 ½ lbs (3 kg). Place the fruit in a bowl with cold water. You do not have to prick them with a fork if you follow this specific process.

6 ½ lbs (3,000 g) carefully chosen plums for preserving
3 ¼ lbs (1,500) peeled, damaged plums
Water

6 vanilla beans
About 7 cups (1 ½ liter) Armagnac

Blanching

1. First, soak the fruit in fresh cold water; make sure that the fruit is completely covered with water. Then add 10 tsp (60 g) salt and 8 tsp (40 g) alum, and mix well.
2. Place the damaged plums in a saucepan with a flat bottom and cover them with water.
3. This mixture should be boiled for 30 minutes, till the plums have fallen apart completely.
4. Pass everything through a strainer and empty back into a copper pot. This process ensures that the blanching bath has the right acid content.
5. When the mixture is boiling, add the carefully chosen plums. Let it come to a boil, then remove it from the stove and let it rest. Place it back on the stove once more. This drastic change in temperature creates small holes in the skin of the plums, which allows the syrup and liquor to soak in more easily.
6. When you preserve, you should always make sure that the fruit maintains its color and shape. Let it rest for about 30 minutes, and thanks to the blanching bath, the plums will turn green again.
7. When the plums have achieved a green color, they should be placed back on the stove and heated once more; however, they should not boil.
8. Now run cold water directly into the pot till the plums are completely cool and blanched all the way through. You can poke the fruit with a fork and it should feel soft on the inside. When all trace of the salt is rinsed away, you can stop.

Preserving

Next, preserve the plums the same way as citrus peels, for 5 days (see Preserved Citrus Peels, p. 107). But add three times more sugar and water since there is a larger quantity of the plums.

DAY 6

1. Carefully pour the plums into a strainer and drain.
2. Place the drained plums in sterilized jars and add a vanilla bean to each jar.
3. Fill the jars to the rim with Armagnac.
4. Screw on the lids and let the plums rest for a couple of weeks before they are served.

Tip!
Reine Claude Plums in Armagnac taste amazing with vanilla ice cream and a piece of almond pie.

Mirabelle Jam

You can make this jam with Reine Claude plums as well. It tastes lovely with fresh baked bread for breakfast or with yogurt. It also works well with matured cheese.

2 ½ lbs (1,200 g) ripe Mirabelle or Reine Claude plums
Juice of 1 lemon
1 ¾ lbs (800 g) sugar

DAY 1

1. Rinse the plums, pit them, and slice them down the middle. If you are using Reine Claude plums, you have to first scald them in boiling water and then place them in cold water and peel the skin off.
2. Pour the lemon juice and sugar into a bowl. Carefully blend everything together, and make sure to really work the sugar in with the fruit.
3. Cover with plastic wrap and let it sit overnight at room temperature.

DAY 2

1. Put the fruit into a pot and boil while constantly removing foam from the surface with a spoon.
2. Boil to 220°F (105°C), till the fruit is starting to turn transparent and the mixture starts forming jelly. Make sure to remove the foam during boiling so that the jelly is completely clear, and brush the inside of the pot with a brush dipped in cold water to prevent sugar crystals from forming in the finished jam.
3. If you do not use a thermometer, perform a jam test on a cold plate, see p. 20.
4. Pour into sterilized jars right away. Screw the lids on immediately and turn the jars upside down a couple of times.

Makes about 3 ¼ lbs (1500 g) jam.

Tip!
Make the same jam, but add a vanilla bean, or you may add some rosemary, orange thyme, or cinnamon basil.

Mirabelle or Reine Claude Jelly with Cognac

Instead of adding apple jelly or apple juice to help the jelly stiffen, you can replace a third of the plums with red or white currants or unripe gooseberries.

2 ¾ lbs (1,300 g) plums of your choice
(2 lbs [1,000 g] net weight)
Juice of 1 lemon
½ cup (100 g/1 dl) cognac
1 ½ cup (350 g/3 ½ dl) apple juice or ½ lb (250 g) Apple Jelly, see p. 16–17.
An equal amount of sugar as the weight of the juice

1. Wash and cut open the plums, and remove the pits.
2. Place in a pot with lemon juice, cognac, and apple juice or apple jelly. Cover with water and let it simmer under a lid for 25 minutes, till the fruit is starting to fall apart.
3. Empty into a strainer and help squeeze out all of the liquid by pressing with the back of a spoon.

4. Pour the fruit mass into a strainer lined with cheesecloth and let it drain on its own until it is completely dry, about 1 hour.
5. Weigh the juice and add as much sugar as the weight of the juice.
6. Pour back into the pot and let it boil while constantly removing foam with a spoon. Brush the inside of the pot with a brush dipped in cold water to avoid sugar crystals forming in the jelly. Remember to remove all the foam so that the jelly becomes clear.
7. Boil to 220°F (105°C), or perform a jelly test, see p. 20.
8. Pour directly into sterilized jars and screw the lids on immediately. Turn the jars upside down a couple of times.

Mirabelle Jam with Acacia Honey

A fabulous-tasting jam with a honey-infused aroma.

2 ¾ lbs (1,300 g) Mirabelle plums, preferably yellow
Juice of 1 lemon
1 lb (400 g) sugar
1 ½ cups (500 g) acacia honey

Prepare the same way as Mirabelle Jam, above, but replace some of the sugar with honey.

Tip!
You may also caramelize the honey to create a more refined taste. Let the honey boil till it's golden brown. Add the lemon juice and the plums. Boil until it passes a jam test, see p. 20.

Preserved Mirabelle or Reine Claude Plums

Mirabelle or Reine Claude plums may be preserved the same way you would citrus zest.

2 lbs (1,000 g) plums, Mirabelle or Reine Claude

1. Choose plums of similar size that are barely ripe. Prick them with a fork all the way down to the pit, to prevent the skin from splitting during the preserving process.
2. Blanch the plums for a couple of minutes until they are soft all the way through.
3. Cool them under running water.

Candy the plums by following the exact steps of Preserved Citrus Peels, see p. 107.

Blanc-Manger aux Prunes Reine Claude.

Blanc-Manger aux Prunes Reine Claude

This was a classic dessert at the Savoy Hotel in Malmö, both in the dining room and the banquet hall. The Bavarois-like almond ring, filled with sour plums, and the contrasting Kirschwasser makes this one of the best desserts I know. We would serve the dessert with baskets of drained caramel, which were garnished with beautiful petit fours.

8–10 servings

1 ring pan, 9 ½ inches (24 cm) in diameter
2 tbsp (10 g) of powdered sugar to dust pan

Plum Compote

2 lbs (1,000 g) green Reine Claude plums
3 cups (325 g) sugar
2 cups (500 g/5dl) water
Juice of 1 lemon
1 vanilla bean, preferably Bourbon

Blanc-Manger

2 tbsp powdered gelatin (8 sheets)
2 ½ oz (75 g) sweet almonds
2 bitter almonds
⅔ cup (75 g) sugar
1 vanilla bean, preferably Bourbon
2 cups (500 g/5 dl) whole-fat milk
6 egg yolks (120 g)
⅔ cup (75 g) sugar
½ cup (10 cl) Kirschwasser
2 ½ cups (500 g/5 dl) heavy cream

For Decoration:

2 fresh, non-treated red roses

DAY 1
Plum Compote

1. Rinse the plums and remove the stems. Poke them all the way through to the pit with a fork.
2. Mix sugar and water in a saucepan that holds 9 cups (2 liters), and add the lemon juice.
3. Slice the vanilla bean down the middle and scrape out the seeds with a knife.
4. Boil everything to 234–240°F (112–114°C), or perform a flight test, see p. 14.
5. Add the plums to the syrup, and let them simmer till they feel soft when you poke them with a fork.
6. Put it all into a bowl and let it cool. Cover with plastic wrap and let it rest in the fridge overnight so that the plums fully absorb the flavors.

Blanc-Manger

1. Dissolve the gelatin in water as per the instructions on the package, if using powder, or soak the gelatin sheets in generous amounts of water for at least 10 minutes.
2. Bring 2 cups (500 g) water to a boil. Add the almonds and let them boil for one minute. Next, rinse the almonds in cold water and let them drain in a strainer.

3. Shell the almonds and mix them with ⅔ cup (75 g) sugar in a food processor till you have a smooth paste. You have now made a classic marzipan.
4. Slice open the vanilla bean down the middle with a knife. Scrape out the seeds and place it in a saucepan.
5. Add the milk to the saucepan and let it come to a boil while stirring. Next, add the almond paste and let it boil till the paste is melted.
6. Lightly beat the egg yolks and ⅔ cup (75 g) sugar. Stir in the almond and milk mixture. Mix well.
7. Pour the whole mixture back into the saucepan and warm the cream to 185°F (85°C).
8. Add the dissolved gelatin to the cream. If using sheets, remove the gelatin sheets from the water and let them drain. Then add them to the cream and stir till they are completely melted.
9. Pour the cream through a fine strainer into a large metal bowl.
10. Cool the cream in a cold water bath, till its temperature is about 65°F (18°C).
11. Add the liquor to the cream mixture and whisk the heavy cream until stiff peaks form.
12. Fold half of the cream mixture in with the whipped cream, using a whisk. Follow by adding the rest; be careful so that the whipped cream doesn't lose its volume.
13. Rinse the ring pan with cold water and let it dry. Sift some powdered sugar into the pan (this helps the cream release from the pan easily).
14. Add the cream to the pan and shake so that the cream spreads out evenly. Cover with plastic wrap and let it sit in the freezer overnight.

Continued on p. 48

Plum marmalades.

DAY 2 (About 3 hours before serving)

1. Dip the pan in warm water and make sure that the cream is now starting to release.
2. Turn cake out onto a plate.
3. Let the plums drain in a strainer.
4. Fill the center of the cake with the plums and decorate with roses.

Crispy almond flakes are great with this. *Photo on p. 45.*

Prune plums are blue or blue-violet, small, oval, and have a pointed top. They are sweet and their flesh is quite firm. The season for prune plums starts in September and October. They have a strong aroma, are firm, and do not release much juice during cooking.

In Europe prune plums are commonly used for pies. They may also be soaked in red wine syrups with Christmas spices, or be boiled into jam and marmalade that tastes amazing with toasted bread. They are also good for soaking in cognac.

Added Flavor

Spices: vanilla, cinnamon, ginger, cloves, bay leaves, star anise, and various peppers

Wine and spirits: red wine, port wine, madeira and glögg, rum, and cognac.

Lemon

Fruit combinations: pears, apples, figs, apricots, and chestnuts

---

Prune Plum Jam

This tasty marmalade is frequently served for breakfast in Alsace, France.

2 ¾ lbs (1,300 g) prune plums
(2 lbs [1,000 g] net weight)
1 ¾ lbs (800 g) light muscovado sugar
Juice of 1 lemon

DAY 1

1. Rinse the plums and remove the stems. Cut them down the middle and remove the pits.
2. Place the pitted plums in a metal bowl with the sugar and lemon juice, and blend well. Let it rest at room temperature for 24 hours.

DAY 2

1. Place everything in a pot and bring to a boil. Stir constantly, and remove foam now and then with a spoon. Brush the inside of the pot with a brush dipped in cold water to prevent sugar crystals from forming.

2. Let it boil to 222–224°F (106–107°C), or perform a jam test on a cold plate, see p. 20.
3. Pour directly into sterilized jars and immediately screw the lids on. Turn the jars upside down a couple of times.

Makes about 3 ¼ lbs (1,500 g) jam.

Prune Compote with Pecan Nuts and Cinnamon

Follow the same process as above except add ⅔ inch (1 cm) of a cinnamon stick and stir in about 5 oz (150 g) pecans at the end of the boiling time.

Seedless Prune Compote Marmalade

Fantastic as a doughnut filling, a side for desserts, or with yogurt in the morning. This jam is commonly used in Austria and Hungary as a filling for cakes.

2 ¾ lbs (1,300 g) prune plums
(2 lbs [1,000 g] net weight)
2 cups (500 g) water
6 whole cloves
4 star anise
1 ¾ lbs (800 g) light muscovado sugar
Juice of 1 lemon

1. Rinse the plums and remove the stems. Cut them down the middle and remove the pits.
2. Place the pitted plums in the water and add the cloves and star anise. Bring it to a boil. Continue boiling until the plums are falling apart.
3. Pass through a strainer. Boil the plum purée, sugar, and lemon juice for about 15 minutes. Let it boil to 220°F (105°C). Verify with a jam test on a cold plate, see p. 20.
4. Pour directly into sterilized jars and screw the lids on immediately. Turn the jars upside down a couple of times.

Makes about 2 ¾ lbs (1,300 g) marmalade.

Prune Preserve with Red Wine and Spices

These delicious prune plums may be served cold with cinnamon or caramel ice cream. I tasted prune preserve with red wine and spices for the first time at the house of the famous chef Alain Chapel, right outside of Lyon.

2 lbs (1,000 g) prune plums
1 orange, zest and juice
1 lemon, zest and juice
2 vanilla beans, preferably Bourbon
2 cinnamon sticks of real cinnamon, ⅓ inch (1 cm) long
4 star anise
6 cups (1,500 g/1 ½ liters), from the Rhone Valley if possible
1 ⅔ cups (400 g/4 dl) freshly brewed tea, Earl Grey
⅔ cup (120 g) muscovado sugar
¾ cup (260 g) acacia honey

1. Rinse the plums, remove the stems, and poke them with a fork.
2. Rinse the orange and the lemon. Cut them in half and squeeze out the juice.
3. Cut the zests into small pieces and boil them three times, each for 5 minutes, and change the water each time. This is to get rid of the bitter taste.
4. Cut the vanilla bean down the middle and scrape out the seeds.
5. Pour all of the spices, wine, citrus zests, vanilla, tea, sugar, and honey into a pot.
6. Let it boil for 10 minutes. Next, add the plums and let it come to a boil. Let the mixture simmer for 5 minutes.
7. Scoop directly into sterilized jars and immediately screw on the lids.
8. If you wish, you may place the jars in a water bath in the oven at 175°F (80°C) for 20 minutes in order to sterilize them. Keep them in the fridge once they have stiffened completely.

Prune Plum Tart

In Switzerland this tart is called Zwetschgenvähe. Friday used to be cleaning day, and so there was no time to prepare a complicated dinner. Therefore, dinner would be soup with a fruit tart as dessert. I remember that on those days there would be a long line at the Confiserie Honold in Zurich. Tarts with prune plums, apricots, rhubarb, pears, and sour cherries were the most common, and of course the apple tart with Belle de Boskoop apples.

This tasty dessert is not overly sweet and is especially good when it's still lukewarm, with some lightly whipped cream. The tart is so delicious it seemingly melts in your mouth.

Makes about 8 servings.

Springform tart pan, 10 inch (26 cm) diameter and about 1 inch (2 cm) tall
2 tbsp (25 g) butter, softened, and 3 tbsp (25 g) flour for the pan

Pâte Sablée

3 cups (400 g) all-purpose flour
14 tbsp (200 g) unsalted butter, softened
½ cup (125 g) sugar
About 5 egg yolks (100 g)
1 lemon
Pinch of salt

3 ⅓ lbs (1,500 g) prune plums
1 ¾ oz (50 g) finely ground almonds

Cinnamon Sugar

½ cup (100 g) sugar
1 tbsp (10 g) freshly ground real cinnamon

Apricot Topping

7 oz (200 g) apricot jelly
¼ cup (50 g) water

Pâte Sablée

This is the technique we used at the Confiserie Hanold to ensure that the dough was not overworked. (You may freeze any leftover dough and use it at another time). Start preparing the dough at least 2 hours beforehand.

1. Spread the flour out in a circle on the table and place the softened butter and salt in the middle.
2. Rinse and grate half of the lemon, by using the finer side of the grater.
3. Place the egg yolks on top of the butter.
4. Blend butter, sugar, yolks, lemon zest, and salt into an even batter. Collect the flour from the sides of the bowl and work it into dough. Wrap the dough in plastic wrap and let it rest in the fridge for an hour.
5. Coat the springform pan with the soft butter and shake some flour around the dish so that it sticks. Empty out any leftover flour and place the dish in the fridge.
6. Cut the rinsed plums down the middle and remove the pits. Cut the plum halves three times with a knife.
7. Roll the dough out, ⅓ inch (3 mm) thick and put it in the pan. Work it so that it covers the sides of the pan and poke the bottom with a fork. Trim off any extra dough and keep this in the freezer for a future baking session.
8. Place the pan in the refrigerator, and let it rest for at least 30 minutes.
9. Set the oven to 375°F (190°C).
10. Bake the crust until light brown, about 10 minutes.
11. Remove the half-baked crust from the oven and sprinkle finely chopped almonds on top.
12. Place the plums in the crust, until the whole bottom is covered. Sprinkle the cinnamon sugar on top and bake for about 36 minutes, till the dough is golden brown and the plums are soft.
13. Lift the tart from the dish, with the help of a wide spatula, and let it cool on a cooling rack.
14. Bring the apricot jam and water to a boil and brush it on top of the tart.

Serve this delicious tart with lightly whipped cream.

Jelly Doughnuts

Prune marmalade tastes fantastic with some really good jelly doughnuts. The Austrians initially used apricot marmalade, while the Germans used raspberry marmalade. In Sweden the most common filling is apple jam, and if the jam is good, the doughnuts taste amazing. Unfortunately, the apple jam is often full of pectin and water instead of apples. On Saturday mornings, when my grandmother returned from the market, I would often get a jelly doughnut or a sugar bun with vanilla for breakfast, just when I got out of bed. I can feel the sugar in my mouth just thinking about it.

Makes about 30 doughnuts.

Starter Dough

⅔ cup (175 g/1 ¾ dl) whole milk
3 ¾ tsp dry active yeast (25 g cake yeast)
2 cups (250 g) all-purpose flour

Batter

2 cups (250 g) all-purpose flour
7–8 egg yolks (150 g)
¼ cup (50 g) sugar
½ tbsp (10 g) real vanilla sugar
Grated zest of 1 lemon
10 tbsp (150 g) unsalted butter
1 ⅔ tsp (10 g) sea salt

4 ¼ cups (1 liter) safflower or canola oil for frying

Jam of choice for filling

½ cup (100 g) sugar
Pinch of real vanilla sugar
1 ½ tbsp (10 g) freshly ground real cinnamon

Starter Dough

1. Warm the milk to 95°F (35°C). Crumble down the yeast and whisk till the yeast dissolves. Stir in the flour and work the dough for at least 5 minutes by hand or with a food processor.
2. Cover the elastic starter dough with plastic wrap and place it at room temperature in a place free from drafts. Let it rise to double its size, about 30–40 minutes (the rising time is shorter than most recipes because the amount of dough is smaller).

Batter

1. Mix the ingredients with the starter dough and work it into elastic dough for about 20 minutes by hand or with a food processor. You should be able to roll the dough out thinly when you have finished working it.
2. Cover the dough with plastic wrap and let it rise for 30 minutes.
3. Turn the dough out onto the table and punch the dough down to push the air out. Knead the dough for about 10 minutes.
4. Cover with plastic wrap and let it rest for 20 minutes.
5. Roll the dough out with the help of some flour and slice into about 30 pieces, with the help of a spatula. Shape pieces into round balls. Each ball should be about the size of a golf ball (about 40 g).
6. Sift a little bit of flour over a baking sheet lined with parchment paper or a kitchen towel. Place the dough balls on top, cover them with a kitchen towel, and let them rise to double their size, about 60 minutes.

Frying

1. Heat the oil to 350°F (180°C) in a sturdy pot that holds about 13 cups (3 liters). Use a thermometer to test the temperature.
2. Place 3 or 4 doughnuts in the oil at a time. Fry them for 2 minutes on one side till they are golden brown. Turn the doughnuts over with a fork and fry them until the other side is golden brown as well.
3. Scoop them up with a slotted spoon and let them drain on a paper towel. If you want to make sure that they are cooked all the way through, you can use a thermometer and verify that the middle temperature is 206–208°F (97-98°C).
4. Pour the jam into a paper cone or a pastry bag.
5. Cut a small hole in the front of the doughnuts and fill them by inserting the tip of the pastry bag into the hole and squeezing the jam inside. Mix sugar, vanilla sugar, and freshly ground cinnamon and roll the doughnuts in the mixture right away.

Serve as fresh as possible with a cup of strong coffee or a glass of German Eiswein (ice wine).

Cherries

Cherries have been cultivated in China for more than 4,000 years. They were known among the Greeks and are described as early as 300 years BCE. Cherries are divided into two groups, sweet cherries and sour cherries.

Sweet cherries (*Prunus avium*), grow wild in most of Europe. They are also cultivated in a variety of places in Sweden. Sweet cherries can be white yellow, yellow, yellow red, and dark red—almost black. They are commonly eaten fresh.

Sour cherries (*Prunus cerasus*) come from Asia and exist in Europe only through cultivation. The trees do not grow as large as the sweet cherry trees, and the fruits are sour and dark red, like the North Star and Morello, or they are light red, like Montmorency. The sour cherry is usually cooked before it is served. In most cases these cherries need to be pitted as well. Cherries do not have high pectin content and therefore need apple juice or currant juice in order to form jelly more effectively.

Flambéed cherries jubilee with vanilla parfait was commonly served when I first started out as a restaurant pastry chef. When I later worked onboard a cruise ship, we would serve Baked Alaska, which we call glace au four, which would always be served with a side of warm cherries. This dessert was traditionally served at the Captain's Welcome Dinner on our cruises around the world, always with a side of burning hot cherries. This culinary sensation was first made in Monte Carlo with a meringue-baked ice cream that was warm on the outside and cold on the inside. The meringue would isolate the ice cream, similar to the sugar cake described below.

Added Flavor

Spices: all of the classic spices, such as cinnamon, ginger, nutmeg, vanilla, and tonka bean.
Herbs: fresh ginger, lemongrass, and rosemary.
Sugar: all varieties, brown if possible.
Spirits and wine: Kirschwasser, cognac, Armagnac, red wine, and port wine.
Fruit combinations: apples, pears, peaches, and apricots, as well as all kinds of red berries and gooseberries.

Cherry Jam with Almond and Rum

7 oz (200 g) sweet almonds,
   for instance, Spanish Marcona
2 ¾ lbs (1,300 g) sour cherries
   (2 lbs [1,000 g] net weight)
2 lbs (1,000 g) light muscovado sugar
¾ cup (200 g/2 dl) red wine

½ cup (100 g/1 dl) dark rum
1 ½ cup (350 g/3 ½ dl) apple juice or
   ½ lb (250 g) apple jelly, see p. 16–17
Juice of 1 lemon
⅓ inch (1 cm) cinnamon stick

1. Bring water to a boil in a small saucepan and add the almonds. Scald them for 1 minute. Run them under cold water and remove the shells.
2. Pit the rinsed cherries and remove the stems.
3. Pour sugar, wine, rum, apple juice, and lemon juice in a pot. Boil and brush the inside of the pot with a brush dipped in cold water to avoid sugar crystals.
4. Boil to 234–240°F (112–114°C) or do a sugar test, see p. 14.
5. Add the berries, almonds, and cinnamon. Boil for 20 minutes or till the berries are starting to turn transparent and the jam starts to form jelly and forms wrinkles on the surface. Remove the foam so that the jam becomes beautifully clear and brush the walls of the pot to keep the sugar crystals from forming in the jam.
6. At about 222–224°F (106–107°C), the jam is ready. You can also do a jam test on a cold plate, see p. 20.
7. Pour half of the jam into sterilized jars so that they are half full, and let it rest for 15 minutes.
8. Bring the remainder of the jam to a boil once more and scoop it into the jars all the way up to the rim. Immediately screw on the lids and turn the jars upside down a couple of times. (This is to prevent the berries floating to the surface; when you turn it upside down, the berries spread out more evenly in the jar.)

Makes about 4 ½ lbs (2,000 g) jam.

Cherry Jam with Currants and Armagnac

Black currants have high pectin content, so in this recipe there is no need for apple juice or apple jelly to get the jam to form gel.

2 lbs (1,000 g) dark red sour cherries
(1 ¾ lbs [800 g] net weight)
1 lb (500 g) black currants
1 ¾ lbs (800 g) sugar
1 ½ cup (350 g/3 ½ dl) water
Juice of 1 lemon
½ cup (100 g/1 dl) Armagnac

1. Pit the rinsed cherries and remove the stems from the currants.
2. Pour sugar, water, and lemon juice into a pot. Boil and brush the inside of the pot with a brush dipped in cold water to prevent sugar crystals.
3. Boil to 234–240°F (112–114°C), or do a sugar test, see p. 14.
4. Add the berries and Armagnac. Boil until the berries are starting to look transparent. Be meticulous about removing the foam, so that the jam comes out clear, and brush the inside of the pot often to prevent the formation of sugar crystals.
5. At 222–224°F (106–107°C) the jam is usually ready, or do a jam test on a cold plate, see p. 20.
6. Scoop directly into sterilized jars. Screw the lids on right away and turn the jars upside down a couple of times.

Makes about 3 ¼ lbs (1,500 g) jam.

Sour Cherry Jam

A tasty and wonderfully tart jam that goes well with cheesecakes and whipped cream cakes. My sister, Gunilla, grows sour cherries in her garden, and she makes use of them quite often, especially for sour cherry pie.

2 ¾ lbs sour cherries (1,300 g)
(2 lbs [1,000 g] net weight)
1 ¾ lbs (800 g)
1 ½ cups (350 g/3 ½ dl) water
Juice of 1 lemon
1 ½ cups (350 g/3 ½ dl) apple juice or ½ lb (250 g) apple jelly, or currant jelly or juice.

1. Pit the rinsed berries.
2. Boil sugar, water, and lemon juice in a pot to 234–240°F (112–114°C), or perform a sugar test, see p. 14.
3. Add the sour cherries and the apple or red currant jelly or juice.
4. Boil while stirring. Remove foam and continually brush the inside of the pot with a brush dipped in cold water to prevent sugar crystals.
5. When the surface of the jam starts to wrinkle and the berries are turning transparent, it is time to perform a jam test or measure the temperature with a thermometer. At 222–224°F (106–107°C), the jam is usually ready. Also perform a jam test on a cold plate, see p. 20.

Scoop jam directly into sterilized jars. Screw the lids on immediately and turn the jars upside down a couple of times.

Makes about 4 lbs (1,800 g) jam.

Cherry Cordial

Make cherry cordial the same way you would make strawberry cordial, see p. 74. Replace the strawberries with sour cherries like morellos or Montmorency.

Cherries in Cognac

Used for pralines, desserts, and pastries.

2 lbs (1,000 g) dark red cherries, preferably morellos
2 vanilla beans
2 cups (500 g/5 dl) cognac or Kirschwasser
½ lb (300 g) sugar
10 crushed cherry stones

1. Rinse the cherries and dry them carefully.
2. Blend everything together in a large glass jar.
3. Shake the jar well to combine and let it sit at room temperature for two months.

After two months, store it in the fridge and use it for desserts and pralines.

Cherries Jubilee

Serve this with vanilla parfait or with glace au four, or Baked Alaska, as it is called in English.

6 servings

1 lb (500 g) sour cherries, preferably morellos
½ cup (125 g) sugar
½ cup (100 g/1 dl) red wine
⅓ inch (1 cm) real cinnamon stick
2 tbsp (50 g) currant jelly, see p. 79
¼ cup (6 cl) Kirschwasser or cognac

Thickener

¼ cup (6 cl) Kirschwasser or cognac
Pinch of cornstarch

1. Rinse the cherries carefully and let them dry.
2. Boil sugar and red wine with cinnamon to 234–240°F (112–114°C), or perform a sugar test, see p. 14.
3. Sift the syrup over the cherries in a flaming pan and let it come to a boil. Add the currant jelly.
4. Dissolve the cornstarch in some of the liquor and whip with a whisk into a thickener. Bring everything to a boil.
5. Carry the pan to the dinner table; pour the liquor on top and set on fire.

Clafoutis aux Cerises

Photographer Klas Andersson and his wife have a favorite dessert—cherry clafoutis. It is usually made during the summer months with especially ripe black cherries. During wintertime you can make a version with pears instead, which is just as good, as long as you get a hold of some truly ripe Williams pears and a few drops of Eau de vie de poires Williams from Alsace.

Serve it warm with lightly whipped, lightly sweetened cream or freshly made vanilla ice cream. *Photo on p. 56.*

6–8 servings

1 round pan, 9 ½ inches (24 cm) in diameter
3 tbsp (50 g) butter for the pan

1 ⅓ lbs (600 g) truly ripe, pitted black cherries
1 vanilla bean, preferably Bourbon
¾ cup (150 g/1 ½ dl) whole milk
¾ cup (150 g/1 ½ dl) heavy whipping cream
1 ½ cup (180 g) muscovado sugar, yellow
3 eggs (150 g)
3 egg yolks (60 g)
1 ½ tbsp (2 cl) Kirschwasser or cognac

Cinnamon Sugar

3 tbsp granulated sugar
½ tsp ground cinnamon

1 ½ cups (3 dl) heavy whipping cream
1 ½ tbsp (25 g) granulated sugar

1. Set the oven to 390°F (200°C).
2. Butter the pan, by spreading the softened butter with a brush.
3. Rinse the cherries and remove the stems. Remove the pits with the help of a cherry/olive pitter or a small knife. Put the cherries in the pan.
4. Cut the vanilla bean down the middle and scrape out the seeds into a small saucepan.
5. Add milk, whipping cream, sugar, eggs, and yolks. Warm while stirring to 185°F (85°C). Flavor with the alcohol (Kirschwasser is the absolute best for this).
6. Pour the cream over the cherries and bake for 18–20 minutes, until it is golden brown.
7. Sprinkle the cinnamon sugar on top and whisk the cream with the sugar until it forms soft peaks. Serve right away while the cream is still warm.

Schwarzwälder Kirschtorte

This German tart is amazingly tasty. In English it is usually referred to as *Black Forest Cake* and it was extremely popular when I worked at sea and we offered this on the menu. The taste of cherries should be overpowering. And at the same time, it should taste like chocolate and Kirschwasser. Don't prepare this tart with a different alcohol; you won't achieve the same taste with any other liqueur.

Makes about 15 servings.

1 springform, about 10 inches (26 cm) in diameter
2 tbsp (25 g) butter, for preparing the pan

Tart Crust – Wienerchokladanslag

2 tbsp (30 g) butter
5 eggs (250 g)
2 egg yolks (50 g)
1 ¾ cups (200 g) sugar
1 cup (100 g) all-purpose flour
²/₃ cup (75 g) cornstarch
4 tbsp (25 g) cocoa powder, preferably Valrhona

Cherry Compote

¾ cup (150 g/1 ½ dl) cherry cordial
3 tbsp (15 g) cornstarch
1 small piece of cinnamon stick
½ lb (250 g) sour cherries, from a jar or frozen are fine

Kirschwasser Syrup for Soaking the Crusts

½ cup (65 g) powdered sugar
¼ cup (50 g/½ dl) water
⅓ cup (85 g/85 ml) Kirschwasser

Chocolate Cream

1 ¼ cup (250 g/2 ½ dl) heavy whipping cream
3 ½ oz (100 g) dark chocolate, Valrhona Grand Cru Guanaja 70%
2 tbsp (30 g/3cl) whole milk

Cream and Kirschwasser Filling

1 ¼ cup (250 g/2 ½ dl) heavy whipping cream
1 tbsp (15 g) sugar
1 tbsp (15 g/15 ml) Kirschwasser
¼ tbsp gelatin (1 sheet)

For Decoration

7 oz (200 g) milk chocolate, preferably Valrhona Jivara Lactee 40%
1 ½ cup (300 g/3 dl) heavy whipping cream
1 ½ tbsp (20 g) sugar
16 jarred cherries in syrup or Kirschwasser
3 tbsp (20 g) powdered sugar

DAY 1

Tart Crust—Wienerchokladanslag

1. Set the oven to 390°F (200°C).
2. Set a saucepan with water on the stove and let it come to a boil.
3. Melt the butter and set it aside. Sift flour, cornstarch, and cocoa together.
4. Set a 10 inch (26 cm) cake ring on a piece of parchment paper, or use a springform pan prepared with 2 tbsp of softened butter.
5. Whisk eggs, yolks, and sugar together in a large metal bowl and warm the mixture over the boiling water, stirring constantly, until it reaches 113–122°F (45–50°C).
6. Remove the bowl from the water bath and whisk the mass with an electric beater, till it is light and airy, and you see smatterings in the foam.
7. Sift the flour mixture and cocoa powder over the egg foam and gently fold it in with a silicone spatula. It should be a light and airy mass.
8. Empty the mass into the springform and spread the batter to the edges so that the bottom becomes completely even.
9. Bake for 25 minutes or until the batter feels firm on the outside when you touch it with your hand. Use a toothpick to check that it is baked all the way through.
10. Take the springform out of the oven and sprinkle 1 tbsp of granulated sugar on top. Turn the tart bottom out on a piece of parchment paper and let it cool.

Cover with plastic wrap and let it sit in the fridge overnight.

Compote

1. Mix the fruit cordial and cornstarch with a whisk in a small saucepan. Add the cinnamon stick and let it come to a boil while stirring.
2. Add the cherries and let it come to a boil once more. Switch to a wooden ladle to stir with.
3. Transfer the mixture to a bowl and remove the cinnamon stick so that the cinnamon taste doesn't become too overwhelming.
4. Cover with plastic wrap and let it cool. Store in the fridge overnight.

DAY 2

1. Cut the tart bottom into three equally thick layers with a serrated knife.
2. Place a circle-shaped piece of parchment paper at the bottom of the springform.
3. Spread a layer of compote over one layer of the crust and carefully place it in the springform with the compote facing up.
4. Place the next layer on top and press down. Brush half of the Kirschwasser syrup over the layers.

Chocolate Cream

1. Lightly whip the cream. Melt the finely chopped dark chocolate in the microwave in a small bowl.
2. Stir now and then, and check the temperature. It should be about 140°F (60°C). Add the milk and whisk together into a smooth cream. Place it back in the microwave and heat it up once more. The temperature should be 130°F (55°C). Carefully fold the chocolate into the lightly whipped cream with a silicone spatula.
3. Spread the chocolate cream evenly on top of the tart bottom with a spatula.

Fill with Cream and Kirschwasser

1. Dissolve the gelatin in water, following the directions on the package (or soak the gelatin sheet in cold water for at least 10 minutes).
2. Whip the sugar and cream into a light foam.
3. Remove the gelatin sheet and melt it in a bowl in the microwave at a temperature of 113–122°F (45–50°C), or melt it in a small saucepan on the stove.
4. Stir in the alcohol with the help of a silicone spatula.
5. Fold into a third of the cream and stir into a smooth batter.
6. Carefully fold in the rest of the cream.
7. Transfer the cream into the springform and spread evenly with a spatula.
8. Add the third crust layer on top and press it down evenly with the help of a baking sheet or a plate.
9. Brush the layers with the rest of the Kirschwasser syrup.
10. Cover with plastic wrap and freeze for at least 3 hours or overnight.

For Decorating

1. Finely chop ⅓ of the chocolate.
2. Place the rest of the chocolate in a bowl and melt it in the microwave. Make sure that the temperature does not go above 122°F (50°C). Warm a clean baking sheet to 113–122°F (45–50°C) and spread a layer of the chocolate evenly onto the baking sheet with the help of a spatula.
3. Let the baking sheet chill in the fridge for 30 minutes. Then, take the sheet out and let it rest at room temperature for 10 minutes.
4. Scrape shavings of the chocolate with the help of a large knife and place them on a plate in the fridge so that they harden.
5. Whip the sugar and cream to soft peaks.
6. With the help of a knife, unstick the cake from the springform.
7. Add ⅔ of the cream on top of the tart and spread it out as evenly as possible.
8. Lift the tart with your hand placed underneath, and sprinkle the edges with the finely chopped chocolate.
9. Put the rest of the cream into a pastry bag. Squeeze out decorative rounds, as pictured, around the edge of the tart. Decorate with the drained and dry cherries, and lastly sift some powdered sugar on top using a little strainer.

Let the tart thaw for 3 hours in the fridge and the last 30 minutes at room temperature. *See photo p. 57.*

Clafoutis aux Cerises. In the jars, raspberry jam.

Schwarzwälder Kirschtorte (Black Forest Cake).

Raspberries

Rubus idaeus

Wild raspberries may be found in all parts of Sweden. Thinking back to our childhoods, we might remember the small raspberry worms found in wild raspberries. The small worms are harmless, but not very appetizing. In the carefully monitored world of cultivated raspberries, these worms are rare. Raspberries ripen in July and the beginning of August. The practice of cultivating raspberries is actually quite new. Raspberries were not cultivated on a large scale until the late 1800s, first in the United States and later in Western Europe.

There are many different varieties of cultivated raspberries, large and small, dark and light, that have varying shapes. The wild raspberry has the most intense aroma. Yellow raspberries (*Rubus idaceus f. chlorocarpa*) are unfortunately very rare. But you might find them in certain older gardens. The raspberry belongs to the family Rubus, along with Arctic raspberries, blackberries, and cloudberries. Sometimes these varieties are combined and create new hybrids.

The raspberry is, after the arctic raspberry, the berry with the richest aroma. And since raspberries are so readily available, it is easy to prepare generous amount of jams, juices, and jellies, not to mention all kinds of good desserts, ice creams, sorbets, tarts, and pastries. In 2004, we started making raspberry marmalade with dark chocolate at Olof Viktors in Glemminge. The marmalade was instantly popular.

As long as you make sure that the berries are not overly ripe, you will end up with beautiful jams and marmalades. Adding 25 percent red currants or unripe gooseberries will make a fresh and clear raspberry jelly. You may use frozen raspberries for all of these recipes.

When I glance through my recipe book, which I started working on at the age of fifteen, I find the following note: Raspberry jam is the most useful jam for a pastry chef.

Raspberry Jam

17 lbs (8,000 g) sugar
16 cups (4,000 g) water
Boiled to 280°F (139°C)
22 lbs (10,000 g) raspberries
1 ¼ cup (300 g) lemon juice

Empty the boiling syrup into a pot with the previously boiled berries and lemon juice. Boil everything to 224°F (107°C), or perform a strong thread test. Back then, we would boil enough jam to last us an entire year.

Added Flavor

Herbs: basil, pineapple sage, fruit sage, lemon verbena, and lemongrass.
Citrus fruits: lemon, lime, and orange.
Wine and spirits: sweet dessert wine, red wine, rum, cognac, and Armagnac.
Berries and fruits: all red berries, blackberries, melon, pears, bananas, peaches, nectarines and apricots.

Classic Raspberry Jam

Rinse but do not soak the raspberries, as they lose much of their juice if you do.

2 lbs (1,000 g) raspberries
1 ¾ lbs (800 g) sugar
Juice of 1 lemon

DAY 1

Mix the raspberries with the sugar and lemon juice. Cover with plastic wrap and let it sit in the fridge overnight.

DAY 2

1. Pour the berries into a pot and bring to a boil.
2. Keep stirring while boiling and brush the inside of the pot with a brush dipped in cold water to prevent sugar crystals from forming. Remove the foam with a spoon to make sure that the jam ends up clear.
3. Boil to 222–224°F (106–107°C). The jam should then be wrinkly on the surface and the berries should look transparent, which is a sign that the jam is almost ready, or you may do a jam test on a cold plate, see p. 20.
4. Pour the jam directly into sterilized jars and immediately screw on the lids. Turn the jars upside down a couple of times.

Makes about 3 ⅓ lbs (1,500 g) jam.

Varieties

You may use the recipe above as a base for the following varieties:

- Raspberry jam with half gooseberries is very good. Preferably with some added cinnamon and, if you wish, some grated ginger (2 tbsp [20 g]).
- Raspberry jam with half red currants and with some pineapple sage added at the end of the boiling time.
- Raspberry jam with half bananas and a cinnamon stick is just delicious.
- Raspberry jam with blanched, finely chopped basil and some lemon zest is a fresh variation.
- Raspberry jam with half apricots (without pits) with shelled almonds and vanilla.
- Raspberry jam with a quarter black currants gives a more fresh and refined flavor.
- Also see Muskmelon Jam with Raspberries, p.136.

Seedless Raspberry Marmalade

A marmalade rich in aroma and perfect for those who don't enjoy raspberry seeds. This marmalade is great as a filling for doughnuts, cakes, tarts, and other pastries.

2 ¾ lbs (1,250 g) raspberries
2 ¼ lbs (1,000 g) sugar
Juice of 1 lemon

1. Blend the raspberries in a mixer and run through a strainer.
2. Bring the purée, sugar, and lemon juice to a boil in a pot while constantly stirring (the mixture burns easily when the jam is strained).

3. Boil to 220°F (105°C). Continually brush the inside of the pot with a brush dipped in cold water to avoid sugar crystals forming. Remove all foam with the help of a spoon. Perform a jam test on a cold plate, see p. 20.
4. Pour directly into sterilized jars and screw on the lids right away. Turn the jars upside down a couple of times.

Makes about 3 ⅓ lbs (1,500 g) marmalade.

Raspberry Jelly

This is incredibly flavorful and fresh-tasting. Keep in mind that the raspberries should not be overly ripe.

1 ⅓ lbs (750 g) raspberries
½ lb (250 g) red currants or unripe gooseberries
½ vanilla bean· preferably Tahiti
Juice of 1 lemon
1 cup (250 g/2 ½ dl) water
Amount of sugar equal to the weight of the strained juice from step 4

1. Put raspberries, red currants or gooseberries, lemon juice, and water in a pot with the sliced and scraped vanilla bean.
2. Bring everything to a boil and let it simmer under a lid for 15 minutes.
3. Pour into a fine strainer and squeeze all of the juice out by pressing with the back of a spoon. Empty the mass into a strainer lined with cheesecloth and let it drain on its own for 60 minutes.
4. Weigh the drained juice and add an equal weight in sugar.
5. Let it come to a boil while carefully removing foam, and brush the inside of the pot with a brush dipped in cold water to avoid sugar crystals in the jelly.
6. Perform a jam test on a cold plate at 220°F (105°C). If the jelly is not stiff, continue boiling to 222–224°F (106–107°C).
7. Pour directly into sterilized jars and screw on the lids right away. Turn the jars upside down a couple of times.

Makes about 2 lbs (1,000 g) jelly.

Classic raspberry jam, raspberry and melon jam, and raspberry jelly.

Classic Raspberry Sauce

During the sixties, when I first started working in restaurants, raspberry sauce was the basic sauce for many desserts. One of our tastiest desserts was called *Pêche à la Savoy*, which consisted of an almond-macaroon pastry with champagne sorbet on top and one whole poached white peach in vanilla syrup. The whole dessert was covered with raspberry sauce and garnished with a veil of white cotton candy and crushed candied violets.

Peach Melba is one of the world's most famous desserts. It was first created by the king of chefs, Auguste Escoffier at the Savoy Hotel in London. He made it for the opera singer Nellie Melba. The dessert consists of a vanilla-poached peach on a bed of vanilla ice cream, covered with raspberry sauce.

1 lb (500 g) raspberries
1 ⅓ cups (150 g) powdered sugar
Juice of ½ lemon
6 tbsp (150 g) currant jelly, see p. 79
4 tbsp (6 cl) Kirschwasser

1. Blend together the raspberries, powdered sugar, and lemon juice, and run through a strainer.
2. Strain the currant jelly, and combine it with the raspberry mixture and the Kirschwasser to form a thick sauce.

Tip!
The raspberry sauce should cover the peach without dripping off too much.

Raspberry Cordial
See strawberry cordial p. 74

Raspberry Sorbet

During the sixties, we at the Hotel Savoy in Malmö would deliver a unique raspberry sorbet to the historic fortress Falsterbohus in Falsterbo, Sweden. The waiters would perfume the sorbet with framboise eau de vie before serving.

6–8 servings

1 ⅓ lbs (600 g) raspberries
1 ¾ cups (200 g) powdered sugar
Juice of ⅓ lemon
1 cup (250 g/2 ½ dl) red wine Côtes-du-Rhône, preferably from the wine house Jaboulet
⅔ cup (150 g/1 ½ dl) water

1. Blend the raspberries, powdered sugar, and lemon juice into a purée. Run through a strainer and add the water and wine.
2. Freeze the sorbet in an ice-cream maker until it feels firm. If you don't have an ice-cream maker, place the blend in the freezer and stir now and then till it looks firm.
3. A sorbet should always be served newly frozen, and if it is to be served as an intermediate course, remember to serve it in a frozen glass before you add the spirits.

Tip!
Replace half of the raspberries with black currants and add some black currant liqueur, crème de cassis, instead of the wine.

Blackberries

Blackberries are relatives of raspberries and part of the Rubus family. There are many different blackberry varieties in existence; the most common are sweet blackberries (Rubus plicatus), which grow on large and thorny shrubs. The berries have to be picked at the right time, because if they are not completely ripe they feel hard and have a sour taste. If they are overly ripe, on the other hand, they feel watery. Swedish blackberries ripen from the end of August to late September. Blackberries grow wild in both Europe and North America. Certain blackberries without thorns are cultivated in gardens. Crosses between blackberries and other berries do exist. The boysenberry, for instance, is a cross between the raspberry and the blackberry. The berries taste great fresh if they are ripe; if not, they might feel too hard.

Blackberries are very suitable for jam, marmalade, and jelly, as well as compote, sorbet, ice cream, and parfait. Blackberry biscuit with punch cream is a yummy traditional dessert that I sometimes make. It consists of a thin shortcrust with high edges, which after baking is filled with vanilla cream and covered with seedless blackberry compote. Bring the juice to a boil and add ¼ tbsp (1 sheet) of gelatin per ½ cup (1 dl) of jelly. Cool the jelly and brush over the dessert. It makes a great finish after crayfish or fried duck with browned chanterelles.

Added Flavor

Spices: vanilla, cinnamon, red chili.
Herbs: orange thyme; orange, lemon, and cinnamon basil; rosemary.
Sugar: preferably light muscovado sugar
Wine and spirits: red wine, cognac, Armagnac, and rum.

Blackberry Jam

This tasty and classic jam is just as good with your bowl of breakfast cereal as with pancakes or toast.

2 lbs (1,000 g) blackberries
1 ¾ lbs (800 g) sugar
1 ¼ cups (300 g/ 1 ½ dl) water
Juice of 1 lemon

1. Squeeze the lemon.
2. Rinse the berries carefully and let the water drain off.
3. Pour sugar, water, and lemon juice into a pot and boil. Brush the inside of the pot with a brush dipped in cold water to prevent sugar crystals from forming the finished jam.
4. Boil to 234–240°F (112–114°C), or perform a sugar test by hand; see Boiling Sugar, p. 14.

5. Add the berries and boil slowly. Stir now and then, remove any foam that might form with a spoon, and brush the inside of the pot with cold water.
6. Boil to 222–224°F (106–107°C), or do a jam test on a cold plate, see p. 20.
7. Pour directly into sterilized jars and screw on the lids right away. Turn the jars upside down a couple of times.

Makes about 3 ⅓ lbs (1,500 g) jam.

Blackberry Jam with Dark Chocolate

Follow the recipe above for Blackberry Jam.
Add 12 oz (350 g) finely chopped Valrhona Grand Cru Manjari or Marabou dark chocolate at the end of the boiling time, and stir till it has melted completely.

Blackberry Marmalade with Apple and Candied Chestnuts

Begin by making the half-candied chestnuts, so called demi-confits. You may buy the chestnuts in the shell and prepare them yourself. You may also buy them shelled and vacuum-packed, or frozen.

For Candied Chestnuts

5 cups (650 g) chestnuts
(1 lb/500 g net weight)
2 cups (500 g/5 dl) water
1 lb (500 g) sugar
1 ½ lbs (650 g) green apples
(1 lb/500 g net weight)
2 cups (500 g/5 dl) water
Juice of 1 lemon
1 ¾ lbs (800 g) sugar
1 lb (500 g) blackberries

DAY 1
Preparing Half-Candied Chestnuts

1. Cut the tips of the chestnuts off with a knife and place them in a pan with water. Set in the oven, at 390°F (200°C), for about 30 minutes.
2. Poke the nuts with a knife to make sure that they are soft.
3. Remove them from the oven and let them cool for a little bit. Remove the outer hard shell, as well as the softer shell, carefully with a small knife. Make sure not to break the chestnuts.
   (Alternatively you can use frozen or vacuum-packed shelled chestnuts)
4. Bring the water to a boil with 125 g / 4,5 oz sugar and add the chestnuts. Let everything stew for 15 minutes.
5. Add an additional ½ cup (125 g) of sugar and let the chestnuts stew for another 25 minutes. Repeat this procedure two more times. Pour the chestnuts directly into a sterilized jar and screw on the lid immediately.
6. Let the jar chill in the fridge overnight.

Continued on p. 64

DAY 2

1. Empty the chestnuts into a strainer so that the syrup is drained.
2. Rinse, peel, and core the apples. Cut them into small wedges.
3. Bring the water and lemon juice to a boil in a pot and add the apple wedges. Cover with a lid and let the apples boil on low heat for 20–30 minutes, until they start to come apart.
4. Blend into a purée by using a hand mixer directly in the pot.
5. Add the sugar and blackberries. Boil to 220°F (105°C) while constantly stirring. Remove foam with a spoon. Brush the inside of the pot now and then with a brush dipped in cold water, in order to prevent sugar crystals from forming.
6. Add the chestnuts to the pot and boil to 220–222°F (105–106°C), or perform a jam test on a cold plate.
7. Pour directly into sterilized jars and screw on the lids right away. Turn the jars upside down a couple of times.

Makes about 4 ¾ lbs (2,200 g) marmalade.

Seedless Blackberry Marmalade

A lot of people dislike blackberry seeds; in that case, this marmalade is the perfect solution. This is great as a filling for pastries and tarts, as well as for other desserts.

3 ⅓ lbs (1,500 g) blackberries
(2 lbs/1,000 g net weight)
1 ¾ lbs (800 g) sugar
Juice of 1 lemon

1. Purée the berries in a food processor and run them through a strainer.
2. Pour the purée into a pot with sugar and lemon juice.
3. Boil while carefully stirring and remove foam from the surface with a spoon so that the marmalade ends up clear. Brush the inside of the pot with a brush dipped in cold water to prevent sugar crystals from forming.
4. Boil to 220°F (105°C), or perform a jam test, see p. 20.
5. Pour directly into sterilized jars and immediately screw on the lids. Turn upside down a couple of times.

Makes about 3 ⅓ lbs (1,500 g) marmalade.

Blackberry Jelly

We once served this jelly with game in chocolate sauce for a special performance with Carina and Peter Nordin at the Restaurant named Prinsen (The Prince) in Stockholm. If you wish to use this jelly for cheese or as a side for roast, I recommend adding some rose pepper in the jars.

This recipe follows method 1, see p. 20. You may also follow method 2 when you prepare blackberry jelly; it is really a matter of preference.

2 lbs (1,000 g) blackberries, not too ripe
1 cup (250 g/2 ½ dl) water
Juice of 1 lemon
The equal amount of sugar as drained juice

1. Pour the rinsed and drained blackberries into a pot with water and lemon juice. Let it boil under a lid for 15 minutes.
2. Pour through a strainer and squeeze all of the juice out with the help of the back of a spoon.
3. Next, pour the fruit mass into a strainer lined with cheesecloth and let it drain on its own for about 1 hour or until the mass is completely dry.
4. Weigh the juice. Add the same amount of sugar as the juice weighs.
5. Pour the mixture into a pot and boil while constantly removing foam with a spoon. Brush the inside of the pot with a brush dipped in cold water to prevent sugar crystals from forming.
6. Boil to 220–222°F (105–106°C), or perform a jelly test on a cold plate, see p. 20.
7. Pour directly into sterilized jars and screw on the lids right away. Turn the jars upside down a couple of times.

Makes about 2 lbs (1,000 g) jelly.

Blackberry Compote

This is great for the blackberry biscuit.

2 lbs (1,000 g) blackberries, ripe and large
1 cup (325 g) sugar
2 cups (500 g/5 dl) water
Juice of 1 lemon

1. Wash and rinse the berries.
2. Boil sugar, water, and lemon juice in a pot. Continually brush the inside of the pot with a brush dipped in cold water to prevent sugar crystals from forming. Boil to 234–240°F (112–114°C), or perform a sugar test, see p. 14.
3. Add the berries and bring it all to a boil. Carefully remove all of the foam.
4. Pour directly into sterilized jars and immediately screw on the lids. If you wish to preserve the berries so as to prolong their shelf life, see Preservation on p. 29.

Blackberry Cordial

Make blackberry cordial by following the recipe for strawberry cordial on p. 74. Replace the strawberries with blackberries.

Cloudberries

Rubus chamaemorus

The gold from the swamps of Norrland! The berries ripen at the end of July and beginning of August. The fruits, similar in their shape to raspberries, are first red and later turn yellow when they are fully ripe. They are very rich in vitamin C. Cloudberries grow in marshes and swamps in cool regions of the northern hemisphere, except for Iceland. In Sweden, they mostly grow in the northern areas, but they do occur in the southern regions as well.

Fried Camembert with cloudberry jam has become a Swedish classic, with fried parsley as a welcome side. Freshly cooked waffles or pancakes with cloudberry jam and whipped cream with some warm punch is a delicious dessert after some split-pea soup. While I worked at the Savoy, Fritiof Nilsson Piraten ("the Pirate") and Sten Broman were often seen gulping down sweet treats like these.

Cloudberry parfait and cloudberry soufflé are classically flavorful desserts that people used to enjoy quite often, and they're definitely worth a renaissance. Jam and cheese go great together, for instance, Gorgonzola with cloudberry jam.

Cloudberry Jam

2 lbs (1,000 g) cloudberries
1 ¾ lbs (800 g) sugar
Juice of 1 lemon

DAY 1

1. Rinse the cloudberries carefully.
2. Combine the berries with the sugar and lemon juice in a pot and bring it all to a boil while stirring.
3. Pour into a bowl and let it cool. Cover with plastic and let it sit in the fridge overnight.

DAY 2

1. Pour the fruit mass into a strainer and let the syrup drain off.
2. Boil the syrup in a pot. Brush the inside of the pot with a brush dipped in water to prevent sugar crystals from forming in the jam. Boil to 234–240°F (112–114°C), or do a sugar test, see Boiling Sugar, p. 14.
3. Add the berries to the syrup and boil while stirring. Continue to brush the inside of the pot.
4. Remove the foam so the jam becomes beautifully clear.
5. Boil to 220–222°F (105–106°C), or perform a jam test on a cold plate, see p. 20.
6. Pour the jam directly into sterilized jars, and fill them all the way up to the rim. Screw on the lids right away and turn the jars upside down a couple of times.

Makes about 3 ⅓ lbs (1,500 g) jam.

Seedless Cloudberry Jam

Many find that the cloudberry seeds disturb the taste and prefer a seedless cloudberry jam. Keep in mind that seedless jams burn very easily, so keep stirring along the bottom of the pot at all times. Use a long ladle: even though the jam is strained, it still splashes.

2 ¾ lbs (1,250 g) cloudberries
1 ¾ lbs (800 g) sugar
Juice of 1 lemon

1. Rinse the cloudberries carefully.
2. Mix all of the ingredients together in a food processor; keep the mixer going until the sugar is melted.
3. Pass the mixture through a strainer and pour into a pot.
4. Boil while constantly stirring so that the jam doesn't burn. Brush the inside of the pot with a brush dipped in cold water to prevent sugar crystals from forming. Occasionally remove foam with a spoon.
5. Boil to 220°F (105°C), or perform a jam test on a cold plate, see p. 20.
6. Pour directly into sterilized jars, all the way up to the rim. Immediately screw on the lids and turn the jars upside down a couple of times.

Makes about 3 ⅓ lbs (1,500 g) jam.

Pickled Pine Shoots and Cloudberry Jam.

Cloudberry Jelly

If the cloudberries seem too ripe, you can add 1 ½ cups (350 g) apple juice or ½ lb (250 g) apple jelly to help the jelly stiffen properly, or you may also add ½ lb (250 g) green apples while boiling. Cloudberry jelly tastes good with juniper-marinated reindeer with cream sautéed apples, browned morels, and almond potatoes turned in butter. It is also great with Norwegian brown cheese and flatbread.

2 lbs (1,000 g) cloudberries
1 cup (250 g/2 ½ dl) water
Juice of 1 lemon
As much sugar as the weight of the drained juice

1. Carefully rinse the cloudberries and add them to a pot with water and lemon juice. Bring it to a boil and let it simmer under a lid for 30 minutes on low heat.
2. Drain the juice and let the fruit continue to drain on its own for an hour or until the fruit mass feels dry.
3. Weigh the drained juice and add an equal amount of sugar.
4. Pour the sugar, fruit, and juice into a pot and boil while carefully removing the foam. Brush the inside of the pot with a brush dipped in cold water in order to prevent sugar crystals from forming in the jelly.
5. Boil to 220°F (105°C), or do a jelly test on a cold plate, see p. 20.
6. Pour directly into sterilized jars and immediately screw on the lids. Turn the jars upside down a few times.

Makes about 2 lbs (1,000 g) jelly.

Cloudberry Jelly with Roquefort Cheese and Roasted Walnuts

This delicious jelly with cheese is a nice dish served with some bread and wine. If you can't get a hold of cloudberries, you may use apples or lingonberries instead.

1 batch of cloudberry jelly (apple jelly or lingonberry jelly)
9 oz (250 g) Roquefort cheese
3 ½ oz (100 g) French walnuts
2 tbsp (15 g) powdered sugar

1. Cut the cheese into pieces the size of sugar cubes and freeze them for 1 hour.
2. Roast the walnuts with the powdered sugar in a frying pan, till they are caramelized. Transfer onto a piece of parchment paper and let cool.
3. Fill sterilized jars halfway with the fresh cloudberry jelly. Add a generous half of the cheese and walnuts.
4. Place in the freezer for 5 minutes. Distribute the remaining cheese and walnuts between the jars and cover with the rest of the jelly. Screw on the lids and turn the jars upside down a couple of times.

Pickled Pine Shoots

Very different, and great for the game dinners of the fall.

1 lb (500 g) pine shoots
1 batch of syrup, see Preserved Green Tomatoes p.182

1. Rinse and dry the pine shoots.
2. Bring 4 cups (1 liter) of water to a boil and blanch the pine shoots for 5 minutes. Place them under cold running water right away.
3. Dry the pine shoots on a kitchen towel and put them in small jars so that the jars are half full.
4. Boil the molasses and pour over the shoots.
5. Screw the lids on right away and turn the jars upside down a couple of times.
6. You may sterilize the jars as well, if you wish; see sterilizing p. 29.

Store in the fridge. *Photo on p. 67.*

Arctic Raspberries

Rubus arcticus

The arctic raspberry is the best and finest of the Nordic berries. The bush grows about 6 inches (15 cm) high with large red blossoms in June and dark-red raspberry-like fruits. They mostly grow wild along the Northern coast of Sweden.

The arctic raspberry makes great jam and jelly. When making jam or jelly, follow the same recipe for Seedless Cloudberry Jam and Cloudberry Jelly, p. 67-68.

Stirred Arctic Raspberry Purée

This purée is suitable for parfait, ice cream, mousse, and soufflé. This stirred preserve is just as good with waffles and pancakes as well. The aroma is intensified when you stir the berries while they are raw.

3 lbs (1,350 g) arctic raspberries
Juice of 1 lemon
¼ cup (5 cl) cognac
2 lbs (1,000 g) sugar

1. Rinse and dry the berries. Stir the berries for about 5 minutes until they are completely liquid.
2. Press through a strainer and add the lemon juice, liqueur, and sugar.
3. Stir everything for 60 minutes with an electric mixer until the purée (or jam) sticks together.
4. Pour directly into sterilized jars and screw on the lids right away. Turn the jars upside down a couple of times.

Makes 4 ½ lbs (2,000 g) purée.

Wild Strawberries

Fragaria vesca

Right after the midsummer solstice, the first wild strawberries appear in fields and along roads. Picking wild strawberries and threading them on pieces of grass is a common childhood activity. Less common are green strawberries (*Fragaria viridis*), which are harder to detach from their stems. Another variety is the musk strawberry, where both the plant and the berry are larger.

The wild strawberries have a fantastic aroma. They taste wonderful with ice cream and whipped cream, as a strawberry parfait or sorbet, and in tarts. If you wish to make jam with wild strawberries, you may follow the recipe for Classic Raspberry Jam on p. 59.

Stirred Wild Strawberry Purée

This so-called "cold preservation" gives a fantastic wild strawberry purée, which has a strong aroma. It is great as a base for ice cream, parfait, sorbet, or mousse.

2 lbs (1,000 g) wild strawberries
Juice of 1 lemon
2 lbs (1,000 g) sugar

1. Rinse the wild berries.
2. Purée them in a mixer and press them through a fine strainer.
3. Add the lemon juice and the sugar. Stir with an electric mixer for 60 minutes.
4. Pour directly into sterilized jars and screw on the lids right away. Store in the fridge.

Makes about 4 ½ lbs (2,000 g) purée. *Photo to the right.*

Wild Strawberry Parfait

This recipe may also be used with raspberries, strawberries, blackberries, cloudberries, or blueberries.

8 servings

16 oz (450 g) stirred wild strawberry purée, see above
About 5 egg whites (150 g)
¾ tbsp (10 g) lemon juice
¼ cup (50 g) sugar
2 cups (400 g) heavy whipping cream, whipped

1. First, prepare a stirred wild strawberry purée.
2. Bring the water to a boil.
3. Whisk the egg whites, lemon juice, and sugar in a clean metal bowl. Place the bowl in the water and whisk while it is in the water bath. Whisk till the temperature reaches 130–140°F (55–60°C).
4. Remove from the stove and continue to whisk the mixture. Whisk till it has completely cooled.
5. Fold in the purée and then the whipped cream. Pour into a baking pan and freeze.
6. When serving, release the parfait from the pan by dipping the pan in lukewarm water. Turn out onto a serving plate and decorate with wild strawberries.

Strawberries

Fragaria ananassa

The strawberry was first created in Europe during the 1700s as a combination of other berries. Since then the strawberry has spread all over the world. Cultivators are constantly working to create new and better varieties. Many may not know that the strawberry has more vitamin C than the orange and high amounts of fiber. You can find Swedish strawberries during the summer months; the rest of the year strawberries are imported. It is always possible to buy fresh strawberries. Consider eating fresh strawberries at room temperature. That is when the aroma is the strongest.

Strawberries are an absolute must for midsummer. Later on, the berries give us late summer moments as jam in our desserts or as cordial in the winter. Stirred strawberry cordial during the summer months tastes exquisite. Strawberries are also extremely suitable for sorbet, ice cream, and parfait. The variety Senga Sengana is especially well-suited for jam, ice cream, sorbet, and mousse, since the berries have a rich taste and aroma. Other good varieties are Elsanta, Pajaro, Gariguette, and Selva.

Keep in mind that you should always use fresh strawberries. If they are overly ripe, the jam may end up gluey. If you want to achieve a strawberry jam with a more jelly-like texture, you can replace a quarter to a half of the fruit with red currants, as they have higher pectin content, or add ½ to ¾ lb (250 g–300 g) currant jelly at the end of the boiling time.

Keep in mind:
Never rinse the strawberries after you've removed the leafy top (calyx); instead rinse first and then remove the calyx, so that none of the strawberry juice is lost.

Added Flavor

Spices: You need to be careful here. Vanilla and cinnamon work fine, as well as grated fresh ginger, but not dried.
Herbs: citrus herbs, including citrus verbena and lemongrass, basil, pineapple sage, and fruit sage.
Wine and spirits: sweet dessert wine and red wine, rum, and cognac.

Strawberry Jam

This flavorful, child-friendly jam tastes great with crêpes, pancakes, and waffles. A true Swiss or Frenchman will generously spread strawberry jam on his breakfast toast every morning. If you want to give the jam a more grown-up taste, you may replace half of the strawberries with currants; you will then end up with a fresher taste.

2 ½ lbs (1,150 g) ripe strawberries
(2 lbs [1,000 g] net weight)
Juice of 1 lemon
1 ¾ lbs (800 g) sugar

DAY 1

Rinse and hull the berries. Add the lemon juice and sugar. Mix well. Cover the mixture with plastic wrap and let it marinate at room temperature for 24 hours.

DAY 2

1. Empty the mixture into a pot and bring it to a boil while constantly removing foam. Brush the inside of the pot with a brush dipped in cold water to prevent sugar crystals from forming. Boil until the strawberries start looking transparent and the jam is turning wrinkly on the surface and forming jelly.
2. A strawberry jam with this amount of sugar, unless the berries are too ripe, will usually be ready at 222–224°F (106–107°C), or perform a jam test on a cold plate, see p. 20.
3. Pour directly into sterilized jars and immediately screw on the lids. Turn the jars upside down a couple of times.

Makes about 3 ⅓ lbs (1,500 g) jam.

Strawberry Jam with Candied Lemon Zest and Lemon Thyme.
Follow the instructions for Strawberry Jam, above. At the end of the boiling time, add the zest of two lemons, which have been quick-preserved the day before. See Quick-Preserved Citrus Peels, p. 107. Blanch ⅓ oz (10 g) of lemon thyme in boiling water, and then cool under cold running water. Finely chop and add to the jam at the end of the boiling time.

Strawberry Jam with Vanilla
Follow the instructions for Strawberry Jam above. Add vanilla bean and seeds, preferably Tahiti or Bourbon, during boiling. This creates a round and child-friendly taste. If you add ½ cup (100 g/1 dl) cognac instead, the jam achieves a more grown-up taste.

Strawberry Jam with Preserved Gooseberries

A beautiful and tasty jam.

1 batch of Strawberry Jam, see p. 70
1 lb (500 g) gooseberries, green and unripe
½ lb (250 g) sugar
¾ cup (200 g/2 dl) water

1. Rinse the gooseberries and place them in a bowl.
2. Bring sugar and water to a boil and pour it over the berries.
3. Cover with plastic wrap and let sit overnight.
4. Let the berries drain in a strainer.
5. Stir the drained berries in with the already boiled strawberry jam. Bring everything to a boil.
6. Pour directly into sterilized jars and screw on the lids right away. Turn the jars upside down a couple of times.

Makes about 4 ½ lbs (2,000 g) jam.

Seedless Strawberry Jam

This jam is great as a filling for tarts, as a dessert garnish, and for cookies. Seedless strawberry jam may also be boiled and used to glaze strawberries on strawberry tarts or pies.

Use the same quantities as Strawberry Jam, p.70, except purée the strawberries, sugar, and lemon before marinating. Boil to 220°F (105°C).

Strawberry Jam with Whole Strawberries

This is both beautiful and flavorful while also showing your friends that you can make your own jam. The French call this kind of jam Confiture demi-confit (half-preserve).

1 batch Strawberry Jam, see p. 70

Half-Candied Strawberries
2 ½ lbs (1,150 g) small, ripe strawberries
4 cups (1,000 g/1 liter) water
2 lbs (1,000 g) sugar
Juice of 1 lemon

DAY 1
Prepare the strawberries for the Strawberry Jam (p. 70) and let them marinate for 24 hours.

Half-Candied Strawberries
1. Rinse and hull the berries.
2. Bring the water, ¼ lb of the sugar, and the lemon juice to a boil. Add the berries and let them simmer for 15 minutes.
3. Add an additional ¼ lb sugar and let it simmer for 15 more minutes.

4. Repeat the process two more times.
5. Pour the berries into a bowl and place it in the fridge. Let it sit overnight.

DAY 2
1. Let the candied, whole berries drain in a strainer.
2. Boil the strawberry jam in accordance with the recipe on p. 70.
3. Add the candied, whole berries at the end of the boiling time so that they maintain their shape.
4. Pour into sterilized jars in three rounds, while allowing it to stiffen after each time. This way the berries will not float to the surface and instead will be evenly distributed.
5. Screw the lids on and turn the jars upside down a couple of times.

Makes about 5 ½ lbs (2,500 g) jam.

Strawberry and Banana Jam

Tasty, child-friendly jam that may also be varied with peach or pineapple.

1 ⅓ lbs (600 g) strawberries
1 lb (400 g) sliced bananas
1 ¾ lbs (800 g) sugar
Juice of 1 lemon
⅓ inch (1 cm) real cinnamon stick

Prepare and boil by following the recipe for Strawberry Jam, see p. 70.

Jam with Red Berries and Armagnac

This is a fantastic, fresh, and flavorful jam.

½ lb (300 g) small, ripe, and rinsed strawberries
7 oz (200 g) rinsed currants
½ lb (300 g) raspberries
7 oz (200 g) pitted ripe cherries
Juice of 1 lemon
1 ¾ lbs (800 g) sugar
½ cup (100 g/1 dl) Armagnac

Prepare and boil by following the recipe for Strawberry Jam, see p. 70. Add the liquor at the end of the boiling time.

1 Strawberry Jam with Orange and Green Pepper. 2 Strawberry Jam with Lemon and Basil. 3 Classic Strawberry Marmalade.

Strawberry Marmalade with Cinnamon Basil

You may vary the flavor by using other herbs instead.

2 ½ lbs (1,150 g) strawberries
(2 lbs [1,000 g] net weight)
2 lbs (1,000 g) sugar
Juice of 2 lemons
¾ oz (20 g) cinnamon basil

1. Rinse and hull the berries. Purée them in a mixer with the lemon juice and sugar.
2. Pour into a pot and bring to a boil. To prevent sugar crystals from forming, brush the inside of the pot with a brush dipped in cold water while boiling.
3. Remove foam while the marmalade is boiling so that it ends up clear. Boil to 220°F (105°C), or perform a jam test on a cold plate, see p. 20.
4. Blanch the basil in boiling water and then rinse it under cold running water. Finely chop it and add at the end of the boiling time.
5. Pour directly into sterilized jars and screw on the lids right away. Turn the jars upside down a couple of times.

Makes about 3 ⅓ lbs (1,500 g) marmalade.

Stirred Strawberry Purée

This kind of cold preserving works very well. During the sixties, when I worked at the Savoy Hotel in Malmö, we would pour stirred strawberry purée into sterilized dark bottles, and seal them with corks we had boiled in water and dipped in melted resin. We stored the bottles in a basement; the purée kept for at least a year and tasted just as fresh as when it was bottled. We used it as a flavoring for sorbet, parfait, ice cream, bavarois, and mousse. Raspberries may be prepared and used the exact same way.

2 ½ lbs (1,150 g) ripe strawberries
(2 lbs [1,000 g] net weight)
2 lbs (1,000 g) sugar
Juice of 1 lemon

1. Rinse and hull the berries. Purée the berries in a mixer with the sugar and lemon juice. Whisk for at least 60 minutes with an electric whisk.
2. Scoop into sterilized jars and screw on the lids right away. Store in the refrigerator.

Strawberry Cordial with Reduced Sugar

This strawberry cordial has a short shelf life because of the relatively low amount of sugar. But it has a fresh and appetizing taste. You may use other soft berries the same way. The cordial keeps for about 14 days in the fridge.

4 ½ lbs (2,000 g) strawberries
½ lb (300 g) sugar
Juice of 1 lemon

1. Set the oven to 175°F (80°C).
2. Rinse and hull the berries. Mix them with the sugar and lemon juice for 15 minutes.
3. Pour into a stainless-steel pot and bring to a boil.
4. Cover with the lid and let the mixture sit, without stirring, for 3 hours in the 175°F (80°C) oven.
5. Pour into a strainer and press all of the juice out with the help of the back of a spoon. Empty the fruit mass into a strainer lined with cheesecloth and let it drain on its own until the mass feels dry.
6. Boil the cordial in a saucepan and remember to remove all the foam.
7. Pour the cordial into sterilized bottles and close with the corks right away. Store in the fridge once it has cooled.

Carefully blend in some water and ice and you have a wonderful beverage that tastes like summer.

Tip!
You may also serve this ice-cold as a strawberry consommé with fresh strawberries and vanilla ice cream. If you wish to make strawberry jelly for dessert, add ¼ tbsp (1 sheet) of gelatin per ½ cup (1 dl) of cordial.

Stirred Strawberry Cordial

A wonderfully fresh taste of summer that anyone would love. A generous amount of sugar is needed to extract the aroma from the berries, and the lemon juice is so that it won't be too sweet. You may follow the same recipe and replace the strawberries with other juicy, ripe berries.

4 ½ lbs (2,000 g) ripe strawberries
3 ⅓ lbs (1,500 g) sugar
Juice of 4 lemons

1. Rinse and hull the strawberries and pour them into a mixer with the sugar and lemon juice.
2. Purée for about 5 minutes. Empty the purée into a bowl or a food processor, and whisk with an electric whisk for about 60 minutes.
3. Push the purée through a fine strainer and immediately pour into sterilized bottles.
4. Store in the fridge.

This cordial may last for quite a while if you keep it in the fridge.

Strawberry Coulis

This lovely strawberry sauce is suitable for most desserts. If you want to make a raspberry coulis instead, increase the sugar quantity to ½ lb (250 g).

2 lbs (1,000 g) strawberries
Juice of ½ lemon
¾ cup (180 g) sugar

1. Rinse and hull the ripe strawberries.
2. Mix them in a food processor with the lemon juice and sugar.
3. Push through a strainer.

Store in the fridge.

Preserved Strawberries

Once these strawberries have dried overnight on a rack, I usually dip them in dark chocolate with a high cocoa percentage. You may also candy the berries after they are dry. See candied flowers, p. 208.

DAY 1
1 vanilla bean
2 lbs (1,000 g) sugar
1 ⅔ cups (400 g/4 dl) water
4 tbsp (100 g) honey
3 ½ oz (100 g) small, firm strawberries

DAY 2
½ lb (250 g) sugar

Strawberry Cordial

I first learned to make this delicious cordial in Switzerland. It is just as good with other soft berries such as raspberries, blackberries, blueberries, currants, lingonberries, and cherries. At the restaurant, children loved the strawberry variety. When we prepared cordial with ripe cherries, we would crush 7 oz (200 g) of the pits in a mortar and let them boil to enhance the taste of the cordial. For strawberry cordial, I always try to get a hold of Senga Sengana strawberries, which I believe have an especially rich aroma.

4 ½ lbs (2,000 g) ripe, red strawberries, preferably Senga Sengana
Juice of 4 lemons
3 ⅓ lbs (1,500 g) sugar
2 cups (500 g/5 dl) water

DAY 1
1. Rinse and hull the ripe strawberries.
2. Blend everything in a stainless-steel pot with a lid. Cover with plastic wrap and let it marinate for 24 hours.

DAY 2
1. Set the oven to 175°F (80°C).
2. Set the pot on the stove and bring it to a boil while stirring. Remove any foam that forms.
3. Cover with the lid and place in the oven. Let it sit in the oven for 3 hours so that the juice is fully extracted from the berries.
4. Pour the mass into a strainer and squeeze out all of the juice with the help of a spoon. Pour the fruit mass into a strainer lined with cheesecloth and let it drain on its own.
5. Bring the cordial to a boil once more and make sure to remove the foam.
6. Pour into sterilized bottles and close with the corks right away.
7. Let them cool and store them in the fridge.

Continued on p. 76

Cheesecake with Strawberries. In the background is a rhubarb tart.

DAY 1

1. Cut open the vanilla bean down the middle. Scrape the seeds out with a knife. Place the bean and seeds in a saucepan with sugar, water, and honey. Carefully select your strawberries, but do not rinse them just yet.
2. Boil the syrup while constantly removing foam. Brush the inside of the saucepan with a brush dipped in cold water to avoid sugar crystals.
3. At 250°F (120°C), add the strawberries. Bring to a boil and remove the foam.
4. Let the mixture cool and let it sit in the fridge overnight.

DAY 2

5. Pour the strawberries into a strainer and let the syrup drain off.
6. Add an additional ½ lb (250 g) sugar to the syrup. Bring it to a boil and make sure to remove the foam.
7. Place the strawberries in sterilized jars and pour the boiling syrup on top. Screw on the lids right away.

The strawberries will be fully preserved after a week. At that time, let them drain on a cooling rack.

Tip!

The preserved strawberries may also be placed in jars and covered with Cointreau liqueur. After about 6 weeks, this will be a great dessert.

Half-Preserved Strawberries

Half-preserved strawberries, so-called demi-confit, are a nice ingredient for ice cream or parfait. They will not stiffen if you freeze them, the way regular strawberry pieces will, but instead stay soft. Let the syrup drain off on a rack before you add the berries to ice cream or parfait.

You may replace the strawberries with other fruits or berries for different ice cream flavors.

1 lb (500 g) fresh, small, and ripe strawberries
1 ½ cups (350 g) water
2 lbs (1,000 g) sugar
¾ cup (250 g) honey
2 tbsp (30 g) lemon juice

1. Rinse and hull the berries.
2. Boil the water, sugar, honey, and lemon juice into syrup.
3. Brush the inside of the pot with a brush dipped in cold water to prevent sugar crystals from forming.
4. Remove any foam from the syrup and add the strawberries (or other fruits or berries) to the boiling syrup. Let it simmer for 5 minutes and carefully remove all foam.
5. Scoop into sterilized containers and let the strawberries marinate in the syrup for at least 24 hours. Store in the fridge.

Cheesecake with Strawberries

A lovely cake for a warm summer day in the garden. Remember to take the cream cheese and eggs out of the refrigerator at least an hour before you start baking. That way the filling will be easier to blend and the texture of the finished cake will also end up better. Do not bake in an oven that is too hot, as the cake may become dry and crumbly, instead of creamy and smooth like a real New York cheesecake should be.

1 springform pan, 10 inch (25 cm) diameter with about 1 inch (2 cm) high edges
1 batch of Pâte sablée, see Prune Plum Tart, p. 49

Cheesecake Filling

1 lemon
1 lb (500 g) Philadelphia cream cheese, at room temperature
¼ cup (50 g) sugar
1 tbsp (25 g) real vanilla sugar
2 eggs (100 g), at room temperature

Garnish

About ½ cup (100 g) Currant Jelly, see p. 79, or another jelly
1 lb (500 g) ripe, fresh strawberries
½ cup (100 g) Currant Jelly, or other jelly
1 cup (300 g/3 dl) heavy whipping cream
2 tbsp (30 g) sugar

Pâte Sablée

1. Make the pâte sablée at least one hour beforehand.
2. Work the dough smooth by hand and roll it out to ⅛ inch (2 ½ mm) thick.
3. Roll the dough into the pan and lightly flour the surface.
4. Gently press the dough so that it covers the sides of the pan. Trim off any surplus dough with a knife. Poke the bottom of the dough a few times with a fork. Let it sit in the fridge for at least one hour.

Cheesecake Filling

1. Rinse the lemon and grate the zest with the finest part of the grater.
2. Blend the cream cheese with the lemon zest and the sugars. Add the eggs one at a time and make sure that you blend well before you add the next one.
3. Set the oven to 320°F (160°C).
4. Remove the pan from the fridge and pour the filling on top of the crust. Spread it out evenly.
5. Set the pan in the oven and bake it until golden brown, about 30–40 minutes. Test with a toothpick to make sure it is baked all the way through.
6. Let it cool and release the cake from the pan. Place it on a serving plate.

Garnish

1. Rinse the strawberries and dry them carefully.
2. Spread a thin layer of currant jelly on top of the cake so that the strawberries will stick.
3. Cut the strawberries in half down the middle and arrange them on top of the jelly.
4. Bring ½ cup (1 dl) currant jelly to a boil in a small saucepan. Brush the melted jelly over the berries to give them a little shine.
5. Whip the whipping cream and sugar until peaks form. Scoop the whipped cream into a pastry bag and pipe beautiful rosettes around the cake. If you think the whipped cream is too much, feel free to leave it out.

Photo p. 75

Rose Hips

Rosa canina, Rosa rugosa, and others

Rose hips are nicknamed the "orange of the north" because of their high vitamin C content. Rose hips are very healthy and most Swedes enjoy the taste of rose-hip soup. Botanically, they are actually the fruit of rosebushes. Rose hips from the Glaucous Dog Rose, Dog Rose, and Japanese Rose are the most commonly used. The seeds, which are situated like hairy nuts in the soft fruit flesh, should always be removed before you use the rose hip.

The rose hip is picked from August to October. Picking rose hips is quite challenging because of the thorns on the plants. Use scissors to cut them off the bush and then pit them by using a knife.

The rose hip is very suitable for jelly, marmalade, jam, and of course the Swedish rose hip soup. You can also preserve them the way you would green tomatoes; this is especially good with game. I first started making and selling rose hip marmalade with apple and rose pepper for the Konstrundan (an art exhibition in Sweden) in 2004. It was extremely well-received and was especially popular with cheese.

Added Flavor

Herbs: thyme and rosemary.
Sugar: You can use different kinds of sugar.
Spirits: cognac and whiskey.
Fruit combinations: all citrus fruits.

Rose Hip Marmalade with Rose Pepper

I made this marmalade for the first time for Easter in 2004. People especially enjoyed it with a variety of cheeses, for pâté, and for charcuteries.

3 ½ lbs (1,600 g) rose hips
1 ½ lbs (650 g) apples, green
(1 lb [500 g] net weight)
Juice of 2 oranges
Juice of 1 lemon
1 ¾ lbs (800 g) sugar per 2 lbs (1 kg) of purée
1 tbsp (20 g) rose pepper

1. Put the rinsed and seeded rose hips in a pot. Rinse and core the apples and add them to the pot with the orange and lemon juice.
2. Boil under a lid for 30 minutes, or till all the fruit has softened.
3. Purée in a mixer and press everything through a strainer.
4. Weigh the purée and add 1 ¾ lbs (800 g) sugar per 2 lbs (1 kg).
5. Pour everything back into the pot with the rose pepper. Boil to 220°F (105°C) while stirring constantly. You may also do a jam test on a cold plate, see p. 20.
6. Make sure everything is well blended and then pour into sterilized jars till they are one-third full.
7. Let cool for 15 minutes. Cover the pot with plastic wrap.

Continued on p. 78

8. Bring the remainder of the marmalade to a boil once more and pour it into the jars. (This process is to make sure that the rose pepper doesn't end up on the surface, but is instead evenly distributed throughout the marmalade.) Screw on the lids and turn the jars upside down a couple of times.

Makes about 4 ½ lbs (2,000 g) marmalade.

Rose Hip Jelly with Cognac

4 ½ lbs (2,000 g) rose hips
Juice of 1 lemon
Juice of 1 orange
¾ cup (150 g) cognac
1 ½ cups (350 g/ 3 ½ dl) apple juice or ½ lb (250 g) apple jelly, see p. 16–17
Quantity of sugar equal to the weight of the drained juice

1. Rinse and seed the rose hips. Place them in a pot and cover them with water. Add the lemon and orange juice, the liquor, and the apple juice or apple jelly.
2. Let it boil under a lid for 30 minutes.
3. Pour into a strainer and press carefully with the back of a spoon. Next, pour into a strainer lined with cheesecloth and let it drain on its own until the fruit mass feels dry, about 60 minutes.
4. Weigh the juice and add an amount of sugar equal to the weight of the juice.
5. Boil while removing all foam so that the jelly turns out clear. Brush the inside of the pot with a brush dipped in cold water to prevent sugar crystals from forming. Boil to 220°F (105°C), or perform a jelly test on a cold plate, see p. 20.
6. Pour directly into sterilized jars and screw on the lids. Turn the jars upside down a couple of times.

Makes about 3 ⅓ lbs (1,500 g) jelly.

Preserved Rose Hips
Candy rose hips by following the recipe for Preserved Citrus Peels.

2 lbs (1,000 g) rose hips

Rinse and seed the rose hips. Blanch them for 1 minute in boiling water and cool them under cold running water. Follow the recipe for Preserved Citrus Peels, p. 107.

Rowanberries

Sorbus aucuparia

The rowanberry is tart and somewhat bitter; accordingly, rowanberries shouldn't be consumed raw. The berries are rich in vitamin C. Like apples, they also contain malic acid and pectin. In order for rowanberries to be soft and tasty in jams and jellies, they shouldn't be picked before they've been frozen at some point. They should also be placed in the freezer for an hour before they are used.

Rowanberry Jelly

Very popular when served with game. Prepared the same way as Lingonberry Jelly, see recipe on p. 87. Replace the lingonberries with rowanberries.

Rowanberry Jam with Cognac

Tastes good with roasts and game terrines.

2 ½ lbs (1,200 g) rowanberries
(2 lbs [1,000 g] net weight)
1 ¾ lbs (800 g) light muscovado sugar
Juice of 1 lemon
½ cup (350 g) water
½ cup (100 g/1 dl) cognac
1 ½ cups (350 g/ 3 ½ dl) apple juice or ½ lb (250 g) apple jelly see p. 16–17

1. Rinse the berries.
2. Pour sugar, lemon juice, and water into a pot and bring to a boil. Brush the inside of the pot with a brush dipped in cold water to prevent sugar crystals from forming.
3. Boil to 234–240°F (112–114°C), or perform a sugar test, see p. 14.
4. Add the berries and boil while constantly stirring. Boil till the berries start turning transparent and the jam is starting to form jelly.
5. Brush the inside of the pot and remove the foam with a spoon.
6. At 222–224°F (106–107°C), the jam is ready, or you may scoop some jam onto a cold plate and do a jam test, see p. 20.
7. Pour directly into sterilized jars and screw on the lids right away. Turn the jars upside down a couple of times.

Makes about 3 ¾ lbs (1,700 g) jam.

Currants

Ribes rubrum

Red currants have always been the most common berries in Swedish gardens. There's early evidence of cultivation of the berries around the 1500s. Preserving currants was a known practice by the 1600s. There are many varieties of currants. They should be exposed to as much sun as possible. White currants are the albino version of red currants. They are sweeter and are better for eating uncooked. They can be used for the same purposes as red currants.

Barely ripe red and white currants have very high pectin content and are therefore perfect for jam and jelly. They are also great as a supplement for other berries with lower pectin content, for instance, raspberries, blueberries, and cherries. In Switzerland we would use currant jelly as a base jelly to help make strawberry jam firmer and fresher. Whole clusters of currants as garnish on tarts are both decorative and very tasty. Combinations with apples and pears are also fine. Be careful with spice combinations so that the berries' weak aroma is not overpowered.

Black currants (*Ribes nigrum*) grow wild in Sweden. But there are also many different cultivated varieties with large and juicy berries. Black currants are rich in vitamin C. The leaves can be used to make cordials, preserves, and more. A classic black currant jelly for an old-fashioned Sunday roast is obligatory. Jam also turns out good, but it's a lot of work to remove all of the stems from the berries. Black currant sorbet and black currant mousse is also very popular. Cordial made with black currants has a very sophisticated taste.

Red Currant Jam with Gin

2 ¾ lbs (1,250 g) red currants
¾ cup (200 g) water
1 ¾ lbs (800 g) sugar
½ cup (100 g/1 dl) gin
Juice of 1 lemon

1. Rinse the berries and remove the stems. Place them in a pot with the water and boil them on low heat under a lid for about 20 minutes.
2. Add the sugar, gin, and lemon juice.
3. Boil while constantly stirring and remove the foam now and then. Brush the inside of the pot with a brush dipped in cold water to prevent sugar crystals from forming.
4. Boil to 222–224°F (106–107°C), or perform a jam test on a cold plate, see p. 20.
5. Pour directly into sterilized jars and screw on the lids right away. Turn the jars upside down a couple of times.

Makes about 3 ⅓ lbs (1,500 g) jam.

Red Currant Jelly

4 ½ lbs (2,000 g) red currants, rinsed
2 cups (500 g/5 dl) water
Juice of 2 lemons
Amount of sugar equal to the weight of the drained juice

1. Pour the rinsed berries, the water, and the lemon juice into a pot.
2. Bring to a boil and let it simmer under a lid on low heat for 15 minutes.
3. Empty the boiled fruit into a strainer and let it drain on its own for about 1 hour.
4. Set the oven to 210°F (100°C). Weigh the juice. Put an amount of sugar equal to that weight on a baking sheet with elevated edges. Set the sugar in the oven and warm.
5. Pour the juice into a pot and bring to a boil. Remove foam from the surface.
6. Remove the pot from the stove and add the warmed sugar. Stir till it is completely melted and the surface is starting to wrinkle.
7. Pour directly into sterilized jars and screw on the lids right away. Turn the jars upside down a couple of times.

Makes about 2 lbs (1,000 g) jelly.

Red Currant Jelly with Raspberries

Prepare by following the recipe for Red Currant Jelly, but replace half of the currants with raspberries. This makes a very fresh and tasty jelly. Another variation can be made by replacing half of the currants with strawberries.

Red Currant Jelly with Thai Basil

Prepare by following the recipe for Red Currant Jelly, but add 1 ½ oz (40 g) chopped basil during boiling.

Red Currant Cordial

See Black Currant Cordial on p. 81.

Currant Jelly and Currant Marmalade.

Black Currant Jam with Rum

2 lbs (1,000 g) black currants
1 cup (250 g/ 2 ½ dl) water
Juice of 1 lemon
2 lbs (1,000 g) sugar
¼ cup (50 g/½ dl) dark rum

1. Rinse the currants and cut the stems off with scissors. Pour them into a pot with the water and lemon juice. Let it simmer under a lid for 15 minutes.
2. Set the oven to 210°F (100°C). Pour the sugar onto a baking sheet with elevated edges and place in the oven for about 10 minutes.
3. Remove the pot from the stove and add the sugar and rum. Stir until the jam is starting to form jelly.
4. Pour directly into sterilized jars and screw on the lids right away. Turn the jars upside down a couple of times.

Makes about 3 ⅓ lbs (1,500 g) jam.

Black Currant Jam with Macadamia Nuts and Cognac

2 lbs (1,000 g) black currants
1 cup (250 g/2 ½ dl) water
Juice of 1 lemon
2 lbs (1,000 g) sugar
¼ cup (50 g/½ dl) cognac
7 oz (200 g) macadamia nuts

1. Rinse the berries.
2. Pour them into a pot with the water and the lemon juice. Let it simmer under a lid for 20 minutes.
3. Transfer the contents into a food processor and purée until smooth. Press through a strainer.
4. Pour back into the pot and add the sugar and cognac.
5. Bring to a boil while stirring. Remove foam now and then. Brush the inside of the pot with a brush dipped in cold water to prevent sugar crystals from forming.
6. Boil to 220°F (105°C), or do a jam test on a cold plate, see p. 20.
7. Stir in the nuts.
8. Pour the jam into sterilized jars and screw on the lids right away. Turn upside down a couple of times.

Makes about 3 ⅓ lbs (1,500 g) jam.

Classic Black Currant Jelly

This is the recipe for my mother's black currant jelly.

4 ½ lbs (2,000 g) black currants
2 cups (500 g/5 dl) water
Amount of sugar equal to the weight of the drained juice

1. Rinse the berries carefully. Add the berries and the water to a pot and boil on low heat under a lid for 30 minutes.
2. Pour into a strainer and squeeze all of the juice out by pressing lightly with the back of a spoon. Empty the mass into a strainer lined with cheesecloth and let it drain on its own for 60 minutes.
3. Set the oven to 210°F (100°C). Weigh the strained juice.
4. Find the right amount of sugar and pour onto a baking sheet with elevated edges. Warm the sugar in the oven for 10 minutes.
5. Bring the juice to a boil and remove any foam that may form.
6. Pull the pot off the stove and whisk in the sugar. Keep whisking until the jelly looks wrinkly on the surface.
7. Pour directly into sterilized jars and screw on the lids right away. Turn upside down a couple of times.

Makes about 2 lbs (1,000 g) jelly.

Black Currant Jelly with Forest Raspberries

Replace a quarter of the black currants with barely ripe forest raspberries. This makes a fantastic jelly. Eat it on a slice of freshly toasted brioche or with a croissant and a caffè latte.

Black Currant Jelly with Spirits

Replace ½ cup (100 g/1 dl) of the water with liquor, for instance, calvados, Armagnac, cognac or rum, and prepare exactly as described above.

Black Currant Cordial

You may follow the same recipe to make red currant cordial.

7 oz (200 g) black currants (or red currants), rinsed
4 cups (1,000 g/ 1 liter) water
Juice of 2 lemons
1 ¾ lbs (800 g) sugar per 4 cups (1 liter) strained juice

1. Boil the rinsed berries under a lid with water and lemon juice for 30 minutes.
2. Pour into a strainer and squeeze all of the juice out with the help of the back of a spoon. Empty the berry mass into a strainer lined with cheesecloth and let it drain on its own for about 60 minutes, or until the mass feels dry.
3. Weigh the juice and measure the right amount of sugar accordingly. Bring it to a boil with the juice and remove all the foam.
4. Pour directly into sterilized bottles and cork them right away. Store in the fridge.

Gooseberries

Ribes uva-crispa

The gooseberry first came to Sweden during the 1500s. By the 1800s, hundreds of varieties were cultivated. Interest in the berry started declining at the beginning of the twentieth century when American gooseberry mildew spread all over the country. The cultivated gooseberries of today are a lot more resistant. You can find Swedish gooseberries from June to August.

Today you can find large green gooseberries, which should preferably be used while they are slightly unripe to prevent the skins from feeling rubbery. There are also red gooseberries. The red gooseberries taste great fresh. In the United Kingdom, gooseberry marmalade and gooseberry jelly are popular because of their tart flavor and unique aroma. The gooseberry taste may be compared to the kiwi.

Unripe gooseberries have a high pectin content, which makes them suitable for jelly. Gooseberries also make fine compotes, creams, and pies, not to mention sorbets.

In my recipe book from when I was an apprentice, I have written the following:

Gooseberry Jam for Swiss Roll Cakes

22 lbs (10,000 g) unripe gooseberries
17 lbs (8,000 g) sugar
2 cups (500 g) lemon juice

1. Run the rinsed gooseberries through a meat grinder and place them in a copper pot.
2. Boil the sugar with 40 percent water to 282°F (139°C).
3. Pour it over the fruit mass and lemon juice and boil to a strong thread test.

Added Flavor

Herbs: various kinds of thyme and peppermint.
Dried spices: for instance, cloves, ginger, cinnamon, vanilla, and tonka beans.
Sugar: Yellow and brown cane sugar, for instance, muscovado.
Fruit combinations: red and black currants, apples, pears, raspberries, and strawberries, and also grapefruit and other citrus fruits.

Classic Gooseberry Jelly

2 lbs (1,000 g) unripe green or red gooseberries
1 cup (250 g/2 ½ dl) water
Juice of 1 lemon
Amount of sugar equal to the weight of the drained juice

1. Rinse the gooseberries and place them in a pot with the water and lemon juice. Bring to a boil, cover with a lid and lower the heat. Let it simmer for 15 minutes.

2. Pour into a fine strainer and press with the back of a spoon so that the juice is squeezed out. Pour the juice and fruit mass into a strainer lined with cheesecloth and let it drain on its own until the fruit mass is dry.
3. Weigh the juice and add an equal weight of sugar.
4. Bring to a boil and carefully remove all the foam. Brush the inside of the pot with a brush dipped in cold water to prevent sugar crystals. Boil to 220°F (105°C), or do a jelly test on a cold plate, see p. 20.
5. Pour the jelly directly into sterilized jars. Immediately screw on the lids and turn the jars upside down a couple of times.

Makes about 2 lbs (1,000 g) jelly.

Gooseberry Jelly with Genever or Gin

Replace ½ cup (100 g) of the water with liquor and continue by following the recipe described above.

Gooseberry Jelly with Chili

Add one finely chopped Serrano chili with seeds to the berries, and continue by following the recipe described above.

Gooseberry Jelly with Cinnamon or Ginger

Add a piece of real cinnamon stick or dried ginger while boiling. Continue by following the recipe described above.

Gooseberry Jam

2 ½ lbs (1,100 g) gooseberries, green or red, unripe
1 ½ cups (350 g) water
Juice of 1 lemon
1 ¾ lbs (800 g) sugar

1. Rinse the berries in cold water and cut off any stems.
2. Bring the water and lemon juice to a boil in a pot and add the berries. Let it simmer under a lid for 10 minutes.
3. Stir in the sugar and continue boiling while constantly removing foam. Brush the inside of the pot with a brush dipped in cold water to avoid sugar crystals. Remove the foam with a spoon so that the jelly becomes clear.
4. When the gooseberries are turning transparent and the jam is starting to form jelly, it is time to measure the temperature. Boil to 220–222°F (105–106°C), or perform a jelly test on a cold plate, see p. 20.
5. Pour directly into sterilized jars and screw on the lids right away. Turn the jars upside down a couple of times.

Makes about 3 ⅓ lbs (1,500 g) jam.

Gooseberry Jam with Ginger, Cinnamon, and Whiskey

Follow the recipe for Gooseberry Jam, see above, but add ¾ inch (2 cm) of real cinnamon stick, a large piece of dried ginger, and ½ cup (100 g/1 dl) of Scottish whiskey. This jam tastes especially good on toast.

Gooseberry Jam with Whole Gooseberries

You can also make this tasty gooseberry jam with red currants.

1 lb (500 g) green, unripe gooseberries (or red currants)
½ lb (250 g) sugar
¾ cup (200 g/2 dl) water

1 batch of Gooseberry Jam, see above.

DAY 1

1. Remove the stems of the rinsed berries and place them in a bowl.
2. Boil the syrup and pour it over the berries while still boiling. Cover with plastic wrap and let it sit overnight.

DAY 2

1. Let the berries drain in a strainer.
2. Stir the berries in with the freshly made gooseberry jam and bring it to a boil. Pour into sterilized jars as above.

Makes about 4 ½ lbs (2,000 g) jam.

Gooseberry Jam with Chili

Seedless Gooseberry Marmalade

When I was an apprentice, we often used this marmalade as a filling in Swiss roll cakes.

2 ½ lbs (1,100 g) unripe gooseberries
1 ½ cups (350 g) water
Juice of 1 lemon
2 lbs (900 g) sugar

1. Boil the rinsed berries with the water and lemon juice in a pot. Let them boil under a lid until soft for 15 minutes.
2. Pour into a mixer and mix into a purée.
3. Press the purée through a strainer and add the sugar. Boil everything while carefully removing foam. Brush the inside of the pot with a brush dipped in cold water to avoid sugar crystals.
4. Boil to 220°F (105°C), or perform a jam test on a cold plate, see p. 20.
5. Pour directly into sterilized jars and screw on the lids right away. Turn the jars upside down a couple of times.

Makes about 3 ⅓ lbs (1,500 g) marmalade.

Preserved Gooseberries

Unripe green gooseberries can be preserved by following the recipe for Preserved Citrus Peels, see p. 107

2 lbs (1,000 g) unripe, large gooseberries

Rinse the berries and place in boiling water. Immediately cool under cold running water. They are then preserved the exact same way as citrus peels, see p. 107.

Swiss Roll Cake

Swiss roll cakes are great with gooseberry jam or raspberry jam as a filling. The jam has to be firm so that it doesn't make the cake soggy. Pastry chefs will sometimes spread a thin layer of buttercream over the cake before adding the jam, so as to prevent the bottom from becoming too soft.

For 1 cake

1 baking sheet with elevated edges
Parchment paper
1 ½ tbsp (25 g) sugar

1 ¼ cup (136 g) all-purpose flour
¼ cup (40 g) cornstarch
2 tsp (10 g) baking powder
5 eggs (250 g)
1 ¼ cup (240 g) sugar
½ tbsp (10 g) real vanilla sugar

Filling

½ lb (250 g) jam

1. Set the oven to 445°F (230°C).
2. Sift the flour, cornstarch, and baking powder together on a piece of paper.
3. Place a saucepan with boiling water on the stove.
4. Whisk the eggs and sugar in a clean metal bowl. Place the bowl in the water bath and warm the mixture to 113–122°F (45–50°C), while whisking (use a thermometer).
5. Remove the bowl from the stove and as it cools, whisk the egg mixture by hand or with an electric whisk until it has tripled in volume.
6. Sift the flour blend into the egg mixture and fold it together carefully so that you end up with an even mass. Spread it out evenly on the baking sheet, lined with parchment paper. Bake it until beautifully golden brown, about 7–8 minutes.
7. Sprinkle 1 ½ tbsp (25 g) sugar over the cake and carefully loosen it from the baking sheet with a knife.
8 Turn onto a piece of parchment paper and let it cool for about an hour.
9. Carefully pull the parchment paper off the bottom of the cake. Stir the jam a little and spread it over the cake. Roll the cake and jam up together with the help of the paper. Place a ruler on the paper before you roll the cake together, to help you move the entire cake at one time.

Slice into pieces and serve with freshly brewed coffee.

Lingonberries
Vaccinium vitis-idaea

The lingonberry is the most important berry in Swedish gastronomy. It has been picked and prepared for hundreds of years. Lingonberries ripen in late September and they grow wild throughout Sweden. They contain benzoic acid, which is a natural preservative. This allows lingonberries to keep for a very long time without any artificial additives. In the past, people would bottle lingonberries and pour boiling water on top. This was called lingonberry water and would last for years. (People also did this with gooseberries).

Cranberries (*Vaccinium oxycoccus*) may be prepared the exact same way as lingonberries. They ripen later in the fall, in October and November. The American cranberry is different from the fruit we use in Sweden.

What would traditional Swedish dishes be without lingonberries— meatballs, bacon pancakes, potato pancakes or fried pork? Lingonberry parfait and the classic lingonberry pears should be mentioned as well. Lingonberry jelly with gin is also incredibly good. Other delights include lingonberry sorbet or cranberry sorbet with vodka or gin.

Added Flavor

Spices: ginger, cinnamon, cloves, vanilla, tonka bean, nutmeg, and juniper.
Herbs: basil, lemongrass, and lemon verbena.
Citrus fruits: zest of preserved lemons, oranges, or grapefruit.
Wine and spirits: red wine, gin, Dutch gin, and rum.
Fruit combinations: currants, blackberries, blueberries, apples, figs, chestnuts, and more.

Traditional Swedish Lingonberry Jam

Goes great with many foods and is not too sweet. It has a wonderful jelly-like texture. There is no need for lemon juice to activate the pectin with lingonberries, because the berries activate on their own. Lingonberries keep better than most other berries. You can prepare a cranberry jam by following the same recipe.

2 lbs (1,000 g) lingonberries
1 ½ cup (350 g/3 ½ dl) water
1 ½ lbs (750 g) sugar

1. Rinse the lingonberries. Place them in a pot with the water and let it boil for 10 minutes.
2. Remove the pot from the stove. Add the sugar and stir until it is melted and the surface of the jam is starting to look wrinkled.
3. Pour directly into sterilized jars and screw on the lids right away. Turn the jars upside down a couple of times.

Makes about 3 ⅓ lbs (1,500 g) jam.
If you prefer a less sweet variety, you can decrease the sugar to 1 lb (500 g). The jam will still form jelly and keep for a long while.

Lingonberry Jam with Ginger, Cinnamon, and Rum

Follow the recipe above, except replace ½ cup (100 g/1 dl) of the water with dark rum and add 2 tsp (10 g) freshly ground cinnamon and a pinch of ground ginger.

Lingonberry Jam with Gin

Replace ¼ cup (50 g/½ dl) of the water with gin and add 6 crushed juniper berries in a cloth bag during the boiling. Remove the bag before you add the sugar.

Stirred Lingonberry Jam

Take equal parts rinsed lingonberries and granulated sugar and mix in a food processor for 60 minutes. Pour into sterilized jars and screw on the lids. This makes a very tasty jam that you can keep in the fridge.

Stirred Lingonberries for Game

2 lbs (1,000 g) rinsed lingonberries
½ lb (300 g) sugar

Stir sugar and the berries for 10 minutes. Keep in a jar in the fridge.

Makes about 2 ¾ lbs (1,300 g) jam.

Lingonberry Jelly

Follow the recipe for Black Currant Jelly, see p. 21. If you want, you may flavor with ½ cup (100 g/1 dl) gin, but in that case, subtract ½ cup (100 g/1 dl) of water from the original recipe. Or you may flavor with fresh thyme or rosemary while boiling.

Sun-Dried Cranberries and Candied Chestnuts in Apple Jelly

This tastes fantastic with roast hare in gravy and browned chanterelles. You can find sun-dried cranberries in delicacy stores.

1 batch of Apple Jelly, see p. 16
½ lb (300 g) sun-dried cranberries
½ lb (300 g) candied chestnuts, see Candied Chestnuts, p. 62
1 sprig of rosemary

1. Add the sprig of rosemary during the boiling of the apple jelly.
2. Place the drained and dried chestnuts in rinsed jars and add the cranberries.
3. Pour the apple jelly on top and screw on the lids immediately. Turn the jars upside down a couple of times.

Photo p. 89

Lingonberry and Pear Jam

You may replace the pears with sour apples, for instance, Cox's Orange or Belle de Boskoop.

1 ½ lbs (650 g) firm, ripe green pears
(1 lb [500 g] net weight)
1 lb (500 g) rinsed lingonberries
1 cup (250 g/2 ½ dl) water
Juice of 1 lemon
1 ⅓ lbs (750 g) sugar
⅓ inch (1 cm) real vanilla bean

1. Rinse, peel, and dice the pears.
2. Rinse the lingonberries.
3. Bring the water and lemon juice to a boil in a pot and boil the pears for about 5 minutes, until soft. Add the lingonberries and boil for an additional 5 minutes.
4. Add the sugar and cinnamon stick and boil to 220°F (105°C), or perform a jam test on a cold plate, see p. 20. Remove the foam with a spoon and occasionally brush the inside of the pot with a brush dipped in cold water to avoid sugar crystals.
5. Pour directly into sterilized jars and screw on the lids right away. Turn the jars upside down a couple of times.

Makes about 1 lb (500 g) jam.

Lingonberry Cordial

Follow the recipe for Black Currant Cordial, see p. 81.

Lingonberry Pears

During Christmas in my home, this classic Swedish specialty was served sprinkled with grated candied ginger with a vanilla parfait and Swedish bowknots on the side. See recipe for Swedish Bowknots on p. 225.

4 ½ lbs (2,000 g) ripe pears   Juice of 1 lemon
 2 lbs (1,000 g) lingonberries   ⅓ inch (1 cm) real cinnamon stick
                                     1 ¾ lbs (850 g) sugar
1 ¾ cups (450 g/ 4 ½ dl) water

1. Rinse the lingonberries and boil them with the water and lemon juice.
2. Let it boil on low heat under a lid for 20 minutes.
3. Empty everything into a strainer lined with cheesecloth and let it drain on its own for 60 minutes.
4. Bring the drained juice, cinnamon, and sugar to a boil in the pot and remove from the stove.
5. Peel the pears and lightly scrape the stems. Remove the cores with a small teaspoon.
6. Add the pears to the syrup and let them simmer carefully till they have gone soft, about 20 minutes.
7. Pour the pears and syrup into sterilized jars and immediately screw on the lids. Turn the jars upside down a couple of times.

Lingonberry and Pear Marmalade.

Sun-Dried Cranberries and Candied Chestnuts in Apple Jelly.

Salzburger Nockerl with Lingonberry Cream

Back when I worked on the cruise ship Vista/Fjord, we used to serve this delicious dessert to the difficult passengers who would complain about anything and everything onboard. The chef-steward would write a special order for this dessert to please them. The soufflé-like dessert has to be served immediately and the egg whites have to be completely stiff; if not, it doesn't turn out as good. On the other hand, if you are very meticulous with the recipe, this tastes amazing with some lingonberry cream.

It is very important to crack the egg whites the night before. That way they are stiffer when you whip them the next day.

4 servings

1 oval baking pan, about 8 inches (20 cm) in diameter with ⅔ inch (2 cm) high sides
1 ½ tbsp (20 g) butter for greasing the pan

7 egg whites (about 210 g)
4 egg yolks (about 80 g)
¾ cup (150 g/ 1 ½ dl) whole milk
½ vanilla bean, preferably Bourbon

1 lemon
1 ½ tbsp (10 g) all-purpose flour
1 ½ tbsp (10 g) cornstarch
½ tbsp (10 g) real vanilla sugar
1 tsp lemon juice
⅓ cup (80 g) sugar

Powdered sugar to decorate

Lingonberry Cream
1 ¼ cups (300 g) heavy whipping cream
3 ½ oz (100 g) Lingonberry Jam, see p. 85 (or Raspberry Jam, p. 59)

DAY 1
1. Divide the egg whites and yolks into two separate glass bowls. The egg white needs to be completely free from yolk.
2. Cover with plastic wrap and let stand in the refrigerator until the next day.

Continued on p. 90

DAY 2

1. Cut the vanilla bean down the middle and scrape out the seeds. Bring the milk and the vanilla bean to a boil in a small saucepan. Cover with plastic wrap and let it rest for 30 minutes.

2. Remove the vanilla bean, butter the baking pan, and pour the milk into the pan.

3. *Lingonberry Cream:* Whip the cream until it forms soft peaks and blend it with the jam. Store in the fridge until serving.

4. Set the oven to 480°F (250°C).

5. Grate the rinsed lemon with a fine grater.

6. Sift flour, cornstarch, and vanilla sugar onto a piece of paper.

7. Whip the yolks until frothy and set the bowl aside.

8. Clean a metal bowl (if possible, a copper bowl) with vinegar and salt and rinse it out with water.

9. Pour the cold egg whites into the bowl with the lemon juice and a third of the sugar. Whisk to soft peaks by hand or on medium speed with an electric whisk. Add an additional third of the sugar and increase the speed. Lastly, add the remaining sugar and increase to full speed. Whisk until stiff peaks form.

10. Fold in the yolks and lemon zest with a silicone spatula. Lastly, fold in the dry ingredients and work into a light, smooth, and airy mass.

11. Now, with the help of the silicone spatula, place the filling in the pan in three large dollops, and bake it in the oven until it is beautifully golden brown, 10–12 minutes.

12. Remove the dish from the oven and cover with powdered sugar. Serve right away with the cream on top.

Blueberries

Vaccinium myrtillus

Blueberries are one of the most important berries of the northern hemisphere. The ripe berries are covered with a thin, light-blue wax membrane, which protects the berries from drying up. Certain berries lack this protection and are in that case completely black. Swedish blueberries grow wild in the woods. The blue color is a result of anthocyanin that turns blue. Blueberries ripen quickly and they don't keep long. They are an important nutritional source for the animals in the woods.

There is also an American variety of blueberries, *Vaccinium corymbosum*, which are sold at garden centers. They can't compare to wild blueberries when it comes to flavor. They are not suitable for jam or marmalade since they are lacking in flavor and aroma.

Added Flavor

Spices: Dried spices like ginger, cinnamon, and vanilla go especially well.
Herbs: Herbs with a lemon flavor, such as lemon balm, lemon verbena, and lemongrass, or green mint and many other kinds of herbs that you may add at the end of the boiling time.
Sugar: Raw sugar, such as dark muscovado or cassonade.
Wine or spirits: red wine, cognac, whiskey, and rum can break nicely with the blueberry taste.
Fruit combinations: Red or black currants are good complementary berries as blueberries have a lower pectin-content; other good choices are gooseberries, apples, oranges, and grapefruit.

Blueberry Jam

Blueberries have virtually zero pectin if they get overly ripe. For preserving, it is therefore very important to make sure that you use fresh berries that are not too ripe. My mother always served blueberry jam with rice porridge on Christmas instead of fruit sauce. My father liked blueberry jam for pancakes.

2 lbs (1,000 g) blueberries
1 ¾ lbs (800 g) sugar
1 lemon
1 ½ cups (350 g/3 ½ dl) water

DAY 1

1. Rinse the blueberries.
2. Squeeze the lemon.
3. Pour sugar and water into a pot and add the berries and lemon juice.
4. Bring it to a boil while stirring.
5. Pour into a bowl and let it cool. Cover with plastic wrap and let it sit in the fridge overnight.

DAY 2

1. Pour the berries into a strainer and let the syrup drain off.
2. Pour the syrup into a pot and bring it to a boil. Keep brushing the inside of the pot with a brush dipped in cold water to avoid sugar crystals.
3. Boil the syrup to 234–240°F (112–114°C), or perform hand test, see Boiling Sugar, p. 14.
4. Add the drained berries and let the mixture boil while stirring. Remove foam now and then and brush the inside of the pot with a brush dipped in cold water, to prevent sugar crystals.
5. Measure the temperature when the berries are turning transparent and the jam's surface is beginning to wrinkle. The jam should boil to 222–224°F (106–107°C), or you can do a jam test, see p. 20.
6. Pour directly into sterilized jars and screw on the lids right away. Turn the jars upside down a couple of times.

Makes about 3 ⅓ lbs (1,500 g) jam.

Blueberry Jam with Vanilla

Follow the recipe for Blueberry Jam above.
Add 1 vanilla bean, preferably Bourbon, during boiling.

Blueberry and Chocolate Marmalade

Follow the recipe for Blueberry Jam above.
Add 12 oz (350 g) chopped chocolate, Valrhona Grand Cru Pur Caraïbe or Marabou dark chocolate, directly after boiling.

Blueberry Jam with Rosemary

Follow the recipe for Blueberry Jam above.
Add ¾ oz (25 g) fresh rosemary sprigs during boiling.

Queen's Jam (Drottningsylt)

This fantastic flavor combination of berries with such rich aroma, like raspberries and blueberries, simply can't help being delicious. Tastes great on freshly made waffles with whipped cream, on French toast, or on warm scones.

1 lb (500 g) blueberries
1 lb (500 g) raspberries
1 cup (250 g/2 ½ dl) water
1 ¾ lbs (800 g) sugar
Juice of 1 lemon

DAY 1

1. Rinse the berries.
2. Bring water and sugar to a boil in a pot. Add the lemon juice and the berries. Boil for about 2 minutes.
3. Pour into a bowl and let it cool. Cover with plastic wrap and let it sit in the fridge overnight.

DAY 2

1. Pour the berries into a strainer and let the syrup drain off.
2. Pour the syrup into a pot and bring to a boil. Brush the inside of the pot with a brush dipped in cold water to prevent sugar crystals.
3. Boil to 234–240°F (112–114°C), or perform a hand test, see Boiling Sugar, p. 14.

Continued on p. 94

4. Add the berries and boil everything while stirring. Remove foam with a spoon and brush the inside of the pot now and then.
5. When the berries are turning transparent and the surface is starting to wrinkle, it is time to measure the temperature. At 222–224°F (106–107°C), the jam is ready. Or you may perform a jam test on a cold plate, see p. 20.
6. Pour the jam directly into sterilized jars and screw on the lids right away. Turn the jars upside down a couple of times.

Makes about 3 ⅓ lbs (1,500 g) jam.

Blueberry Jam with Thyme

Remember to avoid overly ripe blueberries, as the jelly won't stiffen properly but will instead become gluey.

1 ⅔ lbs (750 g) blueberries
½ lb (250 g) red currants or unripe gooseberries
Pinch of thyme
Juice of 1 lemon
1 cup (250 g/2 ½ dl) water
Amount of sugar equal to the weight of the drained juice

1. Rinse the berries. Slowly boil them with thyme, lemon juice, and water under a lid for 15 minutes.
2. Empty into a strainer and gently squeeze all of the juice out with the back of a spoon. Next, pour into a strainer lined with cheesecloth and let it drain on its own for about 1 hour.
3. Weigh the juice and pour it into a pot. Add an equal weight of sugar.
4. Boil while carefully making sure to remove all foam from the surface. Boil to 220°F (105°C).
5. Make sure that the jelly is ready with a jelly test. Scoop some jelly onto a cold plate. If it forms a nice gel, it is ready.
6. Pour directly into sterilized jars and screw on the lids right away. Turn the jars upside down a couple of times.

Makes about 2 lbs (1,000 g) jelly.

Blueberry Cordial
See Strawberry Cordial on p. 74. Replace the strawberries with blueberries.

Elder

Sambucus nigra

Elder has a very important place in natural medicine. Both the berries and the flowers are used. Dip the fresh flowers in batter and fry them golden, then let them drain on a paper towel. Sprinkle powdered sugar and serve with ice cream. This makes a delicious summer dessert!

The black-violet berries ripen in September or October. They may be used for cordial, jam, marmalade, and jelly, as well as sorbet or parfait.

Elderflower Cordial

2 lbs (1,000 g) elder flower bouquets
20 lemons
11 lbs (5000 g) sugar
20 cups (5000 g/5 liters) water

1. Rinse the flowers well and let the water drain off.
2. Clean and slice the lemons. Layer them with the flowers in a large pan.
3. Bring water and sugar to a boil in a pot and pour it, while still boiling, over the flowers and lemon slices.
4. Cover with plastic wrap and let it sit in the fridge for 5 days.
5. Pour the juice into a strainer and let it drain. Carefully squeeze out all of the juice with the back of a spoon.
6. Pour the juice into a pot and bring it to a boil. Remove any foam with a spoon and brush the inside of the pot with a brush dipped in cold water to prevent sugar crystals.
7. Pour into sterilized bottles and cork them right away. Store the bottles in the fridge.
8. If you wish to make the cordial keep longer, set the oven to 175°F (80°C) and place the bottles in a boiling water bath for 20 minutes.

Elder Curd
Make Elder Curd the same way as Lemon Curd, see p. 106. Replace the lemon juice with elder juice.
Note! Do not use a copper pot to make curd, as it will turn the curd green.

Elder Parfait

Serve elder parfait with a variety of fresh berries and Almond Tarts. See the recipe for Almond Tarts on p. 225.

6 servings

Round bundt pan/coffee cake pan that holds 4 cups (1 liter)	½ tbsp gelatin (2 sheets)
Powdered sugar for the pan	About 5 egg yolks (100 g)
1 cup heavy whipping cream (250 g/2 ½ dl)	¾ cup (150 g/1 ½ dl) elderflower cordial
	1 lb (500 g) fresh berries

Continued on p. 96

DAY 1

1. Whip the cream to soft peaks and place it in the fridge.
2. Dissolve the gelatin in water according to package directions, or soak the gelatin sheets in a generous amount of water for at least 5 minutes.
3. Pour egg yolks and elderflower cordial into a round metal bowl. Place the bowl in a pot with boiling water and whip vigorously with a whisk until the cream starts to thicken. Remove the bowl from the water bath and measure the temperature. It should be at 185°F (85°C). Push the egg cream through a strainer and whip with an electric whisk.
4. Add the dissolved gelatin or drained gelatin sheets to the warm egg cream and whisk until it forms stiff peaks.
5. When the egg mixture has cooled completely, fold it in with the whipped cream. Pour the mixture into a cleaned round cake pan, which has been covered with a layer of powdered sugar.
6. Freeze overnight.

DAY 2

1. Dip the cake pan in lukewarm water and turn the cake out onto a plate.
2. Fill the hole in the middle with a variety of fresh berries.

Don't serve the parfait too cold. It needs 15 minutes to achieve the perfect texture.

Sea Buckthorn

Hippophae rhamnoides

Warning: Do not confuse Sea Buckthorn with Common Buckthorn (*R. cathartica*). The fruit of Common Buckthorn is toxic and will induce vomiting.

Sea buckthorn is a thorny bush that has its home in Europe and Asia. In Sweden we mostly find sea buckthorn along the coast by the Bothnian Bay. Sea buckthorn is usually sold at garden centers or it can also be grown in gardens. The fruit is juicy, about 1/3 inch (1 cm) long, yellow red, and starts to ripen at the end of August. Sea buckthorn is very rich in vitamin C, vitamin A, and vitamin E. They also contain flavonoids, which act as antioxidants. The berries have an almost exotic taste.

Most sea buckthorn varieties produce berries every year, but the weather will influence the amount. Picking the berries is very time-consuming. The berries are mostly skin, juice, and seeds, and it is difficult to pick them from the bush. When you try to pick them, the juice will often spurt. The best way to pick them is therefore by using scissors to cut them off the bush. Personally, I always use a juicer to squeeze all of the juice out. The juice may then be frozen and used at another time.

Sea buckthorn is suitable for sorbet, parfait, ice cream, cordial, jam, marmalade, and jelly. You may also use it for sea buckthorn soup or curd.

Added Flavor

Spices: mild spices such as vanilla, so that the special flavor is not overwhelmed.
Lemon: to help the stiffening process.
Sugar: regular granulated sugar
Fruit combinations: rowanberries, lingonberries, apples, and currants.

Sea Buckthorn Cordial

2 lbs (1,000 g) sea buckthorn purée, pressed in a juicer
½ cup (100 g) lemon juice
1 ¾ lbs (800 g) sugar

1. Boil everything in a pot with a lid, and place it in the oven at 175°F (80°C). Let it sit in the oven for 30 minutes.
2. Pour everything into cheesecloth and let it drain on its own.
3. Pour into sterilized bottles and cork right away. Store in the fridge.

Sea Buckthorn Jam

2 lbs (1,000 g) sea buckthorn purée, pressed in a juicer
½ cup (100 g) lemon juice
1 ¾ lbs (800 g) sugar

1. Place all of the ingredients in a pot and bring to a boil.
2. Remove any foam and remove any sugar crystals by brushing the inside of the pot with a brush dipped in cold water.
3. Boil to 220°F (105°C). Perform a jam test on a cold plate to make sure that the texture is right, see p. 20.
4. Pour directly into sterilized jars and screw on the lids right away. Turn the jars upside down a couple of times.

Makes about 2 ¾ lbs (1,300 g) jam.

Mixed Jam with Sea Buckthorn

1 lb (500 g) sea buckthorn purée, pressed in a juicer
½ lb (250 g) lingonberries
½ lb (250 g) red currants
1 ¾ lbs (800 g) sugar
1 lemon

DAY 1

1. Place all of the ingredients in a pot and bring to a boil. Pour mixture into a bowl and let it cool.
2. Cover with plastic wrap and let it sit in the fridge overnight.

DAY 2

1. Pour the berry mixture into a strainer and let it drain.
2. Pour the syrup into a pot and bring it to a boil. Remove the sugar crystals that form on the inside of the pot with a brush dipped in cold water. Remove any foam. Boil to 234–240°F (112–114°C) or perform a sugar test, see p. 14.
3. Add the berries and boil to 220°F (105°C), or perform a jam test on a cold plate, see p. 20.
4. Remove foam during boiling.
5. Pour directly into sterilized jars and screw on the lids immediately. Turn the jars upside down a couple of times.

Makes about 2 lbs (1,000 g) jam.

Sea Buckthorn Curd

Don't use a copper pot when you make this curd. If you do, it will turn green. By only using yolks and melting the butter, the water content decreases in the finished curd and it will keep longer compared to when you use whole eggs and solid butter.

About 15 egg yolks (300 g)
½ lb (300 g) sugar
3 ½ oz (100 g) sea buckthorn purée
2 lemons
¼ cup + 1 tbsp (60 g) lemon juice
1 cup (250 g) unsalted butter

1. Whisk the yolks and sugar for about 5 minutes, until fluffy.
2. Wash the lemons and finely grate the zest of one of the lemons.
3. Squeeze the juice out of the lemons.
4. Boil the butter and let the residue that forms on the top sink down.
5. Pour the butter into a saucepan while making sure that the residue is left behind. Add the lemon juice, sea buckthorn purée, and lemon zest, and bring it all to a boil. Pour everything over the whipped yolks and mix well.
6. Pour it back into the pot and let it simmer into a thick cream while stirring.
7. Pass though a chinoise.
8. Pour directly into sterilized jars and screw on the lids right away. Turn the jars upside down a couple of times.

Makes about 2 lbs (1,000 g) curd.

Sea Buckthorn Jelly

If you prepare jelly from sea buckthorn alone, it will most likely turn out a little gluey, so for each 1 lb (500 g) of sea buckthorn purée, you should also add 1 lb (500 g) green apples. That way the jelly ends up more beautiful and not as sour. You may also use unripe gooseberries, lingonberries, or currants.

1 ⅓ lbs (600 g) sea buckthorn purée
1 lb (500 g) green apples
Juice of 1 lemon
1 cup (250 g/2 ½ dl) water
Amount of sugar equal to the weight of the drained juice

1. Clean and slice the apples into thin slices.
2. Pour all of the ingredients into a pot and bring it to a boil. Cover with a lid and let it simmer for 30 minutes.
3. Pour the mixture into cheesecloth and let it drain on its own for about 1 hour, by which time the juice should have drained and the mass should feel completely dry.
4. Weigh the juice and add an equal weight of sugar.
5. Bring to a boil and remove foam.
6. Boil to 220°F (105°C), or perform a jelly test on a cold plate, see p. 20. Pour directly into sterilized jars and screw on the lids right away. Turn the jars upside down a couple of times.

Makes about 2 lbs (1,000 g) jelly.

CIT
FR

Various Citrus Fruits

The term "citrus fruit" covers a multitude of different varieties. There are the larger fruits, including oranges, lemons, grapefruit, and bitter oranges. Then there are also smaller fruits, such as clementines, tangerines, limes, and more. Many newer varieties are now being cultivated all over the world. The actual division between the different kinds is difficult because the fruits are often combined into fertile hybrids. The kumquat fruits forming the genus *Fortunella* are also counted as part of the citrus-fruit family.

The fruits are picked and transported ripe. The balance between sugar and acid is measured before the harvest begins. Citrus fruits have hard skins that consist of a shiny outer peel and a thicker inner layer that is white. You can find citrus oil in the outer peel as well as most of the vitamins. Almost all kinds of citrus fruits are treated with wax so that they won't dry up.

The orange (*Citrus sinensis*) originated in China and first arrived in Europe during the 1500s. However, it was not until the 1800s that oranges were cultivated in Europe, first in Spain and Italy. We import oranges all year round in Sweden. There are blond oranges with yellow flesh and blood oranges with red flesh. The most common orange, which you can eat fresh or squeeze for juice, is usually sold under the names Jaffa and Valencia. The navel orange is seedless. It has a second small orange growing at the apex and they are not as juicy as the other varieties.

The lemon (*Citrus limon*) came from China to Europe during the 1000s as a medicine and spice. There are hundreds of lemon varieties. The common sour lemon usually has few seeds and can be quite small with a smooth peel. You buy that variety for the sake of the juice. There are also other lemons varieties that are larger and have thicker peels; these are usually bought for the sake of their zest. Quality lemons should be heavy in relation to their size, and have a sharp scent. You can roll the fruit between your hands and it will release more juice. The sweet lemon, which is rarer, stems from the Middle East and Turkey. It is sweet and fresh and is cultivated mostly because of its thick, aromatic peel; it is often preserved.

Bright green limes have a thin green peel and contain a very aromatic juice. They belong to the same family as lemons and are used for the same purposes. The limequat, another variety, is a combination of lime and kumquat. They may be eaten raw or be preserved. You can eat the entire fruit.

The grapefruit (*citrus x paradisi*) was first referenced during the 1700s, when you could find the fruit in Puerto Rico. Later, more extensive cultivation of the fruit began in Florida. Grapefruits are a larger fruit that can be blond with a yellow peel or so-called blood grapefruits with a pink flesh and pink peel. The ugli fruit looks like a rugged grapefruit with a rough green peel. It is a hybrid between the orange, the grapefruit, and the clementine. The pomelo (*Citrus*

grandis) is the largest citrus fruit. It has a pear shape and has a yellow-green peel with a thick white inner layer. Its flesh is light yellow and rough with a fresh taste.

The Seville orange (*Citrus aurantium*) has been known in Europe since the late 1000s as a spice, when it first arrived with the Arabs from India. It is too bitter to eat fresh, but it is great for marmalades.

The mandarin orange (*Citrus reticulata*). Certain smaller citrus varieties came to Europe and the United States from China and Japan during the 1800s. They have since been combined into many new hybrids. Among the most common are tangerines, clementines, and mandarins, see p. 110. The kumquat is the smallest of all the citrus fruits, see p. 113.

Very few other fruits are as useful as an ingredient in cooking food and desserts, and as a drink, ice cream, preserve, and so on.

Added Flavor

Spices: vanilla, ginger, cloves, cardamom, cinnamon, tonka beans, black pepper, rose pepper, and more.
Herbs: various varieties of thyme and basil are very suitable, and rosemary is great.
Sugar: Many varieties, both light and dark.
Spirits: cognac, Armagnac, liqueur such as Grand Marnier and Cointreau.

Lemon Cordial

4 cups (1,000 g/1 liter) squeezed lemon juice
3 ⅓ lbs (1,500 g) sugar

1. Clean the lemons and finely grate the peels of 4 of them.
2. Pour lemon juice, zest, and sugar into a pot.
3. Heat to the boiling point and remove all foam. Boil until the cordial looks clear, about 5 minutes.
4. Sift the cordial right away and pour it into sterilized bottles while still warm. Cork right away and store it in the fridge.

Orange Cordial

3 ½ cups (850 g/8 ½ dl) squeezed orange juice
⅔ cup (150 g/1 ½ dl) squeezed lemon juice
3 lbs (1,350 g) sugar

1. Clean the oranges and finely grate the peels of 4 of them.
2. Pour orange and lemon juice, orange zest, and sugar into a pot and continue as described above for Lemon Cordial (steps 3 and 4).

Lime and Orange Marmalade with Cardamom

4 oranges
6 limes
12 cups (3,000 g/3 liters) water
2 lbs (1,000 g) sugar
1 tbsp (20 g) crushed green cardamom

DAY 1
1. Clean the fruit and cut away the ends. Peel them and cut the pith away with a sharp knife.
2. Slice the peel in very thin strips.
3. Remove the seeds and put them in a cloth bag.
4. Slice the fruit as thinly as possible and place it in a pot with the shredded peel. Add the water and bring everything to a boil. Pour into a bowl and let it cool. Cover with plastic wrap and let it sit in the fridge overnight.

DAY 2
1. Empty everything into a pot and let it boil on low heat for 60 minutes.
2. Add the sugar and cardamom. Raise the heat. Remove foam. Brush the inside of the pot with a brush dipped in cold water to prevent sugar crystals.
3. Remove the bag with the seeds. Boil to 220–222°F (105–106°C). Perform a jelly test on a cold plate, see p. 20.
4. Pour directly into sterilized jars and screw on the lids immediately. Turn the jars upside down a couple of times.

Makes about 3 ⅓ lbs (1,500 g) marmalade. *Photo to the right.*

Orange Jam with Grand Marnier

A fantastic jam for breakfast, but also for desserts, tarts, and pastries.

2 lbs (1,000 g) oranges
Juice of 1 lemon
2 lbs (1,000 g) sugar
1 ½ cups (350 g/3 ½ dl) apple juice, see p. 16
½ cup (100 g/10 cl) Grand Marnier

1. Rinse the oranges, place them in a pot with the lemon juice, and cover with water. Bring it to a boil and let it simmer under a lid for 1 hour.
2. Cool the oranges under running water. Slice them into thin slices and then dice them into small squares. Remove all the seeds and place them in a cloth bag so that you can boil them with the jam.
3. Pour all of the ingredients into a pot and bring it to a boil. Let it simmer on low heat for 30 minutes or until the fruit is starting to look transparent and the jam feels jelly-like. Remove any foam so that the jam becomes clear.
4. Brush the inside of the pot with a brush dipped in cold water to prevent sugar crystals. Boil till the oranges are turning transparent and the surface is starting to wrinkle.
5. At 222–224°F (106–107°C), the jam is ready. You may also do a jam test on a cold plate, see p. 20.
6. Pour directly into sterilized jars and screw on the lids right away. Turn the jars upside down a couple of times.

Makes about 3 ⅓ lbs (1,500 g) jam.

English Breakfast Marmalade with Whiskey

It can't get any more traditional than this.

4 dried Seville orange peels
2 grapefruits
4 oranges
2 lemons
12 cups (3,000 g/3 liters) water
3 ½ lbs (1,550 g) dark muscovado sugar
2 tbsp (50 g) grated ginger
¾ cup (200 g/2 dl) Scottish whiskey
2 cups (500 g/5 dl) apple juice or 12 oz (350 g) apple jelly, see p. 16–17

DAY 1

1. Place the Seville orange peels in water so that they can soak overnight.
2. Carefully clean all of the fruits and peel them. Cut away most of the pith on the peels and cut them into very thin slivers.
3. Dice the fruit flesh and remove the seeds. Place the seeds in a cloth bag so that you can boil them with the jam.
4. Put the peel slivers in 12 cups (3,000 g/3 liters) of boiling water and let them boil for 5 minutes. Throw the water out and repeat the process.
5. Blend all of the ingredients, excluding the Seville orange peels, in a pot and bring it to a boil while stirring.
6. Empty into a bowl and let cool. Cover with plastic wrap and let it rest at room temperature overnight.

DAY 2

1. Place the soaked Seville orange peels in boiling water and let them boil for 5 minutes.
2. Repeat the process, and then cool them under cold running water. Slice the peels into thin slivers.
3. Add everything to a pot and boil while stirring. Brush the inside of the pot with a brush dipped in cold water to prevent sugar crystals.
4. Remove any foam that may appear so that the marmalade is completely clear.
5. After 60 minutes, when the peels are starting to turn transparent and the jam is forming jelly, measure the temperature. It should be at 222–224°F (106–107°C). Or you may perform a jam test on a cold plate, see p. 20.
6. Pour directly into sterilized jars and screw on the lids right away. Turn the jars upside down a couple of times.

Makes about 4 ½ lbs (2,000 g) marmalade.

French Orange or Lemon Jam

I use this jam as a filling for chocolate tarts with chocolate mousse. But you may also use it for orange muffins and for other desserts.

Orange Jam

3 ⅓ lbs (1,500 g) oranges
1 lb (500 g) sugar
2 cups (500 g/5 dl) water
3 lbs (1,400 g) sugar
1 ⅔ cups (400 g/4 dl) water

Lemon Jam

The exact same ingredients and quantities, but use lemons instead of oranges.

DAY 1

1. Bring 12 cups (3 liters) of water to a boil in a pot. Blanch the whole oranges for 5 minutes in the boiling water and then place them under cold running water.
2. Cut the oranges (or lemons) down the middle and cut away the ends. Slice them as thinly as possible with a knife.
3. Boil syrup out of 2 cups (500 g) water and 1 lb (500 g) sugar. Add the orange slices and let it simmer on low heat for 2 hours.
4. Pour into a bowl and let it cool. Cover with plastic wrap.

DAY 2

1. Pour the fruit into a strainer and let the juice drain (you may use this as cordial). Purée the fruit in a food processor.
2. Pour 3 lbs (1,400 g) sugar and 1 ⅔ cups (4 dl) water into a pot and boil.
3. Continually brush the inside of the pot with a brush dipped in cold water to avoid sugar crystals. Boil to 234–240°F (112–114°C), or perform a sugar test, see p. 14.
4. Add the orange or lemon purée and boil, while stirring, to 220°F (105°C). Or you may do a jam test on a cold plate, see p. 20.
5. Pour directly into sterilized jars and screw on the lids right away. Turn the jars upside down a couple of times.

Makes about 4 lbs (2,000 g) jam.

Lemon Curd

You may prepare variations of this recipe where you use other citrus fruits and still get great results, but remember that 25 percent of the juice has to be lemon, otherwise the taste becomes flat. Do not use a copper pot for curd, as it will turn out green.

Grated zest of 3 lemons
⅔ cups (150 g/1 ½ dl) lemon juice
About 6 eggs (300 g)
½ lb sugar (300 g)
14 tbsp (1 ¾ sticks/200 g) unsalted butter

1. Rinse the lemons and finely grate the zest.
2. Whisk the eggs and half of the sugar until fluffy.
3. Bring the lemon juice, zest, and the remaining sugar to a boil.
4. Pour the lemon mixture on top of the whisked egg mixture. Mix well with a whisk.
5. Empty the mix into a small saucepan with a thick bottom. Carefully bring to a boil while whisking.
6. Remove the saucepan from the stove and whisk until smooth.
7. Pour the cream through a strainer. Let it cool to 122°F (50°C) and mix in the butter with a hand blender.
8. Pour the cream into sterilized jars right away. Screw the lids on and turn the jars upside down a couple of times.

If you want to prolong its shelf life, you may do the following: Place the jars in a water bath with hot water in the oven at 175°F (80°C) for 20 minutes. Let them cool down and store them in the fridge.

Makes about 2 lbs (900 g) curd.

Grapefruit Jam

8 large blood grapefruits
2 lemons
12 cups (3,000 g/3 liters) water
Amount of sugar equal to the weight of the fruit mass
¾ cup (200 g/2 dl) gin

DAY 1

1. Rinse the fruits in water and cut the ends off.
2. Cut the fruits in half and slice them as thinly as possible, preferably with a food slicer, if you have one.
3. Place the fruit slices in a bowl and cover them with water. Cover with plastic wrap and let it sit at room temperature for 28 hours so that the bitterness is decreased.

DAY 2

1. Drain the water out. Pour fruit and 12 cups (3 liters) of water into a pot and let it come to a boil. Remove any foam and let it simmer for 30 minutes.
2. Pour into a plastic bowl and let it cool. Cover with plastic wrap and keep it in the fridge overnight.

DAY 3

1. Weigh the entire fruit mass and add an equal weight of sugar.
2. Add the liquor and boil while stirring now and then.
3. Remove foam so that the jam is clear.
4. Brush the inside of the pot with a brush dipped in cold water to prevent sugar crystals. Boil to 220–222°F (105–106°C) or perform a jam test on a cold plate, see p. 20.
5. Pour directly into sterilized jars and screw on the lids right away. Turn the jars upside down a couple of times.

Makes about 2 ¾ lbs (1,300 g) jam.

Tip!

You can also use blood oranges the exact same way. In that case, replace the gin with cognac and add a cinnamon stick.

Quick-Preserved Citrus Peels

Good for dipping in chocolate, for soft fruitcakes, and more.

2 lbs (1,000 g) oranges or other citrus fruits
2 cups (500 g/5 dl) water
1 ⅔ lbs (750 g) sugar
2 ½ tbsp (50 g) honey
1 vanilla bean, preferably Tahiti or Bourbon

1. Cut around the fruits and remove the peels. Place them in boiling water and boil under a lid till they are completely soft. This can take 30 to 60 minutes.
2. When the fruits feel soft when you stab them with a toothpick, cool them under cold running water.
3. Scoop up the peel and remove as much of the pith as possible with a spoon.
4. Cut the vanilla bean open and scrape out the seeds. Place the bean and seeds, ½ cup (125 g) sugar, and 2 cups (500 g) water in the pot with the peels and let it simmer for 15 minutes.
5. Add an additional ½ cup (125 g) of the sugar and let it simmer for 15 minutes more. Repeat this process 4 more times until the peels are completely transparent.
6. Add the honey.
7. Scoop the peels onto sterilized glass jars and cover with the boiling syrup. Screw on the lids right away.

If you wish to make *half-preserved* citrus peels, so-called demi-confit, for desserts and ice cream, you repeat the process only 4 times, in other words you need 1 lb (500 g) sugar and 2 cups (500 g) water.

Preserved Citrus Peels

You can use this same method for orange, lemon, or grapefruit peels. All kinds of berries and fruits can be preserved the same way. Through blanching, the pores in the peel and fruit flesh are opened. By not making the syrup too strong right away, the peels absorb the sugar in increments and will not shrink the way they would if we were to add all of the sugar at once. In this classic method of preserving, honey or glucose is added at the very end in order to prevent the syrup from crystallizing. Pastry chefs use hydrometers, so-called sugar thermometers or sugar weights, where the units of measurement are degrees Baumé, and the preservation is finished when the syrup measures 36° Baumé, see Candying on p. 208. The same basic rule applies to all methods of preserving fruit.

DAY 1

2 lbs (1 kg) oranges or other citrus fruit
1 vanilla bean
1 lb (400 g) sugar
2 ½ cups (600 g/6 dl) water

DAY 2	DAY 3	DAY 4	DAY 5
⅔ cup (140 g) sugar	½ cup (120 g) sugar	½ cup (120 g) sugar	½ cup (120 g) sugar 3 ½ tbsp (75 g) honey

DAY 1

1. Clean the fruits in cold water with a brush.
2. Cut the peel into four pieces and peel it off. Squeeze the fruits. You may freeze the juice and use it at another time, for instance, for sorbet.
3. Place the citrus peels in a saucepan. Cover with water.
4. Bring it to a boil and let it simmer for 30 minutes, or till the peels feel soft when you stick them with a knife.
5. Hold the peels under cold running water to end the boiling. Place them on a cutting board and scrape the pith away with a spoon.
6. Rinse the peels in cold water. Let them drain and dry them off.
7. Place the peels in a clean glass jar that holds about 20 cups (5 liters) (pastry chefs will always place them in a *candissoire* with racks, which will keep the peels down, and a tap that allows the syrup to run off during the preserving).
8. Cut the vanilla bean down the middle. Place it in the jar in between the peels.
9. Bring sugar and water to a boil. Pour the syrup over the peels. Let it cool. Screw on the lids and place in the fridge.

DAY 2

1. Pour the syrup into a pot.
2. Add the sugar. Bring to a boil. Pour the syrup over the peels. Let cool. Screw on the lids and place in the fridge.

DAYS 3 AND 4

Repeat the process of day 2.

DAY 5

Pour the syrup and peels into a pot. Add the sugar. Bring to a boil and remove any foam. Add the honey. Pour back into the now cleaned glass jar. Let it cool and store in the fridge. (Use a spoon, not your fingers, when you pick peels out of the jar and they will keep for at least a year.)

Preserved Orange Peels

3 ⅓ lbs (1,500 g) oranges

1. Clean the oranges and cut them in ¼ in (5 mm) thick slices across. Place them in a baking pan and cover with boiling water.

2. Cover with aluminum foil and let them bake in the oven at 300°F (150°C) for 60 minutes. Let them cool completely.

3. Carefully place them in a container and preserve them as described for citrus peels for 5 days.

You may later dry them on a rack and candy them, see Candying on p. 208.

The World's Best Lemon Cake

Tastes wonderful with coffee or tea. I would always serve this lemon cake with the afternoon tea when I worked on the cruise ship Vista/Fjord. The cake is also great as a dessert with fresh berries and lemon sorbet or ice cream.

Remember to take the eggs and butter out of the fridge the day before so that they are at room temperature. This way the batter will not divide. If the eggs are cold, the butter stiffens and the water is pushed out; if the butter isn't at room temperature, it is hard to whip it until it is fluffy.

2 cake pans, 9 x 3 ½ inches (23 x 9 cm), or aluminum foil pans
4 tbsp (60 g) butter to grease the pans
½ cup (50 g) all-purpose flour for the pans

½ cup (100 g) salted butter, softened	1 ⅔ cups (350 g) sugar
2 ½ cups (280 g) all-purpose flour	Pinch of salt
2 tbsp (10 g) baking powder	2 ¾ tbsp (40 g/4 cl) dark rum
2 lemons	¾ cup (150 g/1 ½ dl) whipping cream
About 6 eggs (300 g)	5 oz (150 g) Apricot Jelly, see p. 118

Lemon Glaze

Lemon juice from the 2 lemons above
1 ⅓ cups (150 g) powdered sugar
Preserved Citrus Peels, see p. 107

1. Carefully brush the inside of the pans with the softened butter. Sprinkle the flour evenly into the pans. Shake out any extra flour.
2. Melt the butter in a small frying pan. Set aside.
3. Sift the flour and baking powder together.
4. Wash the lemons, grate the zest, and squeeze the juice.
5. Set the oven to 340°F (170°C).
6. Whisk eggs, sugar, salt, and lemon peels for about 5 minutes, until soft peaks form.
7. Fold in the flour and baking powder with a silicone spatula. Lastly, add the butter, liquor, and whipping cream. Blend till smooth.
8. Fill the pans three-fourths full with the batter and bake for 45 minutes. Insert a knife into the cakes; if nothing sticks to the knife, the cakes are ready.
9. Remove the cakes from the oven and let them rest for 5 minutes. Turn them out onto a cooling rack.
10. Set the oven to 445°F (230°C).
11. Mix the powdered sugar and lemon juice into a glaze.
12. Boil 5 oz (150 g) apricot jelly and brush it all over the cake. Add strips of preserved lemon peels.
13. Place the cooling rack with the cakes in the warm oven for 1–2 minutes with the oven door ajar so that the glaze stiffens. You can decorate with preserved cherries, if you like.

When the cake has cooled, cut into slices.
Photo on p. 112.

Mandarin and Clementine
Citrus reticulata

The clementine is a cross between the mandarin and Seville orange. It got its name from the Algerian priest Pierre Clement, who first grew it in his garden in 1902. The mandarin is sometimes said to come from China and also Mauritius. It is not as common in stores nowadays.

With its intense flavor, the mandarin is fantastic for sorbets and pralines. The outer peel, with its rich aroma, is good for smaller, softer cakes.

Added Flavor

Spices: Be very careful with spices because the taste in itself is so nice; only use vanilla.
Sugar: if wanted, muscovado, light not dark.
Herbs: lemon verbena, lemon and orange thyme.
Spirits: cognac and Armagnac.
Fruit combinations: bananas, pears, and apples, besides all kinds of citrus fruits.

Mandarin Marmalade with Cognac

2 ¾ lbs (1,300 g) mandarins
2 lemons
Amount of sugar equal to the weight of the fruit mass
⅔ cup (150 g/15 cl) cognac

1. Place the mandarins and lemons in water. Remove the peel and put it in boiling water. Let the peel boil for 5 minutes.
2. Cool everything under cold running water and dice the peel.
3. Purée the fruit flesh in a mixer. Remove the seeds.
4. Weigh the fruit purée and add an equal weight of sugar. Pour everything into a pot with the cognac.
5. Bring it to a boil and remove any foam. Occasionally brush the inside of the pot with a brush dipped in cold water to prevent sugar crystals. Continue to remove foam so that the marmalade is clear.
6. Boil to 222–224°F (106–107°C), or perform a jam test on a cold plate, see p.20.
7. Pour directly into sterilized jars and screw on the lids. Turn the jars upside down a couple of times.

Makes about 3 ⅓ lbs (1,500 g) marmalade.

Clementine Marmalade with Grand Marnier

Follow the recipe above with clementines, and replace the cognac with Grand Marnier Rouge.

Preserved Mandarins

You may boil and preserve small mandarins the same way you would kumquats, see Preserved Kumquat, p. 113.

Another option is to poke holes in them and preserve them with the entire peel still on, the same way as preserved apricots, after which you cover them with a fitting liqueur or cognac.

Preserved Clementines or Mandarins

You can preserve any small citrus fruit the same way you preserve citrus peels; see Preserved Citrus Peels, p. 107.

2 lbs (1,000 g) fruit

Poke holes in the fruit with a fork and boil them in water until they have gone completely soft. Rinse them in running water and preserve them by following the recipe for Preserved Citrus Peels, see p. 107.

Boiled Half-Preserved Clementines

You might want to make half-preserved Clementine, so-called demi-confit, for Christmas. Add star anise, vanilla, and a generous amount of Grand Marnier. See Quick-Preserved Citrus Peels, p. 107.

Serve them cold with cinnamon or pistachio ice cream.

Fruitcake

Fruitcake always tastes excellent with afternoon coffee or tea. Unfortunately, in Sweden we mostly bake this cake for Christmas. The glaze with lemon and rum provides a nice contrast. Feel free to bake it 24 hours before you are serving it; this cake keeps fresh for a long time.

Remember to take out the butter and eggs before baking so that the batter doesn't separate. If you blend the marinated fruit with half the flour, they won't sink to the bottom of the cakes.

2 rectangular baking pans, 9 x 3 ½ inches (23 x 9 cm)
2 tbsp (50 g) butter for greasing the pans
6 tbsp (25 g) breadcrumbs for the pans

3 ½ oz (100 g) yellow raisins
2 ½ oz (75 g) chopped preserved succade
4 ½ oz (125 g) preserved chopped orange peels
¼ cup (50 g/½ dl) dark rum
1 lemon
2 ¾ cups (300 g) all-purpose flour
2 tsp (10 g) baking powder
1 cup (250 g) unsalted butter
1 ⅛ cup (225 g) muscovado sugar, light brown
1 tbsp (25 g) real vanilla sugar
3 eggs (150 g)
2 egg yolks (40 g)

Glaze

Juice of 1 lemon, from above list
1 cup (100 g) powdered sugar
1 ½ tbsp (2 cl) rum

For Decorating:

5 oz (150 g) Apricot Jelly, see p. 118
10 preserved red currants or cherries

DAY 1

Place raisins, succade, and orange peels in a bowl and mix in with the liquor. Cover with plastic wrap and let it marinate overnight.

DAY 2

1. Rinse and dry the lemon and grate the outer peel with a grater.
2. Squeeze the lemon and mix the juice with powdered sugar and liquor for the glaze.
3. Set the oven to 390°F (200°C).
4. Grease the inside of the pans carefully with butter. Spread the breadcrumbs between the pans and shake out any extra.
5. Sift the flour and baking powder on a piece of paper.
6. Place the butter, sugar, and lemon zest in a bowl. Stir it with a whisk until light and foamy.
7. Add the eggs and yolks and mix into a smooth batter.
8. Pour half of the flour into the batter and stir it in without overworking.
9. Blend the remaining flour with the marinated fruit until it is all covered in flour. Carefully add the fruit to the batter.

Continued on p. 113

The World's Best Lemon Cake and Fruitcake.

10. Fill the pans three-fourths full with the batter. Place them in the oven and after 5 minutes lower the temperature to 340°F (170°C).
11. Bake the fruitcakes for an additional 35 minutes. Check with a toothpick to see if they're ready.
12. Take the cakes out of the oven and let them rest for 5 minutes.
13. Carefully release the cakes from the pans and place them with the tops facing upwards on a cooling rack to cool.

Decoration:

Set the oven to 445°F (230°C). Boil the apricot jelly and brush it over the cakes. Cover the cakes with the glaze and decorate with the currants or cherries. Place the cakes in the oven with the door ajar until the glaze surface feels dry, 1–2 minutes. *Photo to the left.*

Tip!

For Christmas you can serve the cake with Rumtopf, see p. 218, and vanilla or cinnamon ice cream. A delicious Christmas dessert!

Kumquat

Fortunella japonica (round)
Fortunella margarita (oval)

The kumquat belongs to the Fortunella family. It stems from China and is both closely related to, and counted as part of, the citrus fruit family. The fruit can be both orange and green (the so-called lime kumquat). You can find the round kumquat as a potted plant and it is often marketed as a mini orange tree.

The fruits only weigh about $^1/_3$ oz (10 g). They are imported from South America and Israel, among other places, almost year-round. They are mostly used fresh as a garnish on tarts and desserts. Personally, I like to boil them in syrup and serve with desserts or cheeses. But they also have a wonderful taste in jam.

Preserved Kumquat

Serve with ice cream or dessert.

2 lbs (1,000 g) kumquats
½ lb (300 g) sugar
5 tbsp (100 g) honey

1 cup (250 g/2 ½ dl) freshly squeezed orange juice
Juice of 1 lemon
½ cup (100 g/1 dl) Grand Marnier

Spices

1 clove
⅓ inch (1 cm) real cinnamon stick
1 bay leaf
2 star anise
1 tbsp (10 g) dried coriander
1 vanilla bean, preferably Bourbon

1. Rinse the fruits and poke them all over with a small fork.
2. Place the fruits in boiling water and blanch them for 5 minutes. Cool them under cold running water.
3. Pour sugar, honey, and orange juice with spices into a pot. Cut the vanilla bean down the middle and scrape the seeds out. Add the vanilla bean, seeds, and lemon juice to the pot.
4. Bring the syrup to a boil and add the kumquats. Let it simmer on low heat until the fruit is starting to turn transparent.
5. Add the liqueur.
6. Pour directly into sterilized jars and screw on the lids right away. If you wish, you may sterilize the preserve as well; see Peaches Boiled in Red Wine, p. 126.

Store in the fridge.

Kumquat Marmalade with Whiskey

2 lbs (1,000 g) kumquats
1 ¾ lbs (800 g) light muscovado sugar
Juice of 1 lemon
⅔ cup (150 g/1 ½ dl) peated whiskey

1. Rinse the kumquats.
2. Poke the fruits all around with a fork and boil them in water for 5 minutes.
3. Pour the sugar and lemon juice into a pot and boil to 234–240°F (112–114°C). Brush the inside of the pot with a brush dipped in cold water to prevent sugar crystals.
4. Add the drained fruits and the liquor and boil on low heat while stirring for about 10 minutes. Remove all foam. Continually brush the inside of the pot.
5. Boil until the fruits look transparent and the surface of the marmalade is starting to wrinkle.
6. At 224–226°F (107–108°C) the marmalade is ready. You may also do a jam test, see p. 20.
7. Pour directly into sterilized jars and screw on the lids right away. Turn the jars upside down a couple of times.

Makes about 3 ⅓ lbs (1,500 g) marmalade.

Apricot

Prunus armeniaca

In China, apricots were cultivated as early as 4,000 years ago. Nowadays, they are mostly cultivated around the Mediterranean Sea, in the United States, and in Australia. The plant is related to the plum and the almond, among others. The fruit is characterized by a wood-like kernel in the middle, soft flesh, and a thin peel.

You may eat apricots fresh or prepare them in a variety of ways. They have juicy flesh with an almond aroma. The apricot is reminiscent of the peach in its taste, but when it is boiled, dried, or preserved, the sour, sharp taste, and the powerful aroma exceed both the peach and the nectarine.

Apricots are used for jam, purée, jelly, and marmalade, for so-called sliced fruit marmalade and for compote. They are both conserved and dried. You can also use dried apricots for preserving, but in that case the fruits need to be soaked in water for at least a day before using. Occasionally, you can use the apricot kernels for cooking chutneys or you may preserve them in alcohol. You should never eat a large quantity of apricot kernels as they contain cyanide. They lose bitterness if soaked in water and are often used as a substitute for almond marzipan in a similar confection known as parzipan.

Traditionally, apricots are often used in both confectionaries and restaurant kitchens. I can still smell the intense scent of apricots from when we would boil apricot sauce for the desserts at the Savoy Hotel in Malmö. When I read in my recipe book, which I started at age fifteen, it says the following about apricot jam: we boiled 22 lbs (10 kg) sugar and 10 ½ cups (2 ½ liters) to 265°F (130°C). We then poured this over 27 ½ lbs (12 ½ kg) apricots and 2 cups (½ liter) lemon juice and boiled to a strong thread test. When boiling such large quantities, boiling the sugar first allowed a shorter boiling time altogether.

The apricot jelly is commonly used with glazed pastries. For instance, classic mazarins, Swedish almond tarts, are first brushed with boiling seedless apricot jam before they are glazed; otherwise the pasty absorbs the water in the frosting and the glaze becomes dull. Pastry chefs will also brush fruits with boiling apricot jelly to give them an extra shine. Seedless apricot marmalade is used as a filling.

Added Flavor

Spices: real cinnamon, cassava, vanilla, tonka bean, coriander, cardamom, pepper, and chili.

Herbs: lavender (a classic flavoring in Provence), lemon balm, peppermint, lemon verbena, rosemary, lemon and orange thyme.

Citrus: zest and juice of various citrus fruits; lemon juice helps the pectin in the preserve form jelly.

Wine and spirits: for instance, Kirschwasser enhances the spice flavors.

Tea: All varieties

Bitter almonds: In small quantities to help enhance the flavor of the kernels.

Honey: acacia honey and orange blossom honey. Remember to never use too much honey in jam or marmalades, as they then turn out gluey.

Fruit combinations: half raspberries and apricots, strawberries and apricots, cherries and apricots; even blackberries and blueberries taste nice; red currants make it tangy and tasty.

Other good combinations: almonds, macadamia nuts, walnuts, and pecans.

Classic Apricot Jam

The basic vanilla flavoring gives a nice aroma, while the bitter almonds enhance the natural taste of the kernels in the finished jam. If you want to add herbs then blanch them first by scalding them in boiling water. Then place them directly in cold water. Finely chop them and add them at the end of the boiling time.

6 bitter almonds
2 ½ lbs (1,200 g) fresh apricots, ripe
(2 lbs [1,000 g] net weight)
1 ¼ cups (300 g/3 dl) water
1 ¾ lbs (800 g) sugar
Juice of 1 lemon
1 vanilla bean, preferably Bourbon

1. Bring ½ cup (1 dl) water to a boil and scald the almonds. Place them in cold water right away and remove the shells. Use a mortar to grind them into an even mass.
2. Bring 8 ½ cups (2 liters) of water to a boil and scald the apricots for about 1 minute. Place them in cold water and peel with a small knife. Cut them down the middle and remove the kernels.
3. Pour the sugar and 1 ¼ cups (300 g) water into a pot and bring to a boil on full heat. Brush the inside of the pot with a brush dipped in cold water to prevent sugar crystals.
4. Boil to 234–240°F (112–114°C). Use a thermometer if possible, or perform a so-called marble test, see Boiling Sugar, p. 14.
5. Add the apricots, bitter almonds, and lemon juice. Cut the vanilla bean down the middle and add the seeds to the pot. Boil everything for about 10 minutes. Stir occasionally and remove foam with a spoon.
6. Boil until the apricots are turning transparent and the surface of the jam is starting to wrinkle. The temperature should then be at 222–224°F (106–107°C). The temperature may be higher if the apricots are very ripe and lower if they are not fully ripened. Perform a jam test on a cold plate, see p. 20.
7. Pour directly into sterilized jars and screw on the lids immediately. Turn the jars upside down a couple of times.

Makes about 3 ⅓ lbs (1,500 g) jam.

Apricot Jam with Salted Butter

The original jam of the Confiserie Brändli in Basel was called *Confiture d'apricot au beurre salé*, or apricot jam with salted butter. The jam was served for breakfast with the typical Swiss breakfast breads like Zopf, Weggli, and Croissant. Try to prepare this jam once you have access to really ripe apricots.

¾ lb (750 g) scalded and pitted apricots
1 ½ lbs (750 g) sugar
Juice of 1 lemon
¼ cup (50 g) salted butter
Pinch of fleur de sel

1. Combine the apricots, sugar, and lemon juice in a pot.
2. Bring to a boil and remove any foam with a spoon. Brush the inside of the pot with a brush dipped in cold water to prevent sugar crystals. Boil everything to 222–224°F (106–107°C), or perform a jam test on a cold plate, see p. 20.
3. Lastly, add the salted butter and a pinch of fleur de sel.
4. Pour directly into sterilized jars and screw on the lids right away. Turn the jars upside down a couple of times.

Seedless Apricot Jam

In Sweden, apricot jam is sometimes called marmalade when it is seedless. The Austrians call it *Marillen-Marmelade* and it is generously used in Austrian pastries and desserts. Seedless apricot jam is great as a filling in doughnuts, danishes, pastries, tarts, desserts, and cookies.

Remember to use a long ladle or spoon when you stir the seedless jam as it splashes a lot. It will easily burn unless you stir it constantly.

6 bitter almonds
2 ½ lbs (1,200 g) fresh apricots, ripe
(2 lbs [1,000 g] net weight)
1 ¼ cups (300 g/3 dl) water
Juice of 1 lemon
1 vanilla bean, preferably Bourbon
1 ¾ lbs (800 g) sugar

1. Bring ½ cup (100 g/1 dl) water to a boil and scald the almonds. Place them in cold water right away and remove the shells. Grind them into a smooth mass in a mortar.
2. Bring 8 ½ cups (2 liters) of water to a boil and scald the apricots for 1 minute. Move them directly into cold water and peel them with a small knife. Cut them down the middle and remove the kernels.
3. Boil the water and add the scalded, peeled, and pitted apricots, the ground bitter almonds, and the lemon juice. Boil for 10 minutes under a lid until the apricots have gone completely soft.
4. Pour into a food processor and mix twice. Press the mass through a strainer.
5. Pour the purée back into the pot. Cut the vanilla bean down the middle and add the seeds to the pot.
6. Add the sugar and boil while constantly stirring. Remove any foam with a spoon while boiling. Brush the inside of the pot with a brush dipped in cold water to prevent sugar crystals. Boil to 220°F (105°C), or perform a jam test, see p. 20.
7. Pour directly into sterilized jars and screw on the lids right away. Turn the jars upside down a couple of times.

Makes about 3 ⅓ lbs (1,500 g) jam.

Apricot Jelly

This jelly is very suitable for delicate pastries and desserts. The pastry chef and cook boil this and brush it on fruit slices and glazed pastries so that the glaze maintains its shine.

If you wish to add vanilla, just boil with the vanilla bean without opening it. Vanilla provides a nice aroma. Apricot jelly may be flavored with spices, herbs, or flowers.

2 ½ lbs (1,200 g) apricots
1 cup (250 g) water
Juice of 1 lemon
1 ½ cups (350 g) apple juice or ½ lb (250 g) apple jelly, see p. 16–17
Amount of sugar equal to the weight of the drained fruit juice

1. Scald the rinsed apricots in boiling water for one minute. Cool in cold water and peel with a small knife.
2. Put the apricots in the pot with the water, lemon juice, and apple juice or jelly. Boil under a lid for 30 minutes until the apricots have fallen apart.
3. Pour into a strainer and gently squeeze all of the juice out by using the back of a spoon. Empty the mass into a strainer lined with cheesecloth and let it drain on its own for about 60 minutes, or until the fruit mass feels completely dry.
4. Weigh the juice and add an equal weight of sugar. Place everything in a pot and boil.
5. Carefully remove foam while boiling. Brush the inside of the pot with a brush dipped in cold water to prevent sugar crystals. Boil to 220°F (105°C). Perform a jelly test, see p. 20.
6. Pour directly into sterilized jars and screw on the lids right away. Turn the jars upside down a couple of times.

Makes about 2 ½ lbs (1,100 g) jelly.

Apricot Sauce

This is the recipe we used at the Savoy Hotel in Malmö. We would always add Kirschwasser, and we served it warm or cold with a variety of desserts. The liqueur helps highlight the taste of the kernels from the apricots. This sauce is a base sauce for many delicious desserts and it also goes great with various desserts, both warm and cold. Some classic desserts typically served with apricot sauce are Soufflé Pudding Palmyré and Peach Sultan.

2 ½ lbs (1,200 g) fresh apricots
(2 lbs [1,000 g] net weight)
1 lb (500 g) sugar
Juice of 2 lemons
2 cups (500 g/5 dl) water
1 vanilla bean, preferably Bourbon

1. Bring 8 ½ cups (2 liters) of water to a boil and scald the apricots for about 1 minute. Afterwards, cool in cold water and peel with a small knife. Cut them down the middle and remove the kernels.
2. Bring the water to a boil and add the scalded, peeled, and pitted apricots

with the lemon juice, and boil for 10 minutes under a lid until they have gone completely soft.
3. Pour into a food processor and mix twice. Press the mixture through a strainer.
4. Pour the purée back into the pot. Cut the vanilla bean down the middle and add the seeds to the pot.
5. Add the sugar and boil while constantly stirring. Brush the inside of the pot with a brush dipped in cold water to prevent sugar crystals. Boil to 215–217°F (102–103°C), or do a jam test, see p. 20.
(We would always dip a spoon in the boiling sauce, and when the sauce created a coating on the inside of the spoon, we would finish the boiling and the temperature would be at 215–217°F [102–103°C])
6. Pour the sauce into sterilized jars and screw on the lids right away. Turn the jars upside down a couple of times.

Lightly heat the sauce before serving and flavor with some Kirschwasser or another fitting liqueur.

Makes about 3 ½ lbs (1,600 g) sauce.

Apricot Jam with Almonds

The first time I tasted this combination was for breakfast at the restaurant Waterside Inn in London. It tasted magnificent with their croissants and brioches, which were still warm from the oven. I count this jam as one of my personal favorites. I prefer it on a sliced, freshly baked, toasted brioche, or with a sliced piece of duck liver. I have made many different varieties of this jam over the years.

By marinating them overnight, the apricots become firmer. The fruits absorb the sugar so that they will not fall apart as easily during boiling.

Tip!
If you are able to find fresh almonds, still with the green shell, the jam turns out especially well. Boil them in water until soft before you add them at the end of the boiling time. Green walnuts are also good with this. If you use dried almonds, you may drench the shelled almonds in boiling milk and let them sit for 1 hour. Afterwards, they will taste like fresh.

2 ½ lbs (1,200 g) apricots
(2 lbs [1,000 g] net weight)
2 lbs (1,000 g) sugar
Juice of 1 lemon
6 bitter almonds
1 vanilla bean, preferably Tahiti or Bourbon
7 oz (200 g) sweet almonds, preferably Marcona from Spain

DAY 1
1. Scald the apricots in boiling water and cool them in cold water right away. Peel with a small knife.
2. Place the apricots in the pot with the sugar and lemon juice.
3. Scald the bitter almonds in boiling water and cool them in cold water. Remove the shells.

Apricot Jam with Almonds.

4. Grind the bitter almonds in a mortar and place them in the pot.
5. Cut the vanilla bean down the middle and scrape out the seeds. Add the seeds to the pot as well.
6. Bring everything to a boil while occasionally stirring.
7. Pour directly into a bowl and let it cool.
8. Cover with plastic wrap and place it in the fridge overnight.

DAY 2
1. Pour everything into a strainer and let the syrup drain.
2. Boil the syrup in a pot. Brush the inside of the pot with a brush dipped in cold water to prevent sugar crystals. Boil to 234–240°F (112–114°C) or perform a sugar test, see Boiling Sugar, p. 14.
3. Add the apricots and the almonds. Boil while removing all foam and other impurities, so that the jam becomes clear.
4. Boil to 222–224°F (106–107°C), or perform a jam test on a cold plate, see p. 20.
5. Pour directly into sterilized jars and screw on the lids right away. Turn the jars upside down a couple of times.

Makes about 3 ¾ lbs (1,700 g) jam.

Apricot Jam with Vanilla and Lavender

I was served this delightful jam with breakfast at Fernand Point's wonderful restaurant La Pyramide in Vienne right outside of Lyon, a restaurant that is a gastronomic destination.

You should be able to see the chunks of fruit in this jam. Marinating overnight makes sure that the fruit does not fall apart during boiling.

Follow the same recipe and process as Apricot Jam with Almonds (p. 118–119), but exclude the almonds and increase the vanilla with an additional stick. Add 1 tbsp (10 g) dried lavender flowers at the end of the boiling time.

Apricot Compote with Vanilla

Compotes used to be served as desserts quite commonly and this is a great use of very ripe fruit. If you want you can serve it cold with, for instance, pistachio ice cream that enhances the taste, or with vanilla ice cream.

The well-known chef Paul Bocuse, who is based in the food mecca Lyon, always offers many types of compote on his dessert table.

Makes about 6 servings

2 lbs (1,000 g) ripe apricots
Juice of 1 orange
Juice of 1 lemon
1 cup (175 g) cassonade sugar (raw cane sugar)
1 vanilla bean, preferably Tahiti

1. Scald the apricots in boiling water and place them directly in cold water. Peel with a small knife.
2. Cut the apricots down the middle and remove the kernels. Squeeze the citrus fruits and pour the juice over the apricots with the vanilla seeds and the sugar. Mix well.
3. Cover with plastic wrap and let it marinate for 2 hours.
4. Empty everything into a pot and simmer on low heat for 10 minutes until the apricots feel soft but not overcooked. (Compotes can also be prepared in the oven; sometimes this may work better as the fruits will not fall apart as easily as in a pot on the stove.)
5. Pour directly into a bowl and let it cool. Place in the refrigerator, preferably overnight, so that the fruit really absorbs all the flavors.

You may also pour the compote into sterilized jars and conserve them in a 175°F (80°C) oven in a hot water bath for 20 minutes.

Apricot Chutney

Serve apricot chutney with hot foods and crispy spare ribs. This even tastes good with a curry dish.

2 ½ lbs (1,200 g) apricots
(2 lbs [1,000 g] net weight)
½ lb (250 g) cherry tomatoes
1 lb (500 g) red onions
3 yellow bell peppers
1 red chili
2 tbsp (25 g) grated fresh ginger
2 oranges
1 ¾ lbs (850 g) sugar, muscovado light
2 ½ cups (60 cl) red wine vinegar
⅓ inch (1 cm) real cinnamon stick
3 ½ oz (100 g) yellow raisins
2 tsp (10 g) sea salt

1. Scald the apricots in boiling water. Place them in cold water and peel with a small knife. Cut them down the middle and remove the kernels. Dice the fruit.
2. Scald the tomatoes in boiling water and cool them in cold water right away. Remove the skins with a small knife.
3. Peel and finely chop the red onions.
4. Rinse the bell peppers. Then remove the core and seeds and cut them into small pieces.
5. Rinse and finely chop the chili.
6. Grate the ginger.
7. Rinse the oranges in water, grate the zest, and squeeze the juice.
8. Place everything in a large pot and bring to a boil while stirring. Let it simmer on low heat for about 1 hour until it has a firm texture. Remember to stir as the chutney burns easily.
9. Pour directly into sterilized jars and screw on the lids right away. Turn the jars upside down a couple of times.

Makes about 4 ½ lbs (2,000 g) chutney.

Preserved Apricots

Great for storage if you can get ripe and inexpensive apricots.

2 ½ lbs (1,200 g) apricots, firm and not too ripe
(2 lbs [1,000 g] net weight)
1 ¼ lbs (650 g) sugar
4 cups (1,000 g/1 liter) water
1 vanilla bean, preferably Bourbon
Juice of 1 lemon

1. Scald the apricots in boiling water. Cool in cold water and peel with a small knife.
2. Pour sugar and water into a pot and bring to a boil.
3. Cut the vanilla bean down the middle and add the bean and the seeds in the syrup.

4. Squeeze the lemon and pour the juice into the syrup.
5. Add the apricots and let it all simmer on low heat for about 10 minutes, until the fruit feels soft.
6. Pour directly into sterilized jars and screw on the lids right away. Turn the jars upside down a couple of times.

If you wish to sterilize the jars you can place them in a 175°F (80°C) oven for 20 minutes. This will lengthen their shelf life.

Store in the fridge, basement, or another cool place.

Apricots in Cognac

Wonderful on a cold winter day with ice cream and an almond cake. You can make this with small peaches, nectarines, plums, or sour cherries as well.

First you prepare a so-called demi-confit, or half-preserved apricots.

2 ½ lbs (1,200 g) apricots
(2 lbs [1,000 g] net weight)
Juice of 1 lemon
1 vanilla bean, preferably Tahiti
4 cups (1,000 g/1 liter) water
2 lbs (1,000 g) sugar
7 oz (200 g) sweet almonds, preferably Marcona
3 ¼ cups (75 cl) cognac

DAY 1
1. Scald the apricots in boiling water. Place them in cold water and remove the skins with a small knife.
2. Squeeze the lemon.
3. Cut the vanilla bean down the middle and scrape out the seeds
4. Pour 4 cups (1,000 g/1 liter) water and ½ lb (250 g) sugar into a pot with the lemon juice and vanilla seeds. Bring to a boil. Place the almonds in boiling water and cool under cold running water. Remove the shells.
5. Let the apricots and almonds simmer on low heat for 15 minutes.
6. Add another ½ lb (250 g) of sugar and let it simmer for 15 minutes more.
7. Repeat the process 2 more times so that you end up with syrup composed of 2 lbs (1,000 g) sugar and 4 cups (1,000 g/1 liter) water.
8. Pour directly into sterilized glass jars and screw on the lids right away. Turn the jars upside down a couple of times.

DAY 2
1. Let the apricots and almonds drain in a strainer. Afterwards, carefully place them in beautiful glass jars.
2. Cover completely with cognac.
3. Add the lids and let sit in the fridge for at least a week, to allow the fruit to absorb the liquor.

Tip!
You can later drink the cognac from the preserve as a liqueur for your coffee. Kirschwasser is also great for preserving apricots. This preserve only gets better with time.

Marillenknödel

This is an Austrian specialty, which tastes wonderful if you make it with light dough. Serve this with meat seasoned with horseradish or a wienerschnitzel with lemon and potato salad as a warm plate beforehand, and it feels like you are in Vienna.

The apricot dumpling should be served warm, rolled in toasted crumbs and covered in powdered sugar. On the cruise ship Vista/Fjord, I would often serve these apricot dumplings for lunch. Sometimes I would fill them with blue prunes or ripe strawberries instead.

8 dumplings, 4 servings

8 large, ripe, juicy apricots
8 sugar cubes
¾ lbs (375 g) floury potatoes
(½ lb [250 g] net weight)
1 lemon
1 tbsp (15 g) butter
⅓ cup (45 g) all-purpose flour
1 ½ tbsp (15 g) semolina
Pinch of salt
1 egg yolk (20 g)
½ vanilla bean, preferably Bourbon
1 ¾ tbsp (25 g) butter
1 ½ cup (100 g) breadcrumbs
Pinch of freshly ground cinnamon
¾ tbsp (15 g) real vanilla sugar

Powdered sugar as topping

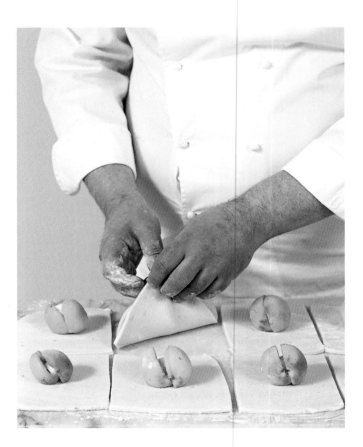

1. Bring 4 cups (1 liter) of water to a boil and scald the apricots for 1 minute. Place them in cold water right away and pull the skins off. Cut a slit on one side, remove the kernels, and replace with a sugar cube. Let them dry on a paper towel.
2. Peel the potatoes. Boil in lightly salted water until they are starting to fall apart. Place them in a strainer and let them drain completely. Press them through a potato press and weigh the right amount.
3. Rinse and grate the zest of half the lemon.
4. Mix the potato, while still warm, with butter, flour, semolina, salt, and lemon zest. Lastly, add the yolk and mix into a dough.
5. Set the oven to 390°F (200°C).
6. Roll the dough out with some flour. Shape into a long cigar and slice it into 8 pieces.
7. Dip your hands in flour and press the dough out. Wrap the apricots in the dough and roll into a bun. Make sure that there are no air pockets in the dumpling, because it might tear.
8. Boil 8 cups (2 liters) of water with a pinch of salt and the half vanilla bean. Add the dumplings and cover with a lid. Place the pot in the oven and let them simmer for 6–8 minutes.
9. Melt the butter in a frying pan and toast the breadcrumbs golden brown with cinnamon and vanilla sugar.
10. Let the dumplings drain before you roll them in the breadcrumbs. Sprinkle some powdered sugar on top and serve.

Peach and Nectarine

Prunus persica

The peach is a very old and culturally significant fruit. It was cultivated in China as early as 2,000 years BCE, and the Romans started cultivating peaches during the first century. Today, peaches are first and foremost cultivated in Southern Europe, California, and South Africa. There are many different varieties of the peach; the nectarine is a variety with thin and smooth skin.

Most peach varieties have juicy fruit flesh. The color may vary depending on the type. Yellow fruits are the most common, but peaches with white flesh are considered the most luxurious. There are also varieties with red fruit flesh. The smooth white peaches are my favorite. Unfortunately, peaches are often unripe, hard, and tough by the time they reach Sweden. They are often harvested too early and therefore do not develop the aroma they should have. A hint of red on the fruit does not necessarily mean it's ripe.

Peaches, which have flesh that sticks to the rough pit, maintain their shape nicely during boiling and are most suitable for preserving and conservation. On a ripe peach, the skin may be pulled off after blanching in boiling water. Unripe peaches will soften during preparation and are often poached in syrup or baked in the oven. Nectarines have juicy flesh. They may have a loose or fastened core, but in contrast to peaches they can't handle long cooking the same way.

Nectarines are most commonly consumed fresh, but are also good in marmalades. They appear in many desserts poached in vanilla syrup. They ripen at room temperature and they have a wonderful scent, but be careful not to squeeze them too much.

I have a lovely marmalade memory from the Riviera at Roger Vergé's restaurant Moulin. With the freshly baked bread they served an apricot and peach marmalade with vanilla, *Confiture d'Apricots et de Pêches à la vanille,* and the jar next to it read *Confiture aux quatre fruits rouges.* It tasted magnificent!

Added Flavor

Spices: ginger, cinnamon, vanilla, tonka bean, and lavender.
Sugar: Feel free to vary with different kinds of cane sugar.
Herbs: Avoid strong-tasting herbs.
Wine and spirits: sweet wines and distilled spirits.
Chocolate: goes well with peaches.
Fruit combinations: bananas, raspberries, strawberries, red and white currants, gooseberries, and pears.

Peach Jam

This jam may be flavored with various blanched herbs at the end of the boiling time, about 4 tbsp (20 g) per 2 lbs (1 kg) of fruit: orange thyme, lemon thyme, pineapple sage, fruit sage, cinnamon basil, lemon verbena, or rosemary fits well. You may also use cloves; if so, add 20 pieces in a textile bag. The jam is very suitable for terrines and pâtés.

Chocolate is also great with this; I recommend Valrhona Grand Cru Manjari.

3 lbs (1,400 g) ripe, fine, firm peaches
(2 lbs [1,000 g] net weight)
1 vanilla bean
1 ¾ lbs (800 g) light muscovado sugar
1 ½ cups (350 g) water
Juice of 1 orange
Juice of 1 lemon

1. Place the peaches in a saucepan with boiling water and let them boil for 1 minute. Next, place them in cold water and remove the skins with a small knife. Squeeze the pits out and cut each peach into 8 wedges.
2. Cut the vanilla bean down the middle and scrape out the seeds. Put the bean, seeds, sugar, and water into a pot. Bring to a boil while brushing the inside of the pot with a brush dipped in cold water to prevent sugar crystals. Boil to 234–240°F (112–114°C), or perform a sugar test, see Boiling Sugar, p. 14.
3. Add peaches and the orange and lemon juice. Boil until the fruit flesh turns transparent and the jam is starting to become a uniform mass.
4. At 222–224°F (106–107°C), the jam is ready, or perform a jam test, see p. 20.
5. Pour directly into sterilized jars and screw on the lids right away. Turn the jars upside down a couple of times.

Makes about 3 ⅓ lbs (1,500 g) jam.

Peach Melba Jam

The dessert Peach Melba consists of vanilla-poached peaches with vanilla ice cream and raspberry sauce. The dessert was created by the king of chefs, Auguste Escoffier, at the Savoy Hotel in London for Nellie Melba, an Australian singer who stayed at the hotel. Toast Melba is a thin, toasted slice of bread, which also carries her name.

1 batch of Raspberry Jam, see p. 58
1 batch of Peach Jam, see above.

1. First fill the jars half full with the freshly boiled raspberry jam and let it stiffen for 30 minutes.
2. Then pour the peach jam on top and screw on the lids immediately. Turn the jars upside down a couple of times.

Makes about 6 ½ lbs (3,000 g) jam.

1 Peach Melba Jam. 2 Peach Jam with Vanilla. 3 Peach Jam with Chocolate.

Peach Marmalade with Chocolate Basil

3 lbs (1,400 g) ripe, firm peaches
(2 lbs [1,000 g] net weight)
2 lbs (900 g) sugar
1 ¼ cup (300 g/3 dl) sweet wine, like Beaume de Venise
1 ½ oz (40 g) chocolate basil
Juice of 1 lemon
Juice of 1 orange

1. Scald the peaches for 1 minute in boiling water. Hold them under cold water and remove the peels with a knife.
2. Push out the pits and place the peaches in a food processor with the wine and the lemon and orange juice. Purée evenly.
3. Pour purée and sugar into a pot and bring to a boil. Let it boil to 220°F (105°C) while carefully stirring. Brush any sugar crystals that appear with a brush dipped in cold water, to prevent them from ending up in the marmalade. Remove foam now and then.
4. Place the basil in boiling water, scoop it up, and quickly cool under cold running water. Squeeze out the water and finely chop the basil. Stir into the boiled marmalade.
5. Pour directly into sterilized jars and screw on the lids right away. Turn the jars upside down a couple of times.

Makes about 3 ⅓ lbs (1,500 g) jam.

Nectarine and Banana Jam

Make a so-called demi-confit, or half-preserve, of the nectarines the first day.

1 ⅓ lbs (600 g) nectarines
(1 lb [500 g] net weight)
1 ¾ lbs (750 g) bananas
(1 lb [500 g] net weight)
1 ¾ lbs (800 g) sugar
Juice of 1 orange
Juice of 1 lemon

DAY 1

1. Scald the nectarines in boiling water for about 1 minute and place them in cold water right away. Peel with a small knife.
2. Cut the nectarines down the middle and remove the pits. Dice into pieces the size of sugar cubes.
3. Boil 2 cups (500 g/5 dl) water with ½ cup (125 g) sugar and add the nectarine cubes. Let them carefully simmer for 15 minutes. Add an additional ½ cup (125 g) sugar and let it simmer for 15 minutes more.
4. Repeat the process an additional 2 times so that you have added 1 lb (500 g) sugar altogether.
5. Pour into a bowl and let it cool. Cover with plastic wrap and set it in the fridge overnight.

DAY 2

1. Empty everything into a strainer and let the nectarines drain.
2. Peel and slice the bananas.
3. Pour the syrup and the remaining sugar into a pot. Boil, brushing the inside of the pot with a brush dipped in cold water to prevent sugar crystals.
4. Boil to 234–240°F (112–114°C). You may also perform a so-called sugar test, see Boiling Sugar, p. 14.
5. Add the bananas and nectarines, and also the orange and lemon juice.
6. Boil while constantly stirring and remove all foam with a spoon. Boil to about 220°F (105°C), or perform a jam test on a cold plate, see p. 20.

Pour directly into sterilized jars and screw on the lids right away. Turn the jars upside down a couple of times.

Makes about 3 ⅓ lbs (1,500 g) jam.

Peaches Boiled in Red Wine

This method is great for pears, plums, apricots, and cherries. Serve with cinnamon ice cream.

3 lbs (1,400 g) sun-ripe peaches
(2 lbs [1,000 g] net weight)
4 cups (1,000 g/1 liter) red wine, preferably like Côtes-du-Rhône
2 ¼ cups (450 g) light muscovado sugar
Juice of 1 orange
Juice of 1 lemon
4 cloves
2 bay leaves
⅓ inch (2 cm) real cinnamon stick
8 black peppercorns
6 whole cloves

1. Place the peaches in boiling water and let them boil for 1 minute. Then place them under cold running water and pull the skins off with a knife. Push the pits out and slice the fruit down the middle.
2. Pour red wine, sugar, orange juice, lemon juice, and the spices into a pot. Bring everything to a boil.
3. Add the peach halves and let them simmer slowly for about 20 minutes until they feel completely soft.
4. Place the peaches in sterilized jars and strain the syrup. Pour the syrup on top and screw on the lids right away.
5. Sterilize the jars in a water bath in a 175°F (80°C) oven for 20 minutes. Once they have cooled, store in the fridge.

Vanilla Poached Peach

This classic preserve is great for desserts with fresh, ripe red berries and ice cream.

3 lbs (1,400 g) sun-ripe peaches
(2 lbs [1,000 g] net weight)
1 ½ lbs (650 g) sugar
Juice of 1 lemon
4 cups (1,000 g/1 liter) water
2 vanilla beans, preferably Bourbon

1. Place the peaches in boiling water and scald them from 1 minute. Hold them under cold running water and remove the peels with a small knife.
2. Pour sugar, lemon, and water into a pot and bring to a boil. Add the split vanilla beans.
3. Add the pitted peach halves and let them poach on low heat until they are completely soft.
4. Pour both the peaches and syrup into sterilized jars. Screw on the lids and place them in a water bath with hot water. Set in a 175°F (80°C) oven for 20 minutes. Once the jars have cooled, store in the fridge.

Preserved Peaches or Nectarines

2 ½ lbs (1,200 g) fruit, not too ripe

1. Scald the fruit for 1 minute, place them in cold water, and remove the peels.
2. Simmer the fruit in water until they are completely soft all the way through. Cool in running water and preserve them by following the recipe for Preserved Citrus Peels, see p. 107.

Pineapple

Ananas comosus

The pineapple belongs to the Bromeliaceae family. The species first existed in the tropical Americas and from there it spread to the islands of the Caribbean Sea, where it was first discovered by Columbus on the island of Guadeloupe in 1493. By the end of the 1500s it had reached Europe. The name in Swedish, "ananas," came through Portuguese from an indigenous word meaning "lovely fruit" in the Guarani language.

When a pineapple is ripe, it should have an intense scent and yellow-brown peel. The fruit should give when you squeeze it and the small leaves should be easily removed. When the fruit is still unripe, it has an uncomfortably strong acid. The pineapple is harvested all year round, but the crops are largest during October and May.

Pineapples ripen at room temperature. You can store them in the fridge, but not below 41°F (5°C), as they will get black frost stains. The weight may vary from 4 ½ to 11 lbs (2 to 5 kilos). Pineapples contain a proteolytic enzyme, bromelain, which helps break down gelatin. You may still use pineapples for mousse and fromage. However, for these purposes it is important that the pineapple is boiled so that the mousse or fromage does not stiffen. The heat kills the enzyme.

Added Flavor

Spices: real cinnamon, cassava, nutmeg, vanilla, Sichuan pepper, black pepper, anise, star anise, dried or fresh ginger, cloves.
Herbs: sage (like fruit sage and pineapple sage), lemon verbena, orange and lemon thyme, lemongrass, and lime leaf.
Sugar: various cane sugars, such as cassonade and muscovado, may provide variety.
Spirits: various rums and tequila.
Citrus: lime juice or lemon juice to help the jam form jelly; juice and flesh of various citrus fruits.
Fruit combinations: mango, papaya, passion fruit, raspberry, or cloudberry.

Pineapple Jam

I first tasted this enjoyable jam with vanilla pudding on the island of Marti-nique. You may create many variations of this base recipe by adding various flavorings.

About 4 ½ lbs (2,000 g) fresh, ripe pineapple
(2 lbs [1,000 g] net weight fruit flesh)
1 ½ lbs (350 g/3 ½ dl) water
1 ¾ lbs (800 g) sugar
Juice of 2 limes

1. Peel the pineapple with a knife so that all brown spots are removed. Dice the fruit.
2. Boil water and sugar in a pot. Brush the inside of the pot with a brush dipped in cold water to prevent sugar crystals. Remove foam with a spoon so that the jam is clear. Boil to 234–240°F (112–114°C) or perform a sugar test, see Boiling Sugar, p. 14.
3. Add the pineapple dices and the lime juice.
4. Boil for about 10 minutes until the pineapple pieces are turning transpa-rent and the surface of the jam is starting to wrinkle.
5. Boil to 224°F (107°C) on the thermometer or perform a jam test on a cold plate, see p. 20.
6. Pour directly into sterilized jars and screw on the lids right away. Turn the jars upside down a couple of times.

Makes about 3 ⅓ lbs (1,500 g) finished jam.

Tip!
If you want to avoid the long boiling time, you may add 1 ½ cups (350 g) apple juice or ½ lb (250 g) apple jelly.

Pineapple Jam with Black Pepper

This goes well with cheeses and with grilled meats, and also as a side for desserts. The pineapple pieces do not fall apart with this method, as they do when they are boiled raw.

About 4 ½ lbs (2,000 g) fresh ripe pineapple
(2 lbs [1,000 g] net weight)
2 lbs (1,000 g) sugar
1 tsp (10 g) crushed black pepper
Juice of 2 limes
6 lime leaves
¼ cup (50 g/½ dl) dark rum
½ lb (250 g) apple jelly or 1 ½ cups (350 g) apple juice, p. 16–17

DAY 1
1. Peel and finely dice the pineapple.
2. Place in a pot with the sugar, black pepper, rum, apple juice, lime juice, and lime leaves.
3. Bring everything to a boil. Pour into a bowl and let it cool.
4. Cover with plastic wrap and let it cool overnight.

DAY 2
1. Let the syrup drain off in a strainer.
2. Pour the syrup in a pot and boil to 234–240°F (112–114°C), or perform a sugar test, see p. 14. Brush the inside of the pot with a brush dipped in cold water to prevent sugar crystals. Remove any foam with a spoon.
3. Add the fruit and boil, while constantly stirring, until the pineapple is turning transparent and the surface is starting to wrinkle. Keep stirring the jam on the edges towards the middle of the pot. Remove foam so that the jam is completely clear.
4. Boil to 222–224°F (106–107°C), or perform a jam test, see p. 20.
5. Pour the jam directly into sterilized jars and screw on the lids right away. Turn the jars upside down a couple of times.

Makes about 3 ¾ lbs (1,700 g) jam.

Pineapple Jam with Rum, Vanilla, Cane Sugar, and Yellow Raisins

This jam has a fantastic flavor and goes with almost anything. It is, for instance, great with cheese or as a filling in crêpes.

About 4 ½ lbs (2,000 g) fresh ripe pineapple
(2 lbs [1,000 g] net weight)
2 lbs (1,000 g) light demerara sugar
Juice of 2 limes
6 lime leaves
1 vanilla bean, preferably Bourbon
½ cup (100 g/1 dl) dark rum
½ lb (250 g) apple jelly or 1 ½ cups (350 g) apple juice, p. 16–17
5 oz (150 g) yellow raisins

Follow the same method as Pineapple Jam with Black Pepper, see above. Add the yellow raisins at the end of the boiling time.
Photo on p. 130.

Pineapple Jam with Mango, Vanilla, and Pineapple Sage

This lovely jam with juicy bits of mango and pineapple, and the vanilla that is enhanced by the sage, tastes great on toast with a cup of tea, or with grilled meat.

About 2 lbs (1,000 g) fresh ripe pineapple
(1 lb [500 g] net weight)
2 lbs (1,000 g) ripe mangos
(1 lb [500 g] net weight)
2 lbs sugar (1,000 g)
Juice of 2 limes
½ lb (250 g) apple jelly or 1 ½ cups (350 g) apple juice, p. 16–17
1 vanilla bean, preferably Tahiti
2 cups (40 g) pineapple sage

DAY 1
1. Peel and dice the pineapple. Peel the mangos and carve out the pits.
2. Blend the fruits in a pot with the sugar, lime juice, apple juice, and vanilla bean.
3. Bring everything to a boil. Then pour into a bowl and let it cool.
4. Cover with plastic wrap and let it cool overnight.

DAY 2
1. Place the pineapple sage in boiling water and later cool under running water. Finely shred the sage.
2. Let the syrup drain in a strainer.
3. Pour the syrup in a pot and boil it to 234–240°F (112–114°C), or perform a sugar test, see p. 14. Brush the edges towards the middle of the pot with a brush dipped in cold water to prevent sugar crystals.
4. Remove any foam with a spoon.
5. Add the fruit and the shredded pineapple sage. Boil while constantly stirring until the pineapple is starting to turn transparent and the surface is wrinkling. Keep brushing the inside of the pot. Occasionally remove foam so that the jam becomes completely clear. Boil to 224°F (107°C), or perform a jam test, see p. 20.
6. Pour the jam directly into sterilized jars and screw on the lids right away. Turn the jars upside down a couple of times.

Makes about 3 ¾ lbs (1,700 g) jam.
Photo on p. 130.

Exotic Pineapple Jam

Tastes great with breakfast and with a basic omelet with sugar instead of salt.

1 ⅓ lbs (600 g) fresh pineapple
(Just under 1 lb [400 g] net weight)
1 lb (500 g) kiwis, green
(Just under 1 lb [400 g] net weight)
3 ½ oz (100 g) passion fruit flesh from about 8 fruits
Juice of 2 limes
1 ¾ lbs (800 g) sugar
½ lb (250 g) apple jelly or 1 ½ cups (350 g) apple juice, p. 16–17

DAY 1
1. Peel the pineapple with a knife and remove the core.
2. Dice the fruit.
3. Slice the kiwis and dice them.
4. Cut the passion fruits down the middle and scoop the flesh out.
5. Squeeze the limes.
6. Pour pineapple, kiwis, passion fruit flesh, lime juice, and sugar into a pot. Bring everything to a boil while stirring.
7. Pour everything into a bowl and let it cool.
8. Cover with plastic wrap and keep it in the fridge overnight.

DAY 2
1. Drain the fruit blend in a strainer.
2. Pour the syrup into a pot and boil. Brush the inside of the pot with a brush dipped in cold water to prevent sugar crystals. Boil to 234–240°F (112–114°C), or perform a sugar test on a cold plate, see p. 20.
3. Pour directly into sterilized jars and screw on the lids. Turn the jars upside down a couple of times.

Makes about 3 ⅓ lbs (1,500 g) jam.

Pineapple Chutney with Banana, Chili, and Coriander

Wonderfully spicy chutney with lots of flavor. Suitable for spicy foods or smoked grilled meat.

3 ⅓ lbs (1,500 g) pineapple
(1 ¾ lbs [800 g] net weight)
1 lb (500 g) bananas, net weight
4 chili peppers, Jalapeño
3 cups (50 g) finely chopped coriander
3 tbsp (25 g) fresh grated ginger
6 tbsp (50 g) crushed garlic
4 cloves
3 tbsp (20 g) green cardamom
½ grated nutmeg
½ lb (300 g) light muscovado sugar
1 ½ cups (350 g/3 ½ dl) white wine vinegar

1. Peel the pineapple with a knife so that every brown spot is removed. Finely chop the flesh.
2. Peel and chop the bananas.
3. Rinse and finely chop the chilies, rinse and finely chop the coriander, and grate the cardamom with a grater.
4. Peel and crush the garlic. Crush the cloves and cardamom in a mortar.
5. Grate the nutmeg.
6. Blend all of the ingredients in a pot and let it come to a boil. Let it boil on low heat for about 60 minutes, until the chutney feels quite firm.
7. Pour directly into sterilized jars and screw on the lids. Turn the jars upside down a couple of times.

Makes about 4 ½ lbs (2,000 g) chutney.

Pineapple chutney tastes good with raw salsas with chili, coriander, lime juice, and sugar.

Pineapple and Orange Jam with Cointreau

Delightfully fresh for the breakfast table or with a dessert.

3 ⅓ lbs (1,500 g) fresh ripe pineapple
(1 ½ lbs [750 g] net weight)
1 ½ cups (350 g/3 ½ dl) freshly squeezed orange juice
Juice of 1 lemon
1 ¾ lbs (800 g) cane sugar
½ cup (100 g/1 dl) Cointreau liqueur
½ lb (250 g) apple jelly or 1 ½ cups (350 g) apple juice, p. 16–17
7 oz (200 g) preserved orange peels, see p.109, finely chopped

Continued on p. 132

DAY 1

1. Peel and finely dice the pineapple.
2. Squeeze the orange and lemon.
3. Pour the pineapple pieces, orange and lemon juice, and sugar into a pot and bring it all to a boil. Pour into a bowl and let it cool. Cover with plastic wrap and set it in the fridge overnight.

DAY 2

1. Pour the fruit mass into a strainer and let the syrup drain off.
2. Pour the syrup into a pot and boil while removing any foam. Brush the inside of the pot with a brush dipped in cold water to prevent sugar crystals. Boil to 234–240°F (112–114°C), or perform a sugar test, see p.14.
3. Add the drained fruit, liqueur, and apple juice or apple jelly. Continue boiling, while removing foam so that the jam becomes clear.
4. Occasionally, brush the inside of the pot with a brush dipped in cold water.
5. At 222–224°F (106–107°C) the jam is ready and the pineapple bits should be transparent. The surface of the jam is starting to wrinkle and form jelly. Perform a jam test on a cold plate, see p. 20.
6. Remove the pot from the stove and add the finely chopped orange peel. Scoop the jam into sterilized jars.
7. Screw the lids on right away and turn the jars upside down a couple of times.

Makes about 3 ¾ lbs (1,700 g) jam.

Pineapple Compote

Serve this compote with some freshly grated coconut on top and some good ice cream and cookies.

Makes about 6 servings

4 lbs (1,800 g) fresh pineapple
(2 lbs [1,000 g] net weight)
1 cup (200 g) sugar
¾ cup (200 g/2 dl) water
1 vanilla bean, preferably Tahiti
4 lime leaves
Juice of 1 lime
¼ cup (50 g/½ dl) dark rum

1. Peel the pineapple with a knife and make sure that all the brown spots are cut away. Cut it into 4 parts and cut out core. Cut in ¼ inch (5 mm) thick slices.
2. Blend sugar and water in a saucepan. Cut the vanilla bean down the middle and scrape the seeds out.
3. Bring the syrup to a boil with the vanilla seeds, lime leaves, and lime juice. Boil to 220°F (105°C).
4. Add the pineapple slices and let them simmer for 5 minutes.
5. Add the liquor.
6. Pour directly into a bowl and let it cool. Cover with plastic wrap and let it rest in a cool place for a couple of hours.

Preserved Pineapple

You can preserve pineapple the same way you would citrus peels, see p. 107. Preserved pineapple is often used for pralines and petit-fours. Preserved pineapple will not freeze in ice cream the way the fresh pineapple does; rather, the pieces stay soft and delicious.

At the Savoy Hotel in Malmö, the ice cream bomb Frou-Frou was very popular. The bomb shape was filled with vanilla ice cream and rum parfait with finely chopped chocolate and a generous amount of drained preserved pineapple bits. It was draped in cotton candy and served on a lighted ice block, standing on serviettes with live flowers—elegant at the time.

If you wish to use canned pineapple instead of fresh, use Del Monte in its own juice. This has a nice quality. (If you use canned pineapple, there's no need to blanch the slices.)

4 ½ lbs (2,000 g) fresh ripe pineapple
(2 lbs [1,000 g] net weight)
1 vanilla bean, preferably Tahiti
Sugar and honey, see Preserved Citrus Peels, p. 107

1. Peel the pineapple with a knife and cut it into wedges. Cut the core out.
2. Place the pineapple pieces in boiling water and move the saucepan, with a lid, into the oven at 300°F (150°C). Let it blanch in the oven until the pineapple bits feel tender, about 30 minutes.
3. Cool the pineapple bits under cold running water so that the boiling stops.
4. Boil the syrup and pour it boiling over the pineapple pieces in a large glass jar. Add the vanilla bean.
5. Cover with a lid right away and let it cool. Keep in the fridge overnight.

Repeat this process for another 5 days, see Preserved Citrus Peels, p. 107. Follow the same schedule until the pineapple is fully preserved.

Banana

Musa x paradisiaca

The banana is one of the oldest cultivated plants. Presumably, they were first cultivated in South Asia and later spread to the east and west. By the 500s, they were already known in Egypt and had spread throughout Africa. The Portuguese brought the plant from West Africa to the Canary Islands in 1402, and during the beginning of the 1500s, it spread around the West Indian Islands.

The cultivation of bananas demands tropical heat and humidity. There are many different varieties of bananas. We import bananas to Sweden year-round. First and foremost, Sweden imports so-called dessert bananas. The yellow kinds are the most common. They have a long and slightly bended shape, and diameter up to 1 inch (3 cm). A banana weighs 3 ½–7 oz (100–120 g), of which the peel is about 30 percent of the weight. Plantains, which are a starchier, less sweet variety of banana, are cultivated in equal quantities as dessert bananas and are commonly used as a basic food in many tropical countries, but are not as suitable for preserving.

When bananas are ripe, they are yellow all over, including the ends. You should also see small brown spots on the peel. If they are too ripe, they will have larger brown spots on the peel and should be consumed right away. Bananas should not be kept in the refrigerator; if exposed to such cold temperatures they turn black and soft. The best storage temperature for bananas is between 50–60°F (12–20°C) in somewhat humid air. The taste is sweet and mild with a pleasant acidity.

Added Flavor

Spices: ginger (fresh and dried), real cinnamon and cassava, nutmeg and nutmeg blossom, cloves, vanilla, various peppers, various chilies.
Herbs: Rosemary, lemon verbena, and various mints.
Spirits: all kinds of rum and arrack.
Sugar: regular white sugar and various kinds of darker cane sugar. Preserved and chopped orange or lemon peels, preserved chopped ginger.
Fruit combinations: dried figs or dates, oranges, limes, mangos, papayas, and passion fruit.

Banana Jam

3 ⅓ lbs (1,500 g) ripe bananas
(2 lbs [1,000 g] net weight)
1 ½ lb (700 g) light muscovado sugar
1 ¼ cups (300 g/3 dl)
2 lime fruits
⅓ inch (1 cm) real cinnamon stick

1. Peel the bananas and slice them. Place them in a bowl.
2. Rinse the lime and grate the zest into the bowl, then squeeze the juice and add that to the bowl as well.

3. Pour sugar and water into a pot. Bring the syrup to a boil and brush the inside of the pot with a brush dipped in cold water to avoid sugar crystals.
4. Boil to 234–240°F (112–114°C), or perform a sugar test, see Boiling Sugar, p. 14.
5. Add the fruit blend and the cinnamon stick.
6. Boil for 10 minutes while carefully stirring (banana jam burns easily once it starts to thicken). Remove any foam while boiling. Continue to brush the inside of the pot with a brush dipped in cold water to prevent sugar crystals.
7. At 220°F (105°C), the banana jam is ready. Perform a jam test on a cold plate to ensure that the texture is right, see p. 20.
8. Pour directly into sterilized jars and screw on the lids right away. Turn the jars upside down a couple of times.

Makes about 3 ⅓ lbs (1,500 g) jam.

Banana Jam with Ginger

Follow the recipe for Banana Jam.
Add a piece of ginger while boiling or add 3 ½ oz (100 g) finely chopped preserved ginger when the jam is ready.

Banana Jam with Lemon Thyme

Follow the recipe for Banana Jam.
Add ⅓ oz (10 g) lemon thyme (or orange thyme) to the blend towards the end of the boiling time.

Banana Jam with Valrhona Chocolate and Barbados Rum

Maria Escalante and I boiled this chocolate jam a couple of years ago and it became very popular at the Chocolatiere Les Trois Roses in Malmö.

Follow the recipe for Banana Jam, above. Add ½ cup (100 g) dark rum during boiling. Take the pot off the stove and stir in 12 oz (350 g) chopped dark chocolate, preferably Valrhona Grand Cru Pur Caraïbe.

Banana Jam with Nectarines and Lavender

1 ⅓ lbs (600 g) ripe nectarines
(1 lb [500 g] net weight)
1 ⅓ lbs [750 g] ripe bananas
(1 lb [500 g] net weight)
2 limes
1 ¾ lbs (800 g) sugar
2 tsp (5 g) dried lavender flowers

DAY 1

1. Scald the nectarines in boiling water and cool them in cold water. Remove their skins with a small knife. Cut the nectarines into small pieces.
2. Peel and slice the bananas. Place them in the pot.
3. Grate the rinsed limes on a grater and squeeze out the juice. Add the zest and squeezed juice to the pot. Add the sugar and bring everything to a boil while stirring. Pour into a bowl right away and let it cool.
4. Cover with plastic wrap and place in the fridge overnight.

Continued on p. 135

1 Banana Jam with Chocolate and Rum. 2 Banana Jam with Lemon Thyme. 3 Banana Jam with Nectarine and Lavender.

DAY 2

1. Drain the fruit blend in a strainer.
2. Pour the syrup and the lavender into a pot.
3. Boil while brushing the inside of the pot with a brush dipped in cold water to avoid sugar crystals. Boil to 234–240°F (112–114°C), see Boiling Sugar, p. 14.
4. Add the fruit and boil to 220°F (105°C) while stirring, or perform a so-called jam test on a cold plate, see p. 20. Remove any foam or impurities with a spoon.
5. Take the pot off the stove and scoop the jam into sterilized jars. Screw on the lids right away and turn the jars upside down a couple of times.

Makes about 3 ⅓ lbs (1,500 g) jam.

Banana Chutney

Fierce chutney for various spicy dishes

7 oz (200 g) dried figs
3 ⅓ (1,500 g) bananas
(2 lbs [1,000 g] net weight)
6 tbsp (100 g) fresh grated ginger
4 pink grapefruits
6 green and red serrano chili peppers
2 ½ cups (600 g/6 dl) white wine vinegar (6 dl / 3 cups)
1 ⅓ lbs (600 g) cassonade sugar, brown
7 oz (200 g) yellow raisins
3 tsp (20 g) sea salt
⅓ inch (1 cm) real cinnamon stick

DAY 1
Dice the figs and soak them in water overnight.

DAY 2
Drain the figs.

1. Peel and slice the bananas. Place them in a pot.
2. Grate the ginger and add to the pot.
3. Squeeze the grapefruit and add the juice to the pot as well.
4. Rinse and finely chop the chili peppers.
5. Blend everything and boil while carefully stirring for about 45 minutes (remember to be diligent with the stirring as the bananas burn easily).
6. Pour directly into sterilized jars and screw on the lids right away. Turn the jars upside down a couple of times.

Makes about 4 ½ lbs (2,000 g) finished chutney.

Melon

Melons have been a familiar fruit for more than 3,000 years. The muskmelon, *Cucumis melo*, is an ancient cultivated variety that is believed to stem from the tropics of Asia. It's been known in Europe since around the 1400s. The watermelon, *Citrullus vulgaris*, stems from the African steppes. Both of the melon varieties are annuals and grow on vines on the ground. They both need a lot of heat.

The watermelon is cultivated in tropical areas. It can weigh up to 33 lbs (15 kg). There are two varieties, one with red fruit flesh and one with yellow. The flesh is very juicy and can contain up to 95 percent water. In Sweden we usually import the melons from Southern Europe from May till the end of September.

Muskmelons, for instance, the cantaloupe, can be cultivated in Swedish greenhouses during the summer months. There are a number of different varieties of muskmelons. Shape and color may vary from round to pointy and oval. The skin can be smooth or ribbed, green or yellow. The fruit flesh can be white, light green, apricot-colored, or red. They can weigh up to 9 lbs (4 kg). They are imported year-round.

Honeydew, cantaloupe, and rockmelons are all varieties of the muskmelon. Honeydew has a sweet and fresh taste; the skin is yellow or green, commonly smooth without ribs. The cantaloupe has its name from the city, Cantalupa, outside of Rome. The round fruits have substantial ribs and a yellow-green shell. The musk fragrance is released when a melon is ripe. Store melons in cool places.

My first memories of the melon is when my mom would buy cantaloupe at the market or "Möllevångstorget" in Malmö. It would be dipped in sugar and eaten fresh, or sometimes it was soaked in port wine and served as a dessert.

Melon Surprise was the main attraction at Hotel Kramer's summer menu, where I worked when I was fourteen. We would scoop out all of the fruit flesh and fill the melon shell with raspberries, cloudberries, melon balls, and melon sorbet. It was then all perfumed with Kirschwasser and served on a lighted and sculpted block of ice with fresh flowers. Dry petit-fours would be served with the dessert.

Added Flavor
Spices: vanilla, ginger, real cinnamon, tonka bean, and nutmeg.
Herbs: lemon verbena, various varieties of basil and thyme.
Citrus fruits.
Wine and spirits: sweet dessert wine, rum, cognac, and Kirschwasser.

Melon Jam

Tastes good on freshly baked bread and as a side with meat or fish, or fruit desserts.

4 lbs (2 kg) melon, for instance, honeydew
(2 lbs [1,000 g] net weight)
2 lbs (2,000 g) sugar
Juice of 2 lemons
Juice of 2 limes
½ lb (250 g) apple jelly or 1 ½ cups (350 g) apple juice, p. 16–17

DAY 1

1. Peel the melon and remove the seeds. Dice the flesh.
2. Place the melon cubes in a bowl with the sugar and citrus juice. Cover with plastic wrap and let it sit at room temperature overnight.

DAY 2

1. Pour everything into a pot and bring to a boil while stirring.
2. Add apple juice or apple jelly and boil while diligently removing any foam. Brush the inside of the pot with a brush dipped in cold water to prevent sugar crystals. Measure the temperature when the fruit is starting to turn transparent and the surface of the jam is wrinkling. At 224–226°F (107–108°C) the jam is ready. Perform a jam test on a cold plate, see p. 20.
3. Pour directly into sterilized jars and screw on the lids right away. Turn the jars upside down a couple of times.

Makes about 3 ⅓ lbs (1,500 g) jam.

Cantaloupe Jam with Raspberries

Ripe Swedish cantaloupe is a fantastic fruit that, combined with raspberries, becomes downright seductive. Freshly baked waffles with this jam will please even the pickiest eater. I made this for the first time during the summer of 2005, and it became one of my absolute favorites that year.

1 ⅓ lbs (600 g) cantaloupe
(1 lb [500 g] net weight)
1 lb (500 g) raspberries
Juice of 1 lemon
1 ¾ lbs (800 g) sugar

DAY 1

1. Rinse and peel the melon and remove the seeds. Dice the flesh into pieces the size of sugar cubes.
2. Clean the raspberries without rinsing them.
3. Squeeze the lemon.
4. Pour everything into a pot with the sugar and bring to a boil while stirring.
5. Pour into a bowl and let it cool. Cover with plastic wrap and let it sit in the fridge overnight.

DAY 2

1. Drain the fruit blend in a strainer.
2. Boil the syrup in a pot. Constantly brush the inside of the pot with a brush dipped in cold water to prevent sugar crystals. Boil to 234–240°F (112–114°C), or perform a sugar test, see Boiling Sugar, p. 14.
3. Add the fruit and boil while constantly stirring. Remove any foam with a spoon.
4. Occasionally brush the inside of the pot. Boil to 224–226°F (107–108°C), or perform a jam test on a cold plate, see p. 20.
5. Pour directly into sterilized jars and screw on the lids right away. Turn the jars upside down a couple of times.

Makes about 3 ⅓ lbs (1,500 g) jam.

Melon jams with various flavors.

Honeydew Jam with Nectarine and Lemongrass

Lovely mild jam with a honey flavor that goes well with both cheese and toast at breakfast.

1 ⅓ lbs (650 g) honeydew
(1 lb [500 g] net weight)
1 ⅓ lbs (650 g) nectarines
(1 lb [500 g] net weight)
Juice of 1 lemon
2 lbs (1,000 g) sugar
½ cup (20 g) lemongrass
½ lb (250 g) apple jelly or 1 ½ cups (350 g) apple juice, p. 16–17

DAY 1

1. Rinse, peel, and remove the seeds from the melon, and dice into pieces the size of sugar cubes.
2. Scald the nectarines in boiling water for about 1 minute. Immediately place them in cold water and remove the peels with a knife.
3. Slice the nectarines down the middle, remove the pits, and dice the flesh.
4. Squeeze the lemon.
5. Place the melon cubes, nectarines, sugar, and lemon juice in a pot and bring to a boil while stirring.
6. Pour into a bowl and let it cool.
7. Cover with plastic wrap and place in the fridge overnight.

DAY 2

1. Pour everything into a strainer and let the syrup drain off.
2. Boil the syrup in a pot. Continuously brush the inside of the pot with a brush dipped in cold water to prevent sugar crystals. Boil to 234–240°F (112–114°C), or perform a sugar test by hand, see p. 14.
3. Add the fruit and apple juice or apple jelly. Boil to 224–226°F (107–108°C), or perform a jam test on a cold plate, see p. 20.
4. When the melon pieces are turning transparent and the surface of the jam is starting to wrinkle, the jam will be close to ready.
5. Blanch the herbs in boiling water and quickly cool in cold water. Finely shred the herbs and add during the last minute of boiling.
6. Pour the jam directly into sterilized jars and screw on the lids right away. Turn the jars upside down a couple of times.

Makes about 3 ⅓ lbs (1,500 g) jam.

Watermelon Jam with Green Serrano Chili Peppers

Great with grilled fish or smoked meats and charcuteries. Goes well with all kinds of cheeses.

4 lbs (1,800 g) watermelon
(2 lbs [1,000 g] net weight)
Juice of 2 limes
2 ½ tbsp (25 g) green serrano chili peppers
1 lemon
1 ¾ lbs (800 g) sugar
½ lb (250 g) apple jelly or 1 ½ cups (350 g) apple juice, p. 16–17

DAY 1

1. Peel the melon with a knife and remove the seeds. Dice the melon into pieces the size of sugar cubes.
2. Squeeze the limes and dice the chilies with the seeds.
3. Pour everything into a bowl and add the sugar. Blend well with a ladle and cover with plastic wrap. Let it marinate for 24 hours in the fridge.

DAY 2

1. Boil the fruit in a pot. Add the apple juice or apple jelly and boil, while stirring, until the fruit bits are turning transparent and the jam surface is starting to wrinkle.
2. At 224–226°F (107–108°C) the jam is ready. Perform a jam test on a cold plate, see p. 20.
3. Pour directly into sterilized jars and screw on the lids right away. Turn the jars upside down a couple of times.

Makes about 3 ⅓ lbs (1,500 g) jam.

Cantaloupe Jam with Papaya and Green Cardamom

A spicy jam that goes well with a variety of things: as a side to various cheeses, on toast for breakfast, or even with grilled duck.

1 ½ lbs (700 g) cantaloupe
(1 lb [500 g] net weight)
1 ¾ lb (800 g) papaya
(1 lb [500 g] net weight)
1 ¾ lbs (800 g) light muscovado sugar
2 tbsp (20 g) crushed green cardamom pods
Juice of 2 limes
½ lb (250 g) apple jelly or 1 ½ cups (350 g) apple juice, p. 16–17

DAY 1

1. Peel and seed the fruits. Dice the flesh.
2. Marinate them in sugar, spices, and lime juice. Cover with plastic wrap and let it sit at room temperature for 24 hours.

DAY 2

1. Pour the fruit mass into a pot and bring to a boil while stirring. Remove any foam with a spoon.
2. Brush the inside of the pot with a brush dipped in cold water to prevent sugar crystals.
3. When the pieces of fruit have turned transparent and the jam is holding together, the temperature should be at 224–226°F (107–108°C), or perform a jam test on a cold plate, see p. 20.
4. Pour the jam directly into sterilized jars and screw on the lids right away. Turn the jars upside down a couple of times.

Makes about 3 ⅓ lbs (1,500 g) jam.

Photo on p. 137.

Preserved Melon

Preserve the same way as citrus peels.

3 ⅓ lbs (1,500 g) melon

Peel, seed, and cut the melon into wedges. Blanch the wedges so that they become completely soft. Cool under running water and preserve them by following the recipe for preserved citrus peels, see p.107.

Melon Jam with Mango

Follow the recipe for Cantaloupe Jam with Papaya and Green Cardamom, but replace the papaya with mango.

Photo on p. 137

Mango
Mangifera indica

The mango has been cultivated for 4,000 years. It was traditionally a cultivated plant in South and East Asia and is now grown in all tropical countries. The mango tree is a tall tree with a sturdy and wide crown. The fruits may be up to 11 ¾ inches (30 cm) long, but are usually around 4 inches (10 cm). The color varies. The skin may be green yellow, green, green red, or yellow red. The fruit flesh is bright yellow or reddish and is often stringy close to the pit.

The mango is imported year-round from a variety of tropical countries. They may weigh from ½ lb (300 g) to 6 ½ lbs (3,000 g), depending on the kind. The fruits are delicate and need to be picked with care. They are imported ripe. You may sometimes be able to determine whether or not the fruit is ripe by inspecting the skin, which should be yellowish. The fruit will also have a strong scent and will easily give in under pressure. Small brown spots are also a sign that the fruit is ripe. The taste is sweet and intense.

My first meeting with the mango was, like most Swedish people, through mango chutney, which I enjoyed eating with chicken curry and other spicy dishes. When the fresh mango first came to Sweden, mango sorbet and mango soufflé became instant favorites.

Added Flavor

Spices: ginger, cloves, cinnamon, vanilla, tonka bean, nutmeg, rose pepper, crushed black pepper, fresh grated ginger.
Herbs: various varieties of thyme, such as lemon and orange thyme, as well as cinnamon basil.
Spirits: for instance, rum and tequila.
Sugar: various cane sugars.
Fruit combinations: raspberries, strawberries, red currants, bananas, melons, papaya, coconut, and so on.

Mango Jam with Lime and Ginger

This jam may be served as a chutney for cheese and smoked or spicy foods. It is also great with toasted bread and tea.

4 lbs (1,800 g) ripe mango
(2 lbs [1,000 g] net weight)
1 ¾ lbs (800 g) light muscovado sugar
Juice of 2 limes
10 lime leaves
2 tbsp (25 g) grated fresh ginger

DAY 1
1. Peel the mangos and cut the flesh away from the pits.
2. Chop the fruit flesh into small pieces and blend with sugar, lime juice, lime leaves, and grated ginger. Cover with plastic wrap.
3. Let it marinate overnight at room temperature.

DAY 2
1. Pour the fruit mass into a pot and boil while removing all foam. Brush the inside of the pot with a brush dipped in cold water to prevent sugar crystals. Boil to 220–222°F (105–106°C), or perform a jam test on a cold plate, see p. 20.
2. Pour directly into sterilized jars and screw on the lids right away. Turn the jars upside down a couple of times.

Makes about 3 ⅓ lbs (1,500 g) jam.
Photo on p. 130.

Mango Jam with Rose Pepper and Coriander

Follow the recipe above, but exclude the lime leaves and ginger. Increase the amount of sugar by ½ cup (100 g).

Purée the fruit mass in a mixer on day 2 and pour into the pot with 5 tbsp (40 g) rose pepper. Add 2 ½ cups (40 g) of blanched and shredded coriander, preferably Thai, at the end of the boiling time.

Mango Jam with Raspberries

Replace half of the mangos with raspberries. Exclude the lime leaves and ginger. Otherwise, prepare by following the recipe for Mango Jam with Lime and Ginger. Another tasty alternative is Mango Jam with Passion Fruit and Raspberries. Use one third of each fruit. Prepare and boil as described in the recipe above.

Mango Chutney

Good with all kinds of spicy dishes.

2 lbs (1,000 g) tamarind fruits
4 lbs (1,800 g) ripe mango
(2 lbs [1000 g] net weight)
1 red bell pepper
4 tbsp (50 g) oz grated fresh ginger
4 tabasco peppers, yellow green, orange, and red
1 ¼ cups (300 g/3 dl) white wine vinegar
1 lb (500 g) dark muscovado sugar
3 ½ oz (100 g) yellow raisins
Pinch of black pepper
Juice of 4 limes
10 lime leaves
Pinch of sea salt

1. Crush the tamarind fruits and boil in 1 cup (250 g/2 ½ dl) water under a lid for 1 hour.
2. Peel and pit the mangoes and cut the flesh off the pits. Remove the core and seeds from the bell pepper and grate the peeled ginger.
3. Pour all of the ingredients, except the salt, into a pot and cover with strained tamarind water. Bring to a boil and remove any foam with a spoon.
4. Brush the inside of the pot with a brush dipped in cold water to prevent sugar crystals.
5. Let boil until the mass thickens, about 40 minutes.
6. Carefully flavor with salt and, if necessary, additional sugar.
7. Pour directly into sterilized jars and screw on the lids right away. Turn the jars upside down a couple of times.

Makes about 4 lbs (2,000 g) chutney.

Papaya
Carica papaya

The papaya stems from central America, but is cultivated in all tropical countries. It is used unripe as a vegetable and ripe as a fruit. It may weigh up to 20 lbs (9 kg), but most commonly it weighs about ½ lb (300 g). The fruit is often pear-shaped, and the color is yellow green or yellow orange. The fruit flesh, 1–2 inches (2 ½–5 cm) thick, is orange, soft, and juicy when the fruit is ripe. The scent is reminiscent of ripe apricots. The papaya needs acidity, or else the taste becomes flat. The black seeds inside of the fruit are removed before consumption. It is imported almost year-round. Unripe fruits ripen at room temperature. Do not store them in the refrigerator.

The papaya may be consumed the exact same way as a melon, with ham and port wine, etc. It is also suitable for sorbet, ice cream, marmalade, jam, and chutney. The fruit and the plant itself contain a proteolytic enzyme called papain. This enzyme is used to tenderize meats and for medical purposes. Papain also breaks down gelatin. Boiling prevents the effects of the enzyme. For instance, if you wish to make a mousse, the purée has to be heated, or else the gelatin loses its function.

Added Flavor
Dried spices: vanilla, cloves, ginger, cinnamon, nutmeg, tonka bean, rose pepper, Sichuan pepper.
Fresh spices: lemongrass, grated ginger, and chili.
Herbs: Various basils.
Citrus fruits.
Sugar: preferably various muscovado sugars.
Spirits: tequila, rum, and arrack.
Fruit combinations: mango, passion fruit, melon, and pineapple, plus coconut.

Papaya Jam with Tequila and Lime

3 lbs (1,400 g) papaya
(2 lbs [1,000 g] net weight)
4 limes
1 ¾ lbs (800 g) light muscovado sugar
⅓ cup (150 g/1 ½ dl) dark tequila
½ lb (250 g) apple jelly or 1 ½ cups (350 g) apple juice, p. 16–17

DAY 1
1. Peel and seed the fruit and dice the flesh into cubes the size of sugar cubes.
2. Rinse the limes and finely grate the zest. Add to a bowl with the papaya cubes.
3. Add the sugar and liquor. Cover with plastic wrap and let it marinate for 24 hours at room temperature.

Papaya Jam with Tequila and Lime.

DAY 2

1. Pour the fruit mass into a strainer and let the syrup drain off.
2. Pour the syrup in a pot and boil to 234–240°F (112–114°C), or perform a sugar test, see p. 14.
3. Carefully remove foam.
4. Brush the inside of the pot with a brush dipped in cold water to prevent sugar crystals.
5. Add the fruit and apple juice or apple jelly. Boil while stirring until the jam has started to form jelly and the fruit pieces are turning transparent.
6. At 224–226°F (107–108°C) the jam is ready. You may also perform a jam test on a cold plate, see p. 20.
7. Pour directly into sterilized jars and screw on the lids right away. Turn the lids upside down a couple of times.

Makes about 3 ¾ lbs (1,700 g) jam.

Papaya and Mango Jam with Rose Pepper and Arrack

1 ½ lbs (700 g) papaya
(1 lb [500 g] net weight)
1 ¾ lbs (800 g) mango
(1 lb [500 g] net weight)
Juice of 2 limes
1 ¾ lbs (800 g) sugar
½ cup (100 g) arrack
½ lb (250 g) apple jelly or 1 ½ cups (350 g) apple juice, p. 16–17
2 ½ tbsp (20 g) rose pepper

DAY 1

1. Peel the papaya and remove the seeds. Dice the flesh into pieces the size of sugar cubes.
2. Peel the mangos and cut the fruit flesh away from the pits. Dice like the papaya.
3. Add the lime juice, sugar, and arrack, and blend well. Cover with plastic wrap and let it sit at room temperature for 24 hours.

DAY 2

1. Empty the fruit into a strainer and let the syrup drain off.
2. Pour the syrup into a pot and boil to 234–240°F (112–114°C), or perform a sugar test, see p. 14.
3. Remove all foam.
4. Brush the inside of the pot with a brush dipped in cold water to prevent sugar crystals.
5. Add the fruit and apple juice or apple jelly. Boil while stirring until the jam has started to form jelly and the fruit pieces are turning transparent. Lastly, stir in the pepper.
6. At about 224–226°F (107–108°C) the jam is ready. You may also perform a jam test on a cold plate, see p. 20.
7. First pour one third of the jam into jars and cover with plastic wrap. Let it sit for 15 minutes, add another third, and let it rest for an additional 15 minutes to stiffen.
8. Warm the jam once more and pour the remaining jam into the jars as well. This way the peppers will not float up to the surface, but be evenly distributed in the jars.

Makes about 3 ¾ lbs (1,700 g) jam.

Preserved Papaya

Papaya is preserved the same way as citrus peels.

2 lbs (1,000 g) papaya

Peel the papaya(s) and cut them into wedges. Blanch in boiling water until they are completely soft. Cool under running water to stop the boiling process. Preserve by following the recipe for Preserved Citrus Peels, see p. 107.

Jackfruit

Artocarpus heterophyllus

The jackfruit is closely related to the breadfruit and belongs to the same family. It is a large fruit with a robust, thorny, green peel. It may weigh up to 110 lbs (50 kilos), but the imported fruits usually weigh significantly less. The jackfruit stems from South Asia but is now cultivated in many tropical countries. The flesh is sweet or tart, depending on the type. You eat the swollen shell that surrounds the seeds. The fruit has a unique aroma, but mostly contains water. It is eaten raw, as ice cream, preserved, and as jam. It may also be dried.

Boiled Jackfruit

I boil this fruit the same way I would lychee fruit, except I double the recipe and add a vanilla bean. First cut away the flesh and chop it into medium-sized bits. Then boil the same way as lychee (see p. 154).

Good to Know

The durian is an egg-shaped fruit from the tree *Durio zibethinus*, which grows in South Asia and especially in Thailand. The fruit is known for its unusual aroma, with a strong flavor and scent that is reminiscent of onions, cheese, and many fruits all mixed together. It can weigh up to 20 lbs (9 kg). The fruit has a thick husk, covered with thorns. The flesh around the seeds tastes fruity and contains 36 percent sugar. The durian is eaten raw, as ice cream, preserved and candied, and may even be used in drinks. It is also fermented into Tempoyak, which is a Malaysian fruit wine..

Photo on p. 165.

Kiwi

Actinidia chinensis

The kiwi is sometimes called the Chinese gooseberry. It originally stems from China, but it got its name from the kiwi bird in New Zealand, where the kiwi fruit is cultivated on a large scale. Today it is cultivated in a variety of places and we import kiwis in large quantities from, among other places, Italy. Kiwis usually weigh 2 ½–3 ½ oz (65–100 g) and they are either yellow or green. They have high vitamin C content and taste tart and sweet. The fruit is ripe when the skin gives in under light pressure. You may store it in the fridge for a couple of days, but it cannot be too cold, as the fruit will become mushy.

Fresh kiwi contains a proteolytic enzyme called actinidin, which dissolves gelatin. Avoid trying to prepare a mousse or jelly with fresh kiwi because it won't stiffen. Boil the kiwi as a purée first and let it cool so that the enzyme loses its functionality. The kiwi is suitable for marmalade, jam, and jelly, as well as sorbet, mousse, and fruit salad.

Kiwi Jam with Lime and Grapefruit

This tart jam is delicious with toast and a cup of tea.

3 lbs (1,400 g) kiwis
(2 lbs [1,000 g] net weight)
2 pink grapefruits
2 limes
2 lbs (1,000 g) sugar
½ lb (250 g) apple jelly, see p. 16

DAY 1
1. Peel the kiwis. Rinse and grate the outer zest of the grapefruits and limes.
2. Finely chop all of the fruit flesh. Pour everything into a bowl and blend well. Cover with plastic wrap and let it sit at room temperature overnight.

DAY 2
1. Pour everything into a pot and slowly boil while constantly stirring. Remove foam from the surface with a spoon. Dip a brush in cold water and brush the inside of the pot sporadically.
2. Boil until the fruit has turned transparent, 224–226°F (107–108°C), or perform a jam test on a cold plate, see p. 20.
3. Pour the jam into sterilized jars and screw on the lids right away. Turn the jars upside down a couple of times.

Makes about 3 ½ lbs (1,650 g) finished jam.

Kiwi Jam with Lime and Grapefruit.

Kiwi Jam with Papaya and Dutch Gin

1 ¾ lbs (800 g) papaya
(1 lb [500 g] net weight)
1 ½ lbs (700 g) kiwis
(1 lb [500 g] net weight)
1 ½ cup (350 g/3 ½ dl) water
Juice of 2 limes
2 lbs (1,000 g) sugar
½ cup (100 g/1 dl) Dutch gin
½ lb (250 g) apple jelly or 1 ½ cups (350 g) apple juice, p. 16–17

1. Peel the papaya and remove the seeds. Cut the fruit into small pieces.
2. Peel the kiwis and dice the fruit flesh.
3. Boil the water and the lemon juice. Add the papaya and let it boil on low heat under a lid for 5 minutes.
4. Pour into a strainer and let the water drain off.
5. Pour the water from the fruit with the sugar into a pot and boil. Keep brushing the inside of the pot with a brush dipped in cold water. Boil to 234–240°F (112–114°C), or perform a sugar test, see Boiling Sugar, p. 14.
6. Add the fruit and liquor, as well as the apple jelly or apple juice. Boil to 224–226°F (107–108°C), or perform a jam test on a cold plate, see p. 20.
7. Pour directly into sterilized jars and screw on the lids right away. Turn the jars upside down a couple of times.

Makes about 4 ½ lbs (2,000 g) jam.

Preserved Kiwi

Kiwi may be preserved the same way as citrus peels.

2 lbs (1,000 g) unripe fruit

Peel and slice the unripe fruits in ¼ inch (5 mm) thick slices. Preserve them without blanching by following the recipe for Preserved Citrus Peels, see p. 107.

Grapes
Vitis vinifera

Wine grapes are recognized as one of the most important cultivated plants. Traces have been found of grapes very similar to the ones cultivated today by the southern coast of the Caspian Sea. These date back 6,000 years. There is a large variety of grapes out there. The majority of harvested grapes are used for wine. Only 10 percent are eaten as fresh fruit and about 5 percent are dried into raisins. Grapes may be green, yellow, red, or blue. There are also seedless varieties.

Wine Jelly

I would personally serve this delicious jelly with duck liver.

2 lbs (1,000 g) green grapes without stems
Juice of 1 lemon
1 cup (250 g/2 ½ dl) white wine, like Alsace
½ cup (100 g/1 dl) cognac
¾ lbs (350 g) apple jelly, see p. 16
Amount of sugar equal to the weight of the drained juice

1. Clean the grapes well. Place them in a food processor with the lemon juice, wine, and cognac. Mix into a purée.
2. Bring to a boil and let it simmer under a lid for 30 minutes.
3. Pour into a strainer lined with cheesecloth and let it drain on its own for about 1 hour.
4. Weigh the juice and add an equal weight of sugar.
5. Add the apple jelly and boil. Remove all foam so that the jelly becomes clear. Occasionally brush the inside of the pot with a brush dipped in cold water. Boil to 220°F (105°C), or perform a jelly test on a cold plate, see p. 20.
6. Pour directly into sterilized jars and screw on the lids right away. Turn the jars upside down a couple of times.

Makes about 1 ¾ lbs (800 g) jelly.

Wine Jelly.

Grape Jam

Feel free to use seedless grapes so you don't have to cut them and rinse out the seeds by hand. If you make jam with green grapes, use a dry white wine. If, on the other hand, you use red or blue grapes, use a heavy red wine, like Bordeaux. In Italy they would also add some yellow mustard seeds.

2 lbs (1,000 g) green grapes, net weight (you can also use red or blue)
1 ½ lbs (700 g) sugar
Juice of 1 lemon
¾ cup (200 g/2 dl) dry, white wine, like Loire (you can also use red wine)

DAY 1
1. Rinse the grapes well and remove the stems. Unless you are working with seedless grapes, cut them down the middle and remove the seeds.
2. Blend the grapes with sugar, lemon juice, and wine. Bring to a boil in a pot. Pour into a bowl and let it marinate for 24 hours.

DAY 2
1. Drain the juice through a strainer. Bring to a boil and remove all foam.
2. Brush the inside of the pot with a brush dipped in cold water to prevent sugar crystals. Boil to 217–220°F (103–105°C), or perform a jam test on a cold plate, see p. 20.
3. Pour directly into sterilized jars and screw on the lids right away. Turn the jars upside down a couple of times.

Makes about 2 ½ lbs (1,200 g) jam.

Tip!
If you want a stronger taste, add ½ cup (100 g/1 dl) cognac. Works well with Roquefort.

Olives
Olea europaea

Olives are mostly cultivated in Mediterranean countries and the Near East. The plum-shaped olive's flesh contains 20–30 percent oil. Unripe green olives are first parboiled and later soaked in brine. Black olives are preserved without blanching. Buy olives with the pits still intact, as they taste better.

Black Olive Marmalade with Pear and Thyme

This marmalade goes great with various cheeses, or as a side with a terrine or antipasto.

1 ½ lbs (650 g) pears
(1 lb [500 g] net weight)
2 cups (500 g/5 dl) water
Juice of 1 lemon
1 lb (500 g) black olives, pitted
5 tbsp (10 g) fresh thyme
1 ¾ lbs (800 g) brown muscovado sugar
½ lb (250 g) apple jelly or 1 ½ cups (350 g) apple juice, p. 16–17

1. Clean, peel, and core the pears. Cut them into wedges.
2. Bring the water to a boil in a pot with the squeezed lemon juice and add the pear wedges.
3. Boil the pears under a lid until soft.
4. Add the chopped, pitted black olives and some crushed thyme.
5. Add the sugar and apple jelly or apple juice.
6. Bring everything to a boil and let it boil on low heat while stirring. Remove foam from the surface with a spoon.
7. Occasionally brush the inside of the pot with a brush dipped in cold water to prevent sugar crystals.
8. Boil to 220°F (105°C), or perform a jam test on a cold plate, see p. 20.
9. Pour directly into sterilized jars and screw on the lids right away. Turn the jars upside down a couple of times.

Makes about 3 ⅓ lbs (1,500 g) marmalade.

In the glass jars, black and green olive marmalade.

Green Olive Marmalade with Mustard Seeds

A delicious marmalade with mature cheeses and as a side with charcuteries.

1 ½ lbs (650 g) green apples, such as Granny Smith
(1 lb [500 g] net weight)
2 cups (500 g/5 dl) water
Juice of 1 lemon
1 lb (500 g) pitted green olives stuffed with pimentos
½ cup (100 g/1 dl) white wine vinegar
2 tbsp brown mustard seeds
1 ¾ lbs (800 g) light muscovado sugar

1. Clean and peel the apples and core them. Cut into small wedges.
2. Bring the water to a boil in a pot with the squeezed lemon juice and add the apple wedges. Boil them under a lid for about 20 minutes, till the apples are falling apart.
3. Finely chop the olives and add them to the pot, along with the vinegar, mustard seeds, and sugar. Boil while constantly stirring and removing foam.
4. Occasionally, brush the inside of the pot with a brush dipped in cold water to prevent sugar crystals.
5. Boil to 220°F (105°C), or perform a jam test on a cold plate, see p. 20.
6. Pour the marmalade directly into sterilized jars and screw on the lids right away. Turn the jars upside down a couple of times.

Makes about 3 ⅓ lbs (1,500 g) jam.
Photo on p. 147

Preserved Green or Black Olives

Preserve the olives the same way as citrus peels.

2 lbs (1,000 g) large green or black olives

Blanch the olives for 5 minutes until they feel soft. Cool them under running cold water.

See Preserved Citrus Peels, p. 107.

Figs
Ficus carica

Figs originated in the Near East. Since the beginning of time, they have been cultivated in the eastern Mediterranean region, including Asia Minor and the Middle East. The fig tree is related to the mulberry plant family. The fruits are pear-shaped and, depending on the variety, green yellow to violet to a soft blue purple when they are ripe. They weigh 1 ¾–2 ½ oz (50–70 g). The fig is mostly imported from Calabria in Italy during the fall and from Brazil the rest of the year.

The fruits contains up to 20 percent sugar. Unripe figs do not taste very good. Ripe figs are sweet with a hint of acidity. The skin is edible as long as it is not too thick. You may squeeze some lemon juice over the fruit. Rub the fig between your hands before you eat it; this makes them juicier.

You may also use dried figs for jam and marmalade, but in that case you should soak them first. Boiled fresh figs in alcohol that is then flambéed tastes great with cheese, prosciutto, and salami.

Added Flavor
Spices: cinnamon, ginger, cloves, various peppers, and bay leaf.
Citrus fruits: both juice and zest.
Sugar: brown sugars.
Fruit combinations: pears, apples, blackberries, prune plums, and sour cherries.

Fig Marmalade with Bay Leaf

I first tasted this marmalade at the restaurant Domaine de Clairefontaine outside of Lyon, with a delicious foie gras. I have done many versions of this recipe over the years, and they all taste good but different. If possible, try to get fresh bay leaves.

2 lbs (1,000 g) reddish fresh figs
Juice of 1 lemon
1 ¾ lbs (800 g) sugar
8 fresh bay leaves or 6 dried

DAY 1
1. Clean the figs and remove the stems. Cut each fig into 6 pieces.
2. Squeeze the lemon.
3. Pour the lemon juice, figs, and sugar into a pot and bring everything to a boil while stirring.

Pour everything into a bowl and let it cool. Cover with plastic wrap and let it sit in the fridge overnight.

Continued on p. 150

Fig Marmalade with Bay Leaf and Fig Marmalade with Chestnuts and Whiskey.

DAY 2

1. Pour the figs into a strainer and let the syrup drain off.
2. Pour the syrup into a pot and boil. Constantly brush the inside of the pot with a brush dipped in cold water to prevent sugar crystals.
3. Boil to 234–240°F (112–114°C), or perform a sugar test, see Boiling Sugar, p. 14.
4. Add the figs and bay leaves. Boil while stirring.
5. Remove any foam from the surface with a spoon. Brush the inside of the pot now and then. When the figs are starting to turn transparent and the jam stays together, it should be at 220–222°F (105–106°C), or perform a jam test, see p. 20.
6. Pour the marmalade directly into sterilized jars and screw on the lids right away. Turn the jars upside down a couple of times.

Makes about 3 ⅓ lbs (1,500 g) marmalade.

Fig Marmalade with Chestnuts and Whiskey

Delicious marmalade for terrines, cheeses, and charcuteries. Will even taste good on a toasted brioche for breakfast. You can buy the chestnuts fresh and prepare them as described in the recipe below. Alternatively, you can buy frozen or vacuum-packed chestnuts, which are already shelled.

2 lbs (1,000 g) chestnuts, fresh
(13 oz [375 g] net weight)
2 cups (500 g) 1 lb water
500 g/ 1 lb sugar
2 lbs (1,000 g) red figs, fresh
1 vanilla bean, preferably Bourbon
Juice of 1 lemon
1 ¾ lbs (800 g) light muscovado sugar
⅓ cup (150 g1 ½ dl) Scotch whiskey

DAY 1

1. Begin by peeling the fresh chestnuts by slitting their pointed end and bake them in a 390°F (200°C) oven for about 30 minutes or until they feel tender when you poke them. Peel away the hard shell with the help of a knife and afterwards carefully remove the inner shell as well. (If you are using pre-shelled chestnuts, you may skip this step.)
2. Preserve the chestnuts; make a so-called demi-confit by half-preserving them so that they don't fall apart during boiling.
3. Boil 2 cups (500 g/5 dl) water with ½ cup (125 g) sugar and let it simmer carefully for 15 minutes.
4. Add another ½ cup (125 g) sugar and let it simmer for an additional 15 minutes.
5. Repeat this process twice more. Next, pour everything into a bowl and let it cool. Cover with plastic wrap and place it in the fridge overnight.
6. Rinse, remove the stems, and finely chop the figs.
7. Cut the vanilla beans down the middle and scrape the seeds out. Place the seeds in a pot with the figs, muscovado sugar, and lemon juice.
8. Bring to a boil while stirring. Pour into a bowl and let cool. Cover with plastic wrap and let it sit in the fridge overnight.

DAY 2

1. Pour the chestnuts into a strainer and let the syrup drain off. Pour the syrup into a bottle and keep it for another time. You will not be needing it for the marmalade.
2. Pour the fig mass into a strainer and let the syrup drain off.
3. Pour the syrup into a pot and let it boil. Brush the inside of the pot with a brush dipped in cold water to prevent sugar crystals.
4. Boil to 234–240°F (112–114°C), or perform a sugar test, see Boiling Sugar, p. 14.
5. Add the figs and liquor and boil while constantly stirring. Remove all foam from the surface and boil to 220°F (105°C). You may also perform a jam test on a cold plate, see p. 20.
6. Add the chestnuts and continue boiling for a little while longer.
7. Pour directly into sterilized jars and screw on the lids right away. Turn the jars upside down a couple of times.

Makes about 4 ½ lbs (2,000 g) finished marmalade.
Photo on p. 149.

Figs in Cognac

You can do half-preserved figs, so-called demi-confit. If possible, use reddish-brown figs. This tasty preserve will keep for years and becomes only better with time. It is traditionally served with whipped cream or ice cream.

If you want to make something extra-good to serve them with, then make a whiskey sauce. Flambé figs in cognac in a lightly heated frying pan with a piece of unsalted butter.

2 lbs (1,000 g) fresh figs
2 cups (500 g/5 dl) water
1 vanilla bean, preferably Bourbon
Juice of 1 lemon
1 lb (500 g) sugar
3 ¼ cups (75 cl) quality cognac

DAY 1

1. Rinse the figs carefully and remove the stems. Poke the figs with a small fork so that they don't burst during blanching.
2. Bring the water to a boil and add the opened and scraped vanilla bean.
3. Add the figs and lemon juice. Let simmer under a lid for about 10 minutes or until the figs feel soft when you poke them with a fork.
4. Add ½ cup (125 g) sugar and let everything simmer for 15 more minutes.
5. Repeat the process twice more until the figs are completely preserved.
6. Scoop onto a large sterilized jar and cover with the lid immediately. Let it cool and place it in the fridge overnight.

DAY 2

Place the drained figs in sterilized jars and pour cognac on top so that they are completely covered. Let them sit for at least 14 days before you serve.

1 Preserved Chestnuts. 2 Preserved Cherries. 3 Figs in Cognac.

Whiskey Sauce

This sauce is great for flambéed figs or with ice cream and fruit desserts.

6 servings

3 ½ oz (100 g) almond paste 50/50
2 ½ oz (75 g) Black Currant Jelly, see p. 21
1 ½ tbsp (4 cl) quality Scottish whiskey
1 ½ cups (300 g/3 dl) light whipping cream

1. Warm the almond paste in the microwave so that it goes soft. Place it in a bowl and add a third of the currant jelly.
2. Add the remaining jelly in two batches and blend into a smooth fluid mass without lumps.
3. Add the whiskey and blend well.
4. Lightly whip the cream and fold it into the fluid mass to make a nice sauce.

Preserved Figs

Figs may be preserved the same way as citrus peels. Preferably use yellow figs, as the violet variety will not come out as beautiful.

2 lbs (1,000 g) figs, preferably yellow

1. Poke holes in the figs with a fork and blanch them for about 5 minutes in boiling water.
2. Cool the figs under cold running water.

Follow the recipe and preserve the same way as Preserved Citrus Peels, see p. 107.

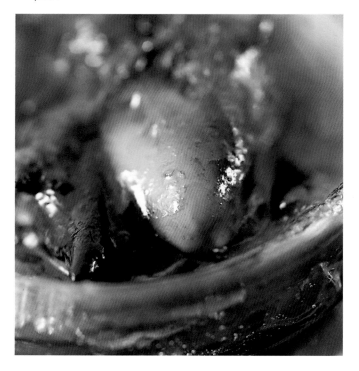

Dates

Phoenix dactylifera

The date palm is an ancient cultivated plant. It was known in the Middle East as early as 3,000 years ago. Dates are cultivated, among other places, in warmer parts of America, in the countries surrounding the Mediterranean Sea, and the Near East. Fresh dates did not become available until more recently. Nowadays, you can find fresh dates year-round. In the fridge they will keep for about 10 days. Fresh dates do not taste as sweet as dried dates. The date fruits are 1 ½ inches (4 cm) long and weigh ⅓ – ½ oz (10–15 g).

In Sweden, dried dates have been imported for a long time, and for Christmas they would be a natural part of the candy assortment. Candied dates, filled with pistachio marzipan, can at that time easily be found in patisseries and they are both very sweet and very tasty.

Date Jam

This jam, just like fresh dates, is especially good with cheese.

3 lbs (1,400 g) fresh dates
(2 lbs [1,000 g] net weight)
1 ¼ cups (300 g/3 dl) freshly pressed orange juice
Juice of 2 lemons
Pinch of saffron
½ cup (100 g/1 dl) Pernod
1 ½ lbs (700 g) sugar
7 oz (200 g) pistachios, preferably from Sicily
½ lb (250 g) apple jelly or 1 ½ cups (350 g) apple juice, p. 16–17

1. Rinse and pit the dates. Chop them into small pieces. Place them in 8 cups (2 liters) of boiling water to blanch and swell so that they will better absorb the syrup. Let them drain.
2. Pour orange juice and lemon juice into a pot with the saffron and Pernod.
3. Add the sugar and bring everything to a boil.
4. Add the drained dates and boil the jam while stirring. Remove all foam from the surface. Boil until the surface is starting to wrinkle. Brush the inside of the pot now and then with a brush dipped in cold water.
5. Add the pistachios and measure the temperature with a thermometer. Make sure that the temperature is 220–222°F (105–106°C), or perform a jam test, see p. 20.
6. Pour the jam into sterilized jars and screw on the lids right away. Turn the jars upside down a couple of times.

Makes about 3 ⅓ lbs (1,650 g) finished jam.

Date Jam.

Physalis

Physalis peruviana

The physalis has its home in South America. It is also called the Cape gooseberry because it was cultivated in South Africa by sailors as a result of its high vitamin C content. The berries are the size of cherries and weigh about an ounce. The straw-colored shell and the enlarged calyx provide effective protection during transportation. The berries can easily be removed from the shell.

The physalis is basically imported all year. The berries are ripe when they have turned yellow. When the berries are still green, they are significantly more tart. The taste is good and sweet, and reminiscent of pineapple. The fruit flesh is yellowish and filled with small seeds.

Physalis is most commonly used as a garnish and dipped in chocolate as pralines, as well as for pies and tarts. You may also dip them in a thick pancake batter and fry them golden brown. I don't recommend any special flavorings for this, as it would just cover the unique taste.

Physalis Jam

3 lbs (1,400 g) physalis fruits
(2 lbs [1,000 g] net weight)
2 lbs (900 g) sugar
Juice of 1 lemon
½ lb (250 g) apple jelly or 1 ½ cups (350 g) apple juice, p. 16–17

1. Clean and rinse the berries in cold water.
2. Pour sugar and lemon juice into a pot and boil to 234–240°F (112–114°C), or perform a sugar test, see p. 14. Constantly brush the inside of the pot with a brush dipped in cold water to prevent sugar crystals.
3. Add the berries and apple juice or apple jelly and boil for about 20 minutes while stirring. Remove all foam so that the jam stays clear.
4. Measure the temperature when the berries are starting to look transparent and the jam has formed jelly. It should be at 224°F (107°C), or perform a jam test on a cold plate, see p. 20.
5. Pour directly into sterilized jars and screw on the lids right away. Turn the jars upside down a couple of times.

Makes about 3 ¾ lbs (1,700 g) jam. *Photo on p. 159.*

Preserved Physalis

You preserve physalis the same way you preserve citrus peels.

2 lbs (1,000 g) fruits

Blanch the fruits in boiling water for 1 minute and cool in cold water.
Preserve the berries the same way you would citrus peels. See Preserved Citrus Peels on p. 107.

Lychee

Litchi chinensis

Lychee and rambutan, *Nephelium lappaceum*, both belong to the same family of Chinese trees. The rambutan is even referred to as the hairy lychee. Lychee was cultivated in ancient China and was considered one of the finest fruits. The fruits grow in clusters with up to 30 fruits in a cluster. The fruits are light brown and turn reddish brown when they ripen. They are spherical or oval and have a diameter of about 1 ¼–1 ½ inches (3–4 cm). The fruits are harvested ripe. Their taste is reminiscent of white currants.

The lychee is imported and may be found all over the world year-round. The fruits are suitable for boiling in syrup for desserts.

Boiled Lychee

You may prepare rambutan the exact same way.

1 lb (500 g) lychee fruits
12 oz (350 g) sugar
2 cups (500 g/5 dl) water
Juice of 1 lime
6 lime leaves
1 star anise

1. Peel the fruits and scoop the fruit flesh out.
2. Combine the sugar, water, lime juice, lime leaves, and star anise in a saucepan and boil to 234–240°F (112–114°C), or perform a sugar test, see p. 14.
3. Boil the fruit and let it simmer for about 5 minutes.
4. Pour into sterilized jars and screw on the lids right away. Store in the fridge.

Serve with ice cream.
Photo on p. 165.

Tamarillo

Cyphomandra betacea

The tamarillo is also called "tree tomato" and belongs to the potato family. But it is considered to be a fruit. The fruits are oval, often with pointy ends. The taste is fresh and tart. Their skin is pretty thick. The fruit has one layer with a firm fruit flesh and then in the middle it has a softer jelly-like flesh. The fruit looks like an orange tomato.

The tamarillo is suitable for marmalade and chutneys. It is reminiscent of the apricot, except with a softer aroma once it is strained.

Tamarillo Jam with Licorice Root

You should be able to find licorice root in specialty stores such as health-food stores.

3 lbs (1,400 g) tamarillos
(2 lbs [1,000 g] net weight)
Juice of 1 lemon
Juice of 2 oranges
2 lbs (1,000 g) sugar
4 licorice roots
⅓ inch (1 cm) cinnamon stick

DAY 1

1. Remove the stems and peel the tamarillos. Cut them down the middle and remove the seeds.
2. Dice the tamarillos and combine them in a pot with squeezed lemon and orange juice, sugar, licorice root, and cinnamon stick.
3. Bring everything to a boil and pour it directly into a bowl. Let it cool, cover with plastic wrap, and keep in the fridge overnight.

DAY 2

1. Place the fruit in a strainer and let the syrup drain off.
2. Pour the syrup into a pot and boil. Brush the inside of the pot with a brush dipped in cold water now and then. Boil the syrup to 234–240°F (112–114°C), or perform a sugar test, see p. 14.
3. Add the fruit and continue to boil. Remove any foam. Brush the inside of the pot with a brush dipped in cold water. Boil to 224–226°F (107–108°C), or perform a jam test on a cold plate, see p. 20.
4. Pour the jam directly into sterilized jars and screw on the lids right away. Turn the jars upside down a couple of times.

Makes about 3 ⅓ lbs (1,500 g) jam.

Passion Fruit, Granadilla

Passiflora edulis

The passion fruit stems from Brazil. The species have a particularly beautiful flower. It first came to Sweden at the end of the 1960s. There are many different varieties. The inside consists of soft flesh, similar to currants, and many small seeds, each surrounded by a mantle of juicy greenish flesh. You may eat both the fruit meat and the seeds. The taste is fresh and rich.

They may be oval or round and 1 ½–2 ¾ inches (4–7 cm) in diameter. The skin is purple to brown or yellow orange, depending on the variety. When they are ripe, the skin should start to wrinkle slightly. They are imported year-round. I usually make sorbets, soufflés, ganache for truffles, and curd from this wonderful fruit.

Passion Fruit Curd

Today you can buy good-quality passion fruit purée frozen. If you want to make your own, you will need about 20 passion fruits for 7 oz (200 g) purée. Cut them down the middle and press them through a strainer. Include some of the seeds; it looks beautiful. Freeze the rest of the seeds for future use.

About 6 eggs (300 g)
½ lb (300 g) sugar
¼ cup (50 g) pressed orange juice
3 ½ oz (100 g) passion fruit purée
1 cup (200 g)

Continued on p. 156

1. Whisk eggs and half of the sugar until fluffy.
2. Boil the orange juice, passion fruit purée, and remaining sugar. Pour it over the egg mixture and whip into a smooth cream.
3. Pour the cream into a saucepan with a thick bottom. Carefully warm while whisking until the cream has thickened and is bubbling.
4. Remove the saucepan from the stove and whip the cream completely smooth.
5. Sift the cream through a strainer. Let the temperature sink to 125°F (50°C). Mix in the butter with a handheld mixer or an electric beater.
6. Scoop into sterilized jars and screw on the lids right away. Turn the jars upside down a couple of times and store them in the fridge.

Makes about 2 lbs (900 g) curd.

Passion Fruit Curd with White Chocolate

Replace the butter with 7 oz (200 g) white chocolate, preferably Valrhona Ivoire.

Passion Fruit Curd with Dark Chocolate

Replace the butter with 6 oz (175 g) dark chocolate, preferably Valrhona Grand Cru Pur Caraïbe.

Passion Fruit Jam with Mango and Lime

1 lb (500 g) passion fruit purée from about 50 fruits (or frozen purée with 50 seeds)
2 lbs (1,000 g) mango
(1 lb [500 g] net weight)
Juice of 2 limes
2 lbs (1,000 g) sugar
½ cup (50 g) white rum
1 ½ cups (350 g) apple juice, p. 17

1. Slice the passion fruits down the middle and pass them through a strainer, unless you are using frozen purée.
2. Peel the mangoes and cut the fruit flesh off the pits.
3. Blend everything in a pot and boil while stirring. Remove all foam. Brush the inside of the pot with a brush dipped in cold water to prevent sugar crystals.
4. Boil while stirring until the mango bits have started to turn transparent and the jam has formed jelly. Boil to 222–224°F (106–107°C), or perform a jam test on a cold plate, see p. 20.
5. Pour the jam into sterilized jars. Screw on the lids and turn the jars upside down a couple of times.

Makes about 3 ¾ lbs (1,700 g) jam. *Photo on p. 130.*

Pomegranate

Punica granatum

The pomegranate is an ancient cultivated plant that most likely has its roots in the Near East and Mediterranean region. The fruit, which is the size of an orange with a diameter of 2 ½–5 inches (7–12 cm), has a prominent calyx. It weighs 1 lb (300–500 g). The color of the skin may vary from reddish yellow to red and yellow brown. The fruit flesh is reddish with small seeds. They are imported during the fall.

The seeds taste tart and slightly sweet, and are reminiscent of red currants. The skin of ripe pomegranates may sometimes crack, which releases an intense scent. When you want to remove the seeds from the fruit, you begin by shaking it: this way the seeds are released. Break the fruit open and the seeds will fall out. One pomegranate will give about ½ cup (1 dl) of seeds. For cordial you may press the fruit on a citrus press. Personally I mostly use pomegranate seeds for garnishing fruit salads.

Pomegranate Jam

3 ½ lbs (1,600 g) pomegranate
(2 lb [1,000 g] seeds, net weight)
Juice of 2 lemons
¾ lbs (350 g) green apples
(½ lb [250 g] net weight)
7 oz (200 g) raspberries
2 ½ lbs (1,200 g) sugar

1. Shake and cut open the pomegranate fruits and shake the seeds out.
2. Press the fruits in a citrus press. Press the lemons as well.
3. Peel the apples and remove the cores. Dice into small cubes.
4. Pour the fruit juice and seeds into a pot and add the apple cubes and raspberries.
5. Let it boil for 10 minutes. Add the sugar.
6. Boil while carefully stirring now and then. Remove all foam to make sure that the jam stays clear.
7. Brush the inside of the pot with a brush dipped in cold water to prevent sugar crystals.
8. When the seeds are turning transparent, the temperature should be at 222–224°F (106–107°C). Perform a jam test, see p. 20.
9. Pour the jam directly into sterilized jars and screw on the lids right away. Turn the jars upside down a couple of times.

Makes about 4 ½ lbs (2,000 g) jam.

Pomegranate Jam and Physalis Jam.

Carambola

Averrhoa carambola

The home of the carambola is most likely Malaysia. Nowadays the fruit is cultivated in many tropical countries. The fruit is oblong, 4–8 inches (10–20 cm), with sharp-edged vertical ridges. Its color is greenish yellow or yellow. It weighs 1 ¾–3 ½ oz (50–100 g). It is imported most of the year.

The fruits are ripe when the transparent fruit flesh turns yellow. When the fruit is really ripe, you can easily pull the peel off. The taste is fresh and tart, reminiscent of sorrel. In countries where it is grown, it is often used for marmalade, jam, or cordial. In Sweden we mostly use it as a garnish. Carambola has a very high vitamin C content.

Carambola Jam with Vanilla and Lemon Verbena

2 ½ lbs (1,100 g) carambola fruit
(2 lbs [1,000 g] net weight)
1 ¾ lbs (800 g) sugar
Juice of 2 limes
1 vanilla bean, preferably Bourbon
¾ oz (20 g) lemon verbena
20 coriander seeds
½ lb (250 g) apple jelly or 1 ½ cups (350 g) apple juice, p. 16–17

DAY 1

1. Rinse the fruits in cold water. Scald them in boiling water for 1 minute and cool them with cold water. Pull the peel off with a small knife.
2. Cut the fruit into small, thin slices and place them in a pot with sugar, lime juice, and vanilla seeds.
3. Bring everything to a boil. Empty into a bowl and let it cool.
4. Cover with plastic wrap and let it sit in the fridge overnight.

DAY 2

1. Pour the fruit into a strainer and let the syrup drain off.
2. Boil the syrup in a pot to 234–240°F (112–114°C), or perform a sugar test, see p. 14. Remove all foam. Brush the inside of the pot with a brush dipped in cold water to prevent sugar crystals.
3. Add the fruit and apple jelly or apple juice and boil while stirring for 20 minutes. When the slices have started to turn transparent and the jam itself is holding together (220–222°F [105–106°C]) the jam is ready. Perform a jam test on a cold plate.
4. Place the herbs in boiling water and then immediately move them under cold water. Finely chop them and add them at the end of the boiling time.
5. Pour directly into sterilized jars and screw on the lids right away. Turn the jars upside down a couple of times.

Makes about 3 ⅓ lbs (1,500 g) jam.

Preserved Carambola Fruit

Carambola slices are preserved the same way as citrus peels.

2 lbs (1,000 g) carambola fruit

Cut the fruit into thin slices of about ⅛ inch (5 mm). Blanch them for 1 minute in boiling water.

Preserve them by following the recipe for Preserved Citrus Peels, see p. 107.

OTHER EXOTIC FRUITS

There are many other exotic fruits that can be used for marmalades, jam, and cordial, and eaten fresh.

Barbary Fig, *Opuntia ficus indica,*

is an oval fruit, about 4 inches (10 cm) long, with a flattened short side. Most likely it stems from the West Indies and Central America, but it could be found in Europe as early as the 1600s. The aroma is tart and reminiscent of the pear. Like the pineapple, kiwi, and papaya, it contains a proteolytic enzyme that breaks down gelatin.

The skin is light green, red, or yellow brown. The surface is covered with tiny, almost invisible thorns that easily puncture your skin. Use gloves when you are handling this fruit. The fruit flesh is light pink. The seeds are eaten as well. The fruit is most commonly eaten fresh, but you can boil jam by following the recipe for pear jam.

Guava, *Psidium guajava,*

is recognized as being among the fruits with the highest vitamin C content. The fruit stems from the tropical areas of the Americas. They grow as big as medium-sized apples or pears, with a greenish-yellow to yellow peel. They weigh about 5 oz (150 g). They are ripe when they release an intense scent and the skin easily gives under pressure.

The fruit flesh may be white green or pink, depending on the variety. In the middle it has small, hard, and spiky seeds embedded in the fruit flesh. The seed are not edible. Guava tastes sweet and tart, and it has a wonderful aroma, like a mixture of pears and figs. The fruit is imported year-round.

Guavas are mostly eaten raw, like apples. They can be prepared as jam, marmalade, sauce, and purée, the same way as apples.

You can make both sliced fruit marmalade and cordial of the fruit as well.

Japanese Persimmon,
Diospyros kaki,

is a development from Israel and the persimmon/kaki fruit, which stems from East Asia. It looks like a tomato with leaves. The color is golden yellow to orange. It weighs 4–14 oz (125–400 g). The diameter is 2–3 inches (6–8 cm). The fruit flesh ranges from orange to red and has a jelly-like texture.

The Japanese persimmon lacks tannin and the fruit flesh is firmer than the kaki fruit, which makes it easier to transport. The fruit is imported from October till March. The fruit tastes sweet and tart and has high sugar content with a hint of vanilla. It is very suitable for jam and marmalade.

Cherimoya, *Annona cherimola,*

originally stems from Peru and Ecuador and has been cultivated since the time of the Incas. The fruit is heart-shaped, the skin matte-green with scale-like markings. The fruit weighs ½ lb (225–300 g). The fruit flesh is cream-white with black seeds. You can boil jam the same way you would prepare pineapple jam.

Mangosteen, *Gacinia mangostana,*

originated in Malaysia. The fruit is the size of a small apple and is flattened at the top and bottom. The thick leathery peel ranges from violet to reddish brown. A thick crown of leaves is fastened along the stem. Beneath the ⅛ inch (5 mm) thick skin is the white fruit flesh divided into 4–5 sections. Its green seeds are embedded in the flesh, and are eaten with the fruit. The fruit flesh melts on your tongue and is very flavorful.

Ginger, *Zingiber officinale,*

is an ancient plant that's been farmed for thousands of years in China and India. In Europe it was both known and used as a spice during the first century. You use the roots. On the outside, they are beige or light brown, while they are light yellowish on the inside. You may find ginger dried, ground, or in whole roots.

Ginger has also been used for medical purposes and as an aphrodisiac. It contains etheric oils with a sharp taste. Another type of ginger that you can buy in Sweden is the galingale. It stems from South Asia, especially Thailand, and is used in Asian cooking.

Preserved and candied ginger has historically been around for hundreds of years. Fresh ginger came to Sweden about fifteen years ago and quickly became popular in Thai and Asian cooking. During the sixties, when I was only beginning to learn my trade, ginger soufflé with foamy zabaione sauce was a common dessert. Ginger sorbet with Drambuie liqueur was another favorite.

In Switzerland we would use ginger for pralines. We cut the preserved ginger in thin slices and dipped them in dark chocolate, and called them "Herren-Pralinen." We would chop it and add it to marzipan or other fillings such as "Fruchtebrot," etc.

Shredded or finely chopped preserved ginger can be very tasty in a marmalade with orange or grapefruit. Applesauce with finely chopped preserved ginger tastes delicious. Lingonberry pears with shredded preserved ginger are also wonderful.

Added Flavor

Spices: nothing but vanilla is needed.
Sugar: regular white sugar.
Lemon: to create a fresh taste.

Preserved Ginger

3 lbs (1,400 g) whole ginger
(2 lbs [1,000 g] net weight)
4 cups (1,000 g/1 liter) water
Juice of 2 lemons
1 vanilla bean, preferably Bourbon
3⅓ lbs (1,500 g) sugar

1. Peel and rinse the ginger. Cut it in pieces the size of quail eggs.
2. Drop the pieces in 4 cups (1 liter) boiling water with the lemon juice and vanilla bean. Cover with a lid and let it simmer until the ginger pieces are completely tender. It usually takes 2–2 ½ hours until they are completely soft. If they are still not ready, just let them boil until you can easily jab a fork through the ginger.
3. Add ½ lb (250 g) sugar and let it simmer for an additional 15 minutes. Add another ½ lb (250 g) sugar and let it simmer for another 15 minutes.
4. Repeat the process 6 times until the ginger is completely transparent.
5. Bring to a boil and remove all foam.
6. Pour into sterilized jars and screw on the lids right away.

This will keep in the fridge for years.

Cheese Soufflé with Preserved Ginger

Get a real mature cheese and you will have an instant crowd pleaser, I promise. This cheese soufflé may be served as a dessert. You can also serve preserved ginger bits with the soufflé, if you don't want to shred it and have it in the actual soufflé.

4 servings

1 soufflé pan, about 8 ½ inch (22 cm) diameter
2 tbsp (25 g) unsalted butter
1 oz (35 g) Parmesan cheese to sprinkle in the pan

Soufflé Batter

3 tbsp (35 g) unsalted butter
⅓ cup (40 g) all-purpose flour
1 cup (200 g/2 dl) whole milk
1 ¾ oz (50 g) Emmentaler cheese, mature
1 ¾ oz (50 g) Parmesan cheese, 4-year
2 ¾ tbsp (4 cl) cognac
About 5 egg yolks (100 g)
Salt, ground white pepper, grated nutmeg, and rose paprika
About 5 egg whites (150 g)
1 tsp lemon juice
¾ oz (25 g) finely shredded preserved ginger

1. Butter the pan and sprinkle the cheese on top. Shake away any extra cheese.
2. Melt the butter in a saucepan. Whisk in the flour. Let it cook for a short time.
3. Whisk in the milk. Bring it to a boil while vigorously stirring. Whisk the batter constantly so that the flour blends in well. The batter should not stick to the edges of the saucepan.
4. Remove the saucepan from the stove and whisk in the cheese till it has completely melted. Stir in the liquor and egg yolks.
5. Flavor with salt, freshly ground pepper, some grated nutmeg, and a pinch of rose paprika.
6. Cover the mixture with plastic wrap and set the oven to 390°F (200°C).
7. Place a baking sheet in the oven so that it warms.
8. Whip the egg whites and lemon in a metal bowl, or if possible a newly cleaned copper bowl, which is rubbed with salt and vinegar and then rinsed with cold water. Whisk to stiff peaks by hand. If you use an electric beater, it will take longer.
9. Fold a fourth of the egg-white foam into the soufflé batter. Use a silicone spatula and fold into a smooth cream.
10. Add the rest of the egg-white foam the same way and turn into a light batter.
11. Place a third of the batter in the pan and sprinkle some diced cheese and shredded ginger on top. Repeat the procedure twice more.
12. Spread the batter evenly with the help of a spatula.
13. Take the baking sheet out of the oven and place the pan on top.
14. Bake for 20–25 minutes and serve right away.

Preserved Ginger, Preserved Jackfruit (top), Preserved Lychee.

Rhubarb

Rheum rhabarbarum

In Sweden you can find rhubarb in almost every garden. It originated in China. In Sweden it was first used for medical purposes during the 1600s, but later became popular as a garden plant during the 1800s. "Turkey rhubarb" was cultivated during the Middle Ages in monastery gardens. Its root was used as a laxative. The edible rhubarb has a significantly shorter history than the medical varieties.

Among the rhubarb varieties are Victoria, which is the most common in Sweden, Elmblitz, and Sutton. Rhubarb is harvested in May in Sweden, but is imported as early as March. In Britain rhubarb is sometimes cultivated in darkness. This variety is called forced rhubarb in English, and glass rhubarb in Swedish, because it is extra crispy and tasty. If you cover a rhubarb plant with a bucket, it becomes more tender.

The taste is tart and it is rich in vitamins. Rhubarb is the first sign of spring and is enjoyed as compote, ice cream, sorbet, cream, and soup, as well as in pies and tarts. It is also suitable for chutney. As a child, rhubarb cream with cold milk was one of my favorites as a snack in summertime.

Added Flavor

Spices: for instance, cinnamon, ginger, cloves, vanilla and tonka beans.
Citrus fruits: juice and zest.
Fruit combinations: black currants, apples, pears, and dried figs.

Classic Rhubarb Jam

One of my best rhubarb memories is from the restaurant Clairefontaine, right outside of Lyon. In the morning I was awakened by the scent streaming from the windows of freshly baked brioches, boiled rhubarb jam, and a fresh pot of coffee.

2 ¾ lbs (1,250 g) rhubarb
(2 lbs [1,000 g] net weight)
2 lbs (1,000 g) sugar
Juice of 2 lemons

DAY 1

1. Rinse and peel the rhubarb stalks and cut the ends and leaves off. Cut into small pieces.
2. Blend all of the ingredients in a bowl and cover with plastic wrap. Let it marinate at room temperature for 24 hours.

DAY 2

1. Pour everything into a pot and boil while slowly stirring. Remove foam with a spoon. Occasionally brush the inside of the pot with a brush dipped in cold water.
2. At 220–222°F (105–106°C), the jam is ready. You may also perform a jam test on a cold plate, see p. 20

Makes about 3 ⅓ lbs (1,500 g) jam.

Rhubarb Jam with Dried Figs

Add 1 lb (400 g) finely chopped, presoaked figs to the Classic Rhubarb Jam. This jam is especially good with cheese.

Rhubarb Jam with Ginger, Cinnamon, and Orange

2 ¾ lbs (1,250 g) rhubarb
(2 lbs [1,000 g] net weight)
1 ¾ lbs (800 g) sugar
Juice of 1 lemon
Juice and zest of 2 oranges
⅓ inch (1 cm) real cinnamon
3 ½ oz (100 g) preserved ginger, see p. 164

DAY 1

1. Rinse, peel, and remove the ends on the rhubarb stalks. Cut them into dice-sized pieces.
2. Blend with sugar, cinnamon stick, lemon juice, orange zest, and orange juice.
3. Cover with plastic wrap and let it marinate overnight at room temperature.

DAY 2

1. Pour the mixture into a pot and boil while stirring. Remove any foam from the surface with a spoon.
2. Occasionally brush the inside of the pot with a brush dipped in cold water.
3. Finely chop the preserved ginger and add to the pot.
4. The rhubarb should now be turning transparent and the surface of the jam should look wrinkly.
5. At 224–226°F (107–108°C), the jam should be ready. Perform a jam test on a cold plate, see p. 20.
6. Pour directly into sterilized jars and screw on the lids right away. Turn the jars upside down a couple of times.

Makes about 3 ⅓ lbs (1,500 g) jam.

Rhubarb Jam with Tahiti Vanilla

Don't use the cinnamon, ginger, and orange. Instead, add the vanilla seeds from 1 vanilla bean during boiling.

Rhubarb Jam with Whole Strawberries

This jam will become a new breakfast favorite! By lightly preserving the berries in advance, they maintain their shape better during boiling. The French call this kind of preserving "demi-confit," half-preserved.

Half-Preserved Strawberries

2 lbs (1,000 g) rinsed and ripe small strawberries, lightly pricked with a fork
4 cups (1,000 g/1 liter) water
2 lbs (1,000 g) sugar

Rhubarb Jam

2 ¾ lbs (1,250 g) rhubarb
(2 lbs [1,000 g] net weight)
Juice of 2 lemons
2 lbs (1,000 g) sugar

DAY 1

1. Boil 2 lbs (1,000 g) water and ½ lb (250 g) sugar in a large saucepan. Add the strawberries and let it simmer carefully for 15 minutes.
2. Remove the saucepan from the stove, cover with a lid, and let sit for 30 minutes.
3. Add an additional ½ lb (250 g) sugar and let it simmer for 15 more minutes.
4. Remove from the stove and cover with plastic wrap. Let it sit overnight.

DAY 2

1. Add ½ lb (250 g) sugar and bring it to a boil. Let simmer carefully for 15 minutes.
2. Add another ½ lb (250 g) sugar and let it simmer for 15 more minutes.
3. The strawberries are now preserved and transparent. Cover with plastic wrap and let them sit overnight.

DAY 3

1. Rinse and peel the rhubarb. Remove the ends and dice into pieces the size of sugar cubes.
2. Pour the rhubarb into a pot with the lemon juice and sugar.
3. Boil while stirring and removing all foam from the surface. Brush the inside of the pot with a brush dipped in cold water now and then. Boil to 220°F (105°C). Add the drained berries and boil to 224–226°F (107–108°C), or perform a jam test on a cold plate, see p. 20.
4. Pour directly into sterilized jars and screw on the lids right away. Turn the jars upside down a couple of times.

Makes about 5 ½ lbs (2,500 g) jam.

Rhubarb Jam with Strawberries

You can also make this jam with rhubarb and raspberries.

1 ¼ lbs (650 g) rhubarb
(1 lb [500 g] net weight)
1 lb (500 g) strawberries (or raspberries)
1 ¾ lb (800 g) sugar
Juice of 1 lemon

DAY 1

1. Rinse and peel the rhubarb and cut the ends off, then dice.
2. Rinse the berries; if you are using strawberries, remove the tops.
3. Blend rhubarb and berries with the sugar and lemon juice in a bowl. Cover with plastic wrap. Let it sit at room temperature overnight.

DAY 2

1. Pour everything into a pot and boil while stirring. Remove foam with a spoon. Brush the inside of the pot with a brush dipped in cold water sporadically during boiling.
2. When the rhubarb is transparent and the surface of the jam is wrinkling, the jam is almost ready. Boil to 224–226°F (107–108°C), or perform a jam test on a cold plate, see p. 20.
3. Pour directly into sterilized jars and screw on the lids right away. Turn the jars upside down a couple of times.

Makes about 3 ⅓ lbs (1,500 g) jam.

Rhubarb Jam with Black Currants

Follow the recipe above, except replace the strawberries or raspberries with black currants. This jam is magnificent with mature cheeses.

Rhubarb Jam with Strawberries, Rhubarb Jam with Raspberries.

Rhubarb Compote

This wonderful spring compote is great served with fresh vanilla or strawberry ice cream and some tasty sandwiches.

6 servings

2 lbs (1,000 g) young pink rhubarb
(about 1 ¾ lbs [800 g] net weight)
1 ⅔ cups (400 g/4 dl) Sauternes or another sweet dessert wine
2 lbs (1,000 g) sugar
Juice of 2 lemons
1 vanilla bean, preferably Bourbon

1. Set the oven to 260°F (125°C).
2. Rinse the rhubarb stalks and cut them into 1 ½ inch (4 cm) long pieces.
3. Place the pieces in a saucepan with the wine, sugar, and lemon juice.
4. Cut the vanilla bean down the middle and scrape the seeds out. Add the seeds to the saucepan.
5. Let everything carefully come to a boil. Cover with a lid and place the whole saucepan in the oven for 5–8 minutes.
6. Pour it into a bowl and place the bowl in cold water to cool.
7. When cooled, cover with plastic wrap and let it sit in the fridge for a couple of hours until it is completely chilled.

Rhubarb Cordial with Lemon and Vanilla

5 lbs (2,400 g) young pink rhubarb
(4 ½ lbs [2,000 g] net weight)
Juice of 2 lemons
1 vanilla bean, preferably Bourbon
2 ½ cups (600 g/6 dl) water
1 ⅓ lbs (600 g) sugar per 4 cups (1 liter) of juice

1. Rinse and chop the rhubarb. Squeeze the lemon. Cut the vanilla bean down the middle and scrape out the seeds.
2. Boil everything in the water under a lid for 15 minutes, until the rhubarb is falling apart.
3. Empty everything into a strainer and squeeze all of the juice out by lightly pressing with a ladle. Pour the fruit onto cheesecloth and let it drain on its own for 60 minutes or until the mass feels dry.
4. Measure 1 ⅓ lbs (600 g) sugar per 4 cups (1 liter) of juice and bring it to a boil. Remove all foam so that the cordial is completely clear. Pour into sterilized bottles.

Rhubarb Tartlets

Wonderfully tasty, with a lovely buttery shortbread crust and a streusel topping. On the cruise ship Vista/Fjord, we called these tartlets Rhubarb Crumble Tarts. We would serve them with strawberry coulis and rhubarb sorbet.

12 tartlets

12 mini tart pans

Rhubarb

2 lbs (1,000 g) young pink rhubarb, preferably forced rhubarb
1 cup (200 g) sugar

Streusel Topping

⅓ cup (65 g) butter, cold
½ cup (65 g) powdered sugar
½ tbsp (10 g) real vanilla sugar
⅔ cup (75 g) all-purpose flour

Pâte Sablée

See Prune Plum Tart, p. 49

Almond Filling

1 ¾ oz (50 g) sweet almonds, preferably Spanish
¼ cup (50 g) sugar
¼ cup (50 g) butter, room temperature
1 egg (50 g) room temperature
1 ½ tbsp (2 cl) dark rum
Pinch of cornstarch

DAY 1

1. Rinse and peel the rhubarb. Cut the stalks in ⅓ inch (2 cm) long pieces.
2. Combine the pieces with the sugar in a bowl and let it marinate for 24 hours.

DAY 2

Pour the rhubarb into a strainer and let the sugar drain off.

Streusel Topping

1. Mix the cold butter with the rest of the ingredients and work it into dough.
2. Squeeze the dough through a potato press and place the crumb in the freezer until use.

Pâte Sablée

1. Work the cold dough smooth with your hands and roll it out ⅛ inch (2 ½ mm) thick.
2. Lift the dough up now and then and sprinkle flour underneath so that it doesn't stick to the table.
3. Carefully roll the dough up and place it on top of the mini tart pans.
4. Sprinkle some flour over the dough and bring the pans together a little.
5. Place a piece of dough in each pan so that they are beautifully lined with dough.

6. Roll over the pans with a rolling pin and place the pans on a baking sheet.
7. Prick the dough in the pans with a fork to prevent the dough from rising.
8. Place in the fridge for at least 30 minutes.

Almond Filling

1. Boil 2 cups (500 g/5 dl) of water in a saucepan. Throw the almonds in and let boil for 1 minute. Empty into a strainer and cool them under cold running water.
2. Shell the almonds. Place them in a food processor and add the sugar.
3. Mix into an almond paste and place in a bowl.
4. Stir in the butter in two halves with a spoon. Mix into a smooth mass.
5. Add the eggs one at a time, making a smooth batter. Lastly add the liquor and cornstarch.

Complete the Tartlets

1. Take the pans out of the fridge.
2. Put the almond paste into a pastry bag or cut a small hole in a plastic bag. Pipe out a ball of the mixture into each pan, about ¾ oz (20 g) of filling in each.
3. Add the rhubarb and cover with the streusel topping.
4. Bake the tartlets golden brown in a 375°F (190°C) oven for about 15 minutes. Release from the pans as soon as they have cooled and let them cool on a cooling rack.

Rhubarb Tart with Egg Punch, as in Alsace

Line a springform pan, about 11 inch (28 cm) diameter, with the pâte sablée dough. Fill with rhubarb, egg punch, and streusel topping. Serve with a strawberry salad and strawberry sorbet.

Egg Punch

3 eggs (150 g)
⅔ cup (75 g) all-purpose flour
2 tbsp (12 g) cornstarch
⅛ cup (25 g/¼ dl) whipping cream
1 tbsp (25 g) real vanilla sugar

Mix everything with a whisk and pass though a chinoise. Don't use the almond paste from the previous recipe: add the rhubarb to the pans, cover with the egg punch and streusel topping. Bake at 355°F (180°C) for about 30 minutes.

Angelica

Angelica archangelica

Angelica is a 3 foot (1 m) tall genus of the parsley family, with greenish-white flowers. It has been grown in gardens since the Middle Ages. It was even used medicinally. Young shoots may be used in jam or candied. The root, angelica root, is very aromatic and is used as a spice in liqueurs.

Candied green angelica, in French *angélique*, is common in France, Italy, and Spain. You cut the stalks into 4 inch (9 cm) long pieces and boil them in water with a generous amount of green food coloring until they are soft and completely green. After this, they are preserved the exact same way as citrus peels. They are used as a garnish on pastries and desserts. You can also boil marmalade with the stalks, and sometimes they're combined with rhubarb. If you only use the angelica, the result will be spicy and good.

Jam with Angelica and Rhubarb

1 ⅓ lbs (600 g) angelica stalks
(1 lb [500 g] net weight)
1 ⅓ lbs (600 g) young pink rhubarb
(1 lb [500 g] net weight)
1 ¾ lbs (800 g) sugar
Juice of 1 lemon

DAY 1

1. Rinse and peel the angelica and rhubarb. Cut them into smaller pieces and blend with sugar and lemon juice.
2. Cover and let it marinate at room temperature overnight.

DAY 2

1. Empty everything into a pot and boil while stirring.
2. Remove any foam from the surface with a spoon. Brush the inside of the pot with a brush dipped in cold water to prevent sugar crystals.
3. Boil to 222–224°F (106–107°C). When the pieces have turned transparent and the surface is starting to wrinkle, do a jam test, see p. 20.
4. Pour directly into sterilized jars and screw on the lids right away. Turn the jars upside down a couple of times.

Makes about 3 ⅓ lbs (1,500 g) jam.

Preserved Angelica

Cut the angelica stalks into 1 inch (3 cm) long pieces and blanch them in boiling water. Cool them under cold running water. Preserve the same way as Preserved Citrus Peels, see p. 107, but add green food coloring so that they turn a bright green color.

Fennel

Foeniculum vulgare

Fennel is best recognized by its taste and scent of anise, even if the leaves look more like dill. It is imported from Italy from October through April. The size may vary. It is crunchy when raw but turns soft and aromatic once it's boiled.

Fennel Jam with Walnuts and Oregano

This jam goes great with cheeses, but can also be a tasty chutney.

1 ¼ lbs (650 g) fennel
(1 lb [500 g] net weight)
1 ¼ lb (650 g) green apples
(1 lb [500 g] net weight)
2 cups (500 g/5 dl) water
Juice of 1 lemon
¼ cup (50 g/½ dl) white wine vinegar
1 cup (100 g) walnuts
1 ½ oz (40 g) fresh chopped oregano
1 ¾ lbs (800 g) light muscovado sugar

1. Rinse and dice the fennel.
2. Rinse, peel, and core the apples. Dice the apples as well.
3. Pour water, lemon juice, and vinegar into a pot with the fennel.
4. Boil under a lid on low heat for 10 minutes.
5. Add the apples and let it boil for another 10 minutes.
6. Add the sugar and boil while constantly stirring. Remove foam with a spoon. Brush the inside of the pot with a brush dipped in cold water to prevent sugar crystals.
7. Boil to 222–224°F (106–107°C), or perform a jam test on a cold plate, see p. 20.
8. Stir in the walnuts and oregano and pour the jam directly into sterilized jars.
9. Screw the lids on right away and turn the jars upside down a couple of times.

Makes about 3 ⅓ lbs (1,500 g) jam. *Photo on p. 176.*

Pumpkin

Cucurbita pepo

The pumpkin belongs to the cucumber family. Some varieties are called squash, zucchini, and decorative pumpkin. They originated in America and came to Europe during the 1500s. The pumpkin may present itself in many different shapes and colors. There are varieties that can grow very large. In regard to cooking, we can divide the pumpkins into categories: summer varieties (soft-shelled) and winter varieties (hard-shelled).

The pumpkin is peeled and cut into sections, and the stringy center and the seeds are removed, after which the fruit flesh is used. Choose an orange variety for marmalades and chutney. Pumpkin is a great ingredient for soups, purées, and pies. The pumpkin pie is a classic in the United States, where it is eaten for Thanksgiving.

The squash bears many names. In Italy it is called zucchini, in France courgette. The most common variety is reminiscent of regular cucumbers. They can be yellow or green.

Added Flavor
Spices: ginger, cloves, cinnamon, nutmeg, nutmeg flower, and tonka bean.
Citrus fruits: zest and juice.
Spirits: whiskey, like bourbon, as well as dark rum.

Pumpkin Chutney

Lovely chutney that goes well with most anything.

2 lbs (1,000 g) orange pumpkin
(1 ¾ lbs [800 g] net weight)
½ lb (250 g) red onion
2 red bell peppers
½ lb (250 g) cherry tomatoes
1 ¾ oz (50 g) fresh ginger
2 lbs (1,000 g) muscovado sugar
5 oz (150 g) yellow raisins
2 cups (50 cl) apple vinegar
2 tbsp (40 g) rose pepper
2 tsp (10 g) sea salt

1. Cut open the pumpkin and remove the skin and seeds. Cut into small pieces.
2. Peel and finely chop the onion.
3. Rinse and core the bell peppers and dice them.
4. Remove the calyxes from the tomatoes and scald them in boiling water. Place them in cold water and remove the peels with a knife.
5. Peel and grate the ginger.
6. Pour all of the ingredients into a pot and boil while stirring on low heat. Boil until the mass is starting to thicken, about 50 minutes.
7. Pour the chutney directly into sterilized jars and screw on the lids right away. Turn the jars upside down a couple of times.

Makes about 3 ¾ lbs (1,700 g) chutney.

Fennel Jam with Walnuts and Oregano.

Squash Jam with Green Kiwi and Lemon Verbena

This jam is especially good with cheese and charcuteries.

2 ½ lbs (1,200 g) squash
(2 lbs [1,000 g] net weight)
1 lbs (600 g) kiwis
(1 lb [500 g] net weight)
1 pink grapefruit
Juice of 1 lemon
1 ¾ lbs (800 g) sugar
¾ oz (20 g) lemon verbena

DAY 1

1. Clean and slice the squash down the middle. Scrape the seeds away and dice the flesh.
2. Peel the kiwis and dice.
3. Peel and dice the grapefruit. Squeeze the lemon.
4. Pour everything into a bowl and blend well.
5. Cover with plastic wrap and let it sit at room temperature for 24 hours.

DAY 2

1. Empty everything into a pot and boil while constantly stirring. Remove foam. Occasionally brush the inside of the pot with a brush dipped in cold water.
2. When the pieces are starting to turn transparent, the temperature should be 224–226°F (107–108°C), or perform a jam test on a cold plate, see p. 20.
3. Pour the jam directly into sterilized jars and screw on the lids right away. Turn the jars upside down a couple of times.

Makes about 3 ⅓ lbs (1,500 g) jam.

Pumpkin Jam with Bourbon, Ginger, and Citrus Fruits

1 orange pumpkin of about 3 lbs (1,350 g)
(2 lbs [1,000 g] net weight)
2 oranges
2 lemons
2 ½ oz (75 g) fresh ginger
1 ¾ lbs (800 g) light muscovado sugar
¼ cup (50 g/½ dl) bourbon

DAY 1

1. Peel and seed the pumpkin. Cut it into small pieces.
2. Rinse the citrus fruits, cut them down the middle, and squeeze the juice out. Cut the peel off with a knife and shred into thin pieces.
3. Add the peels to boiling water and let it boil for 10 minutes. Place in a strainer and hold under cold running water.
4. Peel and grate the ginger.
5. Blend all of the ingredients in a bowl and let it marinate at room temperature for 24 hours.

DAY 2

1. Empty everything into a pot and boil on low heat while constantly stirring for 20 minutes.
2. Remove any foam on the surface with a spoon and occasionally brush the inside of the pot with a brush dipped in cold water.
3. Check the temperature when the pumpkin is starting to turn transparent. It should be at 224–226°F (107–108°C). You may also perform a jam test on a cold plate, see p. 20.
4. Pour the jam directly into sterilized jars and screw on the lids right away. Turn the jars upside down a couple of times.

Makes about 3 ⅓ lbs (1,500 g) jam.

Various chutneys.

Tomato

Solanum lycopersicum

The tomato originated in Peru. It was quite a common cultivated plant in South America by the time the Spanish arrived. The tomato was first cultivated in Europe in the 1540s, and quickly became a commodity in Italy. Today the tomato is cultivated in most parts of the world. Tomatoes are usually divided into two separate groups, namely determinate and indeterminate tomatoes. Within both of these divisions is a great number of varieties that have varying sizes, shapes, and tastes.

Tomatoes are sensitive to cold and should be stored at temperatures between 50–57°F (11–14°C). If you keep them at room temperature, the taste will develop to its fullest. Swedish tomatoes are always a great seasonal delicacy, but tomatoes are imported year-round.

For red jams and marmalades, I prefer plum tomatoes, as they are both tender and rich in aroma. My mother would bake delicious graham biscuits and serve them with tomato marmalade and a cup of strong tea.

Green Tomato Marmalade

Green tomato marmalade may also be flavored with chilies and various almonds and spices. *Photo on p. 181.*

4 ½ lbs (2,000 g) small, firm green tomatoes
(2 lbs [1,000 g] net weight)
2 lemons
2 lbs (1,000 g) sugar
1 cinnamon stick

DAY 1

1. Scald the tomatoes in 12 cups (3 liters) of boiling water. Place them in cold water and pull the skins off with a knife.
2. Scoop the insides out.
3. Grate the rinsed lemon and squeeze the juice out.
4. Blend everything with the sugar and let it marinate at room temperature overnight.

DAY 2

1. Boil the mixture while stirring for about 35 minutes until the marmalade has thickened. Brush the inside of the pot with a brush dipped in cold water to prevent sugar crystals. Remove all foam. The tomatoes should be transparent and the surface of the marmalade wrinkly.
2. At 210°F (100°C), the marmalade is ready. Pour a small amount onto a cold plate and perform a jam test, see p. 20.
3. Pour directly into sterilized jars and screw on the lids right away. Turn the jars upside down a couple of times.

Makes about 3 ⅓ lbs (1,500 g) marmalade.

Tomato Jam with Chilies and Valrhona Manjari Chocolate

During the Christmas season in 2005, this marmalade was incredibly popular at the Maria Escalante Chocolaterie Les Trois Roses in Malmö.

2 ½ lbs (1,100 g) red plum tomatoes
(1 lb [500 g] net weight)
1 ½ lbs (700 g) green apples
(1 lb [500 g] net weight)
2 cups (500 g/5 dl) water
1 ¾ lbs (800 g) sugar
Juice of 2 lemons
2 vanilla beans, preferably Bourbon
⅓ oz (10 g) chili pepper, habanero
12 oz (350 g) dark chocolate, Valrhona Grand Cru Manjari
   or Marabou dark

1. Boil 12 cups (3 liters) of water in a large pot and add the tomatoes. Let them boil for 1 minute.
2. Place the tomatoes in cold water and peel the skin off with a small knife. Slice them down the middle and remove the cores.
3. Peel and core the apples. Cut them into wedges.
4. Boil 2 cups (500 g/5 dl) water in a pot with the lemon juice and two cut and scraped vanilla beans.
5. Add the apples and boil under a lid until the fruit is falling apart.
6. Add the tomatoes, sugar, and the finely chopped chili.
7. Boil while constantly stirring and removing all foam. Occasionally brush the inside of the pot with a brush dipped in cold water. Boil to 220°F (105°C), or perform a jam test on a cold plate, see p. 20. Remove the pot from the stove and stir in the finely chopped chocolate.
8. Pour directly into sterilized jars and screw on the lids right away. Turn the jars upside down a couple of times.

Makes about 4 lbs (1,800 g) jam.

Tomato Jam with Tahiti Vanilla and Marcona Almonds

This jam is the favorite at Olof Viktors bakery in Glemminge, Sweden. The favorite with all cheese plates.

5 lbs (2,200 g) red, ripe plum tomatoes (2 lbs [1,000 g] net weight)
2 lbs (1,000 g) sugar
Juice of 2 lemons
1 vanilla bean, Tahiti
½ lb (250 g) shelled almonds

DAY 1

1. Bring about 12 cups (3 liters) of water to a boil in a saucepan, add the tomatoes, and let them boil for 1 minute. Place them in cold water and peel the skins off with a small knife.
2. Cut the tomatoes down the middle and remove the cores.
3. Finely chop the tomatoes and blend them with the sugar and lemon juice.
4. Cut the vanilla bean down the middle and scrape the seeds out.
5. Cover with plastic wrap and let everything marinate overnight.

DAY 2

1. Pour everything into a pot and boil while stirring. Remove all foam. Boil until the tomatoes have turned transparent and the surface of the jam is wrinkling. Brush the inside of the pot with a brush dipped in cold water.
2. The jam is ready at 224–226°F (107–108°C), or perform a jam test on a cold plate, see p. 20.
3. Remove the pot from the stove. Stir in the shelled almonds.
4. Fill the jars half-full with the jam. Let them sit for 30 minutes.
5. Bring the jam to a boil once more and fill the jars with the remaining jam. Screw on the lids right away and turn the jars upside down a couple of times.

If you fill the jars in this manner, the almonds will not all float up to the surface but will instead be evenly distributed in the jars.

Makes about 2 ¾ lbs (1,300 g) jam.

Preserved Cherry Tomatoes

2 lbs (1,000 g) small, barely ripe cherry tomatoes

1. Poke the tomatoes all over with a fork to keep the skin from splitting. Blanch them in boiling water for 1 minute.
2. Cool the tomatoes under cold running water.
3. Preserve by following the recipe for Preserved Citrus Peels, see p. 107.

Preserved Green Tomatoes

This is a somewhat nostalgic recipe for me. I remember when I would go down to my grandmother's basement to get various preserves from the shelves. Serve with a classic braised steak in cream sauce or with a Swedish "slottsstek." My grandmother would also preserve yellow Mirabelle plums the same way, and sometimes also Reine Claude plums.

2 lbs (1000 g) small, firm green tomatoes
8 cups water (2 liters) water
2 tsp (10 g) fleur de sel

Syrup
¾ cup (2 dl) white wine vinegar, 12%
1 ¼ cups (3 dl) water
½ lb (250 g) light muscovado sugar
1 piece dried ginger
6 whole cloves
12 white peppercorns
6 black peppercorns
⅓ inch (1 cm) cinnamon stick
1 star anise

1. Clean and rinse the tomatoes. Poke them all over with a small fork so that they won't split during boiling.
2. Boil the water and salt and add the tomatoes. Let them simmer for 5 minutes until they have softened.
3. Pour the tomatoes into a strainer and cool them with cold water to halt the boiling.
4. Combine all of the ingredients for the syrup in a pot and bring it to a boil.
5. Add the tomatoes and let everything simmer for about 10 minutes. The tomatoes should be turning transparent.
6. Scoop the tomatoes into jars and bring the syrup to a boil once more. Cover the tomatoes with the boiling syrup and screw the lids on right away. Turn the jars upside down a couple of times.

Preserved Green Tomatoes.

Red Beet

Beta vulgaris subsp. *vulgaris* var. *conditiva*

This tasty root vegetable is often overlooked when we are making jam or marmalade. It probably stems from the Near East. Red beets can be grown in most kinds of fields. There are different varieties with distinctive shapes and colors, including round and long, and yellow in addition to the red.

In Poland they grate red beets and blend them with grated horseradish and some oil and vinegar. It is flavored with salt and pepper as well as French mustard. This makes a great side for meats, poultry, or fried fish.

Added Flavor

Spices: cloves, bay leaves, black currant leaves, thyme, ginger, nutmeg and nutmeg flower, fresh and dried ginger, cumin, star anise, real cinnamon, cassava, spice pepper and other pepper varieties.
Herbs: thyme and oregano.
Sugar: white sugar and various cane sugars.
Vinegar
Lemon to give the jam a fresh taste and to help it form jelly.
Vegetable and fruit combinations: celery, celeriac, apples, and pears.

Red Beet Jam

This jam may be used with game or with good aromatic cheeses.

3 ⅓ lbs (1,500 g) red beets
(2 lbs [1,000 g] net weight)
2 lemons
1 ⅓ lbs (600 g) sugar
1 cup (250 g/2 ½ dl) water
4 whole star anise

1. Rinse and peel the beets. Grate them with a grater, using the large holes.
2. Rinse the lemons and grate the lemon peels directly into the beet mixture.
3. Squeeze the lemons and pour the juice in with the vegetables.
4. Boil the sugar and water in a pot to 234–240°F (112–114°C), or perform a sugar test, see Boiling Sugar, p. 14. Brush the inside of the pot with a brush dipped in cold water to prevent sugar crystals.
5. Add the star anise and beet mixture and boil, while stirring, to 226–230°F (108–110°C), or perform a jam test on a cold plate, see p. 20.
6. Remove any foam with a spoon.
7. Pour directly into sterilized jars and screw on the lids right away. Turn the jars upside down a couple of times.

Makes about 3 ⅓ lbs (1,500 g) jam.

Red Beet Jam with Apple and Gooseberries

Terrific with cheeses, pâtés, and terrines.

Just under 1 lb (400 g) red beets
(⅔ lb [300 g] net weight)
1 lb (500 g) green apples
(Just under 1 lb [400 g] net weight)
⅔ lb (300 g) green gooseberries
1 lemon
1 ½ lbs (700 g) sugar
⅓ inch (1 cm) real cinnamon stick
1 ½ cups (350 g) apple juice

1. Rinse and peel the beets. Grate them with a grater, using the large holes.
2. Rinse and remove the calyxes on the gooseberries.
3. Rinse, peel, and core the apples. Dice them finely.
4. Rinse and grate the lemon peel. Squeeze the lemon juice.
5. Blend everything in a pot and boil while constantly stirring and removing all foam with a spoon. Occasionally brush the inside of the pot with a brush dipped in cold water to prevent sugar crystals. Boil to 224–226°F (107–108°C), or perform a jam test on a cold plate, see p. 20.
6. Pour directly into sterilized jars and screw on the lids right away. Turn the jars upside down a couple of times.

Makes about 3 ⅓ lbs (1,500 g) jam.

Red Beet Jam with Apple and Gooseberries and Red Beet and Pear Jam with Star Anise and Cloves.

Red Beet and Pear Jam with Star Anise and Cloves

Wonderful with game, poultry, and cheese.

1 ¼ lbs (550 g) red beets
(Just under 1 lb [400 g] net weight)
1 ⅔ lbs (750 g) pears
(1 ⅓ [600 g] net weight)
Juice of 1 lemon
2 cups (500 g/5 dl) water
4 whole star anise
4 cloves
1 ¾ lbs (800 g) sugar
½ lb (250 g) apple jelly or 1 ½ cups (350 g) apple juice, p. 16–17

1. Rinse, peel, and grate the red beets.
2. Rinse, peel, and core the pears. Cut them in wedges.
3. Squeeze the lemon.
4. Bring the water, pear wedges, lemon juice, star anise, and cloves to a boil.
5. Let it simmer under a lid for 30 minutes, until the pears are tender.
6. Remove the spices from the pot.
7. Place a pot on the stove and fill with the pear mixture, the grated beets, and the sugar. Lastly, add apple juice or apple jelly and let it boil while removing all foam. Continually brush the inside of the pot with a brush dipped in cold water to prevent sugar crystals. Boil to 222–224°F (106–107°C), or perform a jam test on a cold plate, see p. 20.
8. Pour directly into sterilized jars and screw on the lids right away. Turn the jars upside down a couple of times.

Makes about 3 ¾ lbs (1,700 g) finished jam. *Photo p. 185.*

Red Beet Chutney

Especially suitable for game.

1 lb (500 g) pears
(Just under 1 lb [400 g] net weight)
3 ⅓ lbs (1,500 g) red beets
(2 lb [1,000 g] net weight)
1 ¾ oz (50 g) fresh ginger
⅓ oz (10 g) spice peppers
1 tsp (5 g) black pepper
4 cloves
½ lb (250 g) red onion
2 cups (50 cl) red wine vinegar
4 bay leaves
¾ cup (150 g) cassonade sugar, brown
5 oz (150 g) yellow raisins
1 tsp (10 g) sea salt
1 ¾ oz (50 g) grated horseradish

1. Peel the pears and dice them.
2. Clean the beets and remove the skins. Roughly grate them, and place them in a pot.
3. Peel and grate fresh ginger into the pot. Crush the peppers in a mortar with the cloves and add to the pot as well.
4. Finely chop the red onion.
5. Pour all of the ingredients, except the horseradish, into the pot and bring it to a boil while stirring.
6. Lower the heat and boil slowly while stirring now and then. (Beet chutney burns easily unless you are meticulous with the stirring.)
7. After about 45 minutes it should be thick and ready.
8. Grate and add the horseradish and blend well.
9. Pour directly into sterilized jars and screw on the lids right away. Turn the jars upside down a couple of times.

Make about 3 ⅓ lbs (1,500 g) finished chutney.

My Mother's Preserved Red Beets

I could not resist including this recipe. Red beets are indispensable to Christmas herring salad and my favorite brawn. They are also good in beef stew, which is braised so that you can eat it with a spoon. Small beets are best. Slice them and put them in, larger slices first.

2 ¾ lbs (1,300 g) red beets
(2 lbs [1,000 g] net weight)

Syrup

1 ½ dl / ¾ cup white wine vinegar, 12%
¾ cup (160 g) sugar
2 cups (500 g/5 dl) water
6 whole cloves
1 tsp yellow mustard seeds
1 bay leaf
6 spice peppercorns
⅓ inch (1 cm) horseradish root

1. Clean the beets with a brush, without peeling them or damaging the root tips.
2. Cover the beets with water in a saucepan and boil under a lid until they are completely soft when you poke them with a stick. Boiling time is about 30–50 minutes.
3. Cool the beets in cold water.
4. Peel the beets. Keep the small ones whole and place them in sterilized jars.
5. Boil white wine vinegar, sugar, and water with all of the spices. Cover the beets with the boiling syrup.
6. Screw the lids on right away and place the jars in a hot-water bath in a 175°F (80°C) oven for 20 minutes. This prolongs the shelf life of the preserve. Remember to keep the jars warm, or else they may crack.

Store in the fridge.

Carrot

Daucus carota

The carrot came from Central Asia to Spain during the 1100s. It was bright red or yellow. It was first during the 1600s that the well-known yellow-red carrot was developed in Holland. Carrots can be round, short, chubby, or more elongated. The taste and aroma is very similar between the varieties.

Small and tender carrots are, however, sweeter than the larger ones. The sweetness of the carrot complements almost anything. It also has the advantage of not falling apart during long boiling times. The parsnip is related to the carrot and is even sweeter, with a nutty flavor. The parsnip can be used in jam and marmalade using the same methods as the carrot. This is also true for the rutabaga and the sugar beet. Carrot cake has gained much popularity in cafes and bakeries these days. Carrot ice cream with orange or apricot purée is always a winner.

Carrot Jam

This basic jam can be flavored in a multitude of ways. Orange juice and orange zest are especially good with carrots.

3 lbs (1,400 g) fresh carrots
2 lemons
1 ¾ lbs (800 g) sugar
1 ½ cups (350 g/3 ½ dl) water

1. Clean and peel the fresh carrots. Roughly grate them with a grater.
2. Clean the lemons and grate the zest in with the carrots.
3. Squeeze the lemon juice on top.
4. Boil sugar and water in a pot. Brush the inside of the pot with a brush dipped in cold water to prevent sugar crystals. Boil to 234–240°F (112–114°C), or perform a so-called sugar test, see Boiling Sugar, p. 14.
5. Add the carrot blend and boil for 15 minutes. Keep brushing the inside of the pot.
6. Remove any foam so that the jam becomes clear. When the carrots are starting to turn transparent and the surface is wrinkling, the jam is almost ready.
7. Boil to 220–222°F (105–106°C), or perform a jam test on a cold plate, see p. 20.
8. Pour the freshly boiled jam directly into sterilized jars. Screw the lids on immediately and turn the jars upside down a couple of times.

Makes about 3 ⅓ lbs (1,500 g) jam.

Carrot Jam with Orange and Green Cardamom

This jam is great with pungent cheese and warm scones.

Follow the recipe for Carrot Jam, above.
Add the zest and juice of 4 rinsed oranges and ⅓ oz (10 g) crushed green cardamom. *Photo on p. 188.*

Carrot Jam with Ginger

The jam tastes very Anglo-Saxon with graham biscuits.

Follow the recipe for Carrot Jam, above.
Add a large piece of ginger during boiling.

Carrot and Pear Jam with Pink Grapefruit and Yellow Raisins

This combination creates an exciting taste that goes with most everything.

1 ½ lbs (650 g) young carrots (1 lb [500 g] net weight)
1 pink grapefruit
1 lemon
1 ½ lbs (650 g) pears (1 lb [500 g] net weight)
2 cups (500 g/5 dl) water
1 ¾ lbs (800 g) sugar
½ lb (250 g) apple jelly or 1 ½ cups (350 g) apple juice, p. 16–17
3 ½ oz (100 g) yellow raisins

1. Clean, peel, and roughly grate the carrots.
2. Cut and squeeze the lemon and grapefruit.
3. Clean, peel, and core the pears.
4. Bring 2 cups (500 g) of water to a boil and let the pears boil until tender under a lid, about 30 minutes.
5. Scoop up the pear pieces and place them in a strainer. Let them drain.
6. Boil the pear water with the sugar in a pot. Continually brush the inside of the pot with a brush dipped in cold water to prevent sugar crystals. Boil to 234–240°F (112–114°C). You may also perform a sugar test, see Boiling Sugar, p. 14.
7. Add the softened pears and the grated carrots with the grapefruit juice and lemon juice. Boil while stirring and remove all foam with a spoon. Add the apple juice or apple jelly and sporadically brush the inside of the pot.
8. When the carrots are starting to look transparent and the surface of the jam is wrinkling, it is time to check the temperature. At 220–222°F (105–106°C), the jam is ready, or perform a jam test on a cold plate, see p. 20.
9. Stir in the raisins.
10. Pour into sterilized jars right away and screw on the lids. Turn the jars upside down a couple of times.

Makes about 3 ⅓ lbs (1,500 g) jam. *Photo on p. 188.*

1 Carrot and Pear Jam with Pink Grapefruit and Yellow Raisins. 2 Carrot Jam with Orange and Green Cardamom. 3 Red Onion Marmalade.

Carrot and Mango Chutney

A tart and tasty chutney which goes great with everything from cheese to meat and fish.

1 ⅓ lbs (600 g) young carrots (Just under 1 lb [400 g] net weight)
½ lb (250 g) yellow onion
2 ¾ lbs (1,300 g) ripe mangos (1 ⅔ lbs [750 g] net weight)
2 oranges
2 lemons
7 oz (200 g) yellow raisins
1 lb (400 g) cassonade sugar
1 tsp (10 g) sea salt
½ grated nutmeg
1 ¾ oz (50 g) fresh ginger
¾ lbs (200 g) white wine vinegar
6 red chili peppers

1. Rinse and peel the carrots. Finely grate them.
2. Finely chop the peeled yellow onion.
3. Rinse and peel the mangos. Cut the fruit flesh away from the pit and dice.
4. Clean and grate the oranges and lemons. Squeeze the juice.
5. Pour everything into a pot with raisins, sugar, and salt. Grate the nutmeg and fresh ginger on top.
6. Pour in the vinegar and finely chopped red chili peppers with the seeds.
7. Let everything boil until thick for about 45 minutes, while carefully stirring.
8. Pour the chutney directly into sterilized jars and screw on the lids right away. Turn the jars upside down a couple of times.

Makes about 4 ½ lbs (2,000 g) chutney.

Onion

Allium cepa var. *rapaceum*

The onion has been cultivated since the beginning of time and you can find it in all corners of the world. During the Middle Ages, the onion was considered to have many traits, both as a foodstuff and medical aid. The red onion is related to the yellow onion. It has a milder taste than the yellow onion.

Red Onion Marmalade

This marmalade is very good with meat and fish, as well as pâtés and terrines. You can use all kinds of onions here, and even red cabbage.

2 ½ lbs (1,200 g) red onion (2 lbs [1,000 g] net weight)
¼ cup (50 g/½ dl) canola oil
¾ oz (25 g) fresh ginger
1 tsp (10 g) sea salt
4 cloves
Pinch of Sichuan pepper
½ cup (100 g/1 dl) red wine vinegar
2 cups (500 g/5 dl) mulled wine
¾ cup (150 g) light cassonade sugar

1. Peel and finely chop the onion. Slowly fry it in the oil until it has softened, about 10 minutes.
2. Peel and grate the ginger and add the remaining ingredients. Boil everything slowly for about 30 minutes, until the mass feels firm.
3. Pour directly into sterilized jars and screw the lids on right away. Turn the jars upside down a couple of times. Store in the fridge.

Makes about 1 ¾ lbs (800 g) marmalade. *Photo on p. 188.*

Celeriac

Apium graveolens var. *rapaceum*

Celeriac has been well-known in the northern hemisphere since the 1300s. It originated from the countries surrounding the Mediterranean Sea and was used medicinally. A good celeriac should not be hollow or woody. The flesh should be white to yellowish white and firm.

Celeriac Marmalade with Apple and Walnuts

The celeriac is a root vegetable with a pleasant sweetness that makes it suitable for marmalades. This would also taste good with parsnip instead. This marmalade is great with various cheeses.

1 ½ lbs (650 g) celeriac
(1 lb [500 g] net weight)
1 ½ lbs (650 g) green apples
(1 lb [500 g] net weight)
1 ⅔ cups (400 g/4 dl) water
½ cup (100 g/1 dl) balsamic vinegar
Juice of 1 lemon
1 ¾ lbs (800 g) muscovado sugar, dark
Pinch of sea salt
7 oz (200 g) walnuts

1. Scrub and peel the celeriac and cut it into shreds.
2. Peel and core the apples and cut them into shreds.
3. Boil water, vinegar, and lemon juice in a pot. Add the celeriac and apples and boil until the water starts to evaporate.
4. Add the sugar and salt. Boil while carefully removing all foam so that the marmalade is clear. Continuously brush the inside of the pot with a brush dipped in cold water so that the sugar crystals do not stick.
5. The marmalade is ready when the shreds are turning transparent and the marmalade holds together and its surface is wrinkly. Measure the temperature or perform a jelly test on a cold plate, see p. 20. The correct boiling temperature is 222–224°F (106–107°C).
6. Stir in the walnuts and let the marmalade come to a boil once more.
7. Pour directly into sterilized jars and screw the lids on right away. Turn the jars upside down a couple of times.

Makes about 3 ⅓ lbs (1,500 g) marmalade. *See photo on p.190.*

Beans

Frejol Colado

A Peruvian bean marmalade. This recipe was given to me by Jorge Escalante. In Peru this is eaten cold as a dessert.

6 servings

1 ⅓ lbs (600 g) brown beans
8 cups (2 liters) water for soaking
2 cups (500 g/5 dl) water
3 whole cloves
2 lbs (1,000 g) sugar
13 oz (375 g) unsweetened condensed milk
2 oz (60 g) white poppy seeds

1. Soak the beans in water overnight. Rinse them in cold water.
2. Place the beans in a saucepan with 2 cups (500 g/5 dl) water and the cloves. Boil them under a lid until soft, 30–45 minutes.
3. Let the beans drain in a strainer and purée them in a mixer. Empty the mixture into a saucepan with a thick bottom and add the sugar and condensed milk. Boil while stirring until you are able to see the bottom of the saucepan when you stir. Toast the poppy seeds golden brown in an ungreased pan and add them on top of the marmalade.

Pour everything into a bowl and let it cool. Serve with ice cream or whipped cream to balance the sweetness. *Photo on p. 191.*

Sweet Potato

Ipomoea batatas

The sweet potato is presumably from Peru. It is often confused with the yam. But they belong to two completely different families. The flesh can be yellow or pale with a sweet taste that is reminiscent of chestnuts. Sweet potatoes are best when oven-baked or puréed. They are imported year-round.

To enhance the sweetness, it is common to add cane sugar, honey, and spices. The sweet potato is often used as a purée for pies, desserts, puddings, and sweet potato bread.

Dulce de Camote

This sweet potato marmalade is often served as a dessert in South America. Serve it at room temperature with whipped cream and vanilla ice cream.

2 ½ lbs (1,200 g) sweet potatoes
2 ½ oz (75 g) yellow raisins
2 ½ oz (75 g) dark raisins
3 ½ oz (100 g) pecans
Pinch of freshly ground cinnamon
½ tbsp (10 g/10 ml) dark rum
½ tbsp (10 g/10 ml) dark tequila
1 lb (500 g) dark muscovado sugar
¾ cup (200 g/2 dl) water
1 vanilla bean, preferably Tahiti

1. Set the oven to 390°F (200°C).
2. Clean the potatoes with a brush and bake them in the oven for 1 hour. They should be completely soft when you prick them with a fork. Let them cool for a short while and peel off the skin with a knife. Finely chop the potatoes.
3. Finely chop the raisins and pecans.
4. Pour the potatoes, raisins, pecans, cinnamon, and liquor into a bowl.
5. Pour water and sugar into a pot. Add the sliced and scraped vanilla bean.
6. Boil to 234–240°F (112–114°C), or perform a sugar test, see Boiling Sugar, p. 14.
7. Pour the boiling sugar over the potato mixture and mix into a smooth mass with a wooden spoon.
8. Pour into a bowl and cover with plastic wrap. Let it cool. Store in the fridge overnight.

Makes about 3 ⅓ lbs (1,500 g) marmalade as dessert. *Photo on p. 191.*

Celeriac Marmalade with Apple and Walnuts.

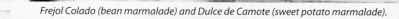

Frejol Colado (bean marmalade) and Dulce de Camote (sweet potato marmalade).

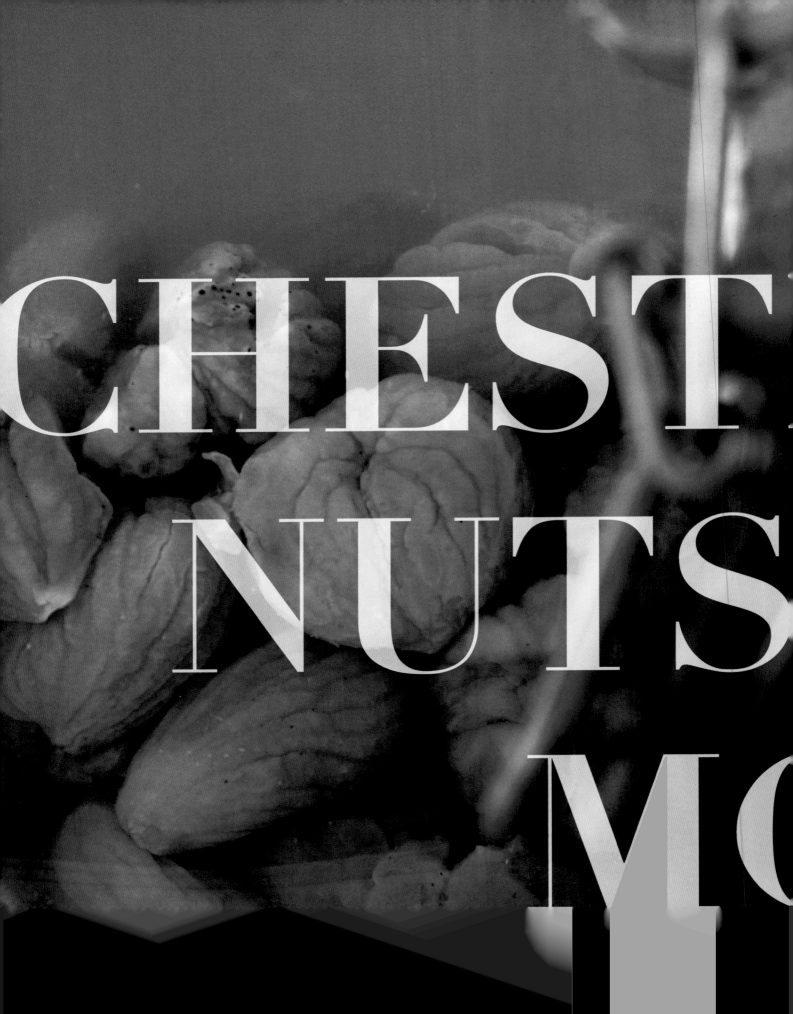

Chestnuts

Castanea sativa

Real chestnuts should not be mistaken for the horse chestnut, which belongs to a different family entirely. The real chestnut with edible meat has its home in the Mediterranean region. The finest are grown in Italy, Spain, and France. When the nuts are ripe, the shells open and the nuts fall down. To make them sweeter, they are often stored for a couple of days so that the starch is turned into sugar. Roasted chestnuts, in Italian *marroni*, in French *marrons*, are common in these countries. Chestnuts are mainly imported during the fall, but nowadays you can find frozen or vacuum-packed chestnuts in many stores.

Chestnuts are rich in starch: 30 percent starch, 23 percent carbohydrates, 6 percent protein, and only 3 percent fat. In Switzerland and France, chestnuts are often used for *marron glacé*, preserved glazed chestnuts, which are commonly used with pralines, ice cream, jam, and purées. During fall in Switzerland, the vermicelli pastry with chestnut purée is a main attraction in patisseries, and large amounts of chestnut purée are prepared for this purpose alone. You should only use large, fine chestnuts for jam, marmalade, and purée.

Peeling Chestnuts

If you are not able to buy frozen or vacuum-packed chestnuts, you will need to peel them yourself. The best way to do this is as follows:

1. Make a slit at the tip of the chestnuts with a small knife, starting at the calyx and bringing the knife all the way around.
2. Set the oven to 480°F (250°C). Place the chestnuts on a baking sheet with edges and add boiling water. Place in the oven. Because of the heat, the skin will pull away from the nut.
3. Bring back out of the oven and remove the inner skin with the help of a knife.

Every 2 ½ lbs (1 kg) of chestnuts will become about ¾ lbs (375 g) peeled.

For Purée

1. Place the chestnuts in boiling water so that they are just covered. Boil until they are starting to fall apart.
2. Place the chestnuts in a strainer and let them drain.

Chestnut Jam

In French this is called *confiture de châtaigne*. When we made glazed chestnuts at the Confeserie Brändli in Basel, there would be a lot of leftovers from chestnuts that broke. We used these to make this jam or puréed them. This jam is great as a dessert with whipped cream or vanilla sauce and an almond tart. Sometimes we would stir them in ganache for pralines.

3 ⅓ lbs (1,500 g) chestnuts, peeled and boiled
2 lbs (1,000 g) demerara sugar
1 ⅔ cups (400 g/4 dl) water
1 vanilla bean, preferably Bourbon

1. Grind the boiled chestnuts in a food processor or blender.
2. Boil sugar, water, and the scraped vanilla bean to 234–240°F (112–114°C), or perform a sugar test, see Boiling Sugar, p. 14.
3. Add the chestnut mash and bring it all to a boil. Let it boil on low heat while constantly stirring for about 20 minutes. The jam should start to hold together and no longer stick to the walls of the pot. While boiling, brush the inside of the pot with a brush dipped in cold water to prevent sugar crystals.
4. Pour the jam directly into sterilized jars and screw the lids on right away. Turn the jars upside down a couple of times.

Makes about 5 lbs (2,300 g) chestnut jam. *See photo below and p. 197.*

Sweet Chestnut Purée

This is the so-called vermicelli purée. Pipe the cold purée over ice cream or onto meringue with whipped cream. Great as a fall dessert!

About 6 ½ lbs (3,000 g) chestnuts
(2 lbs [1,000 g] peeled chestnuts)
2 tbsp (50 g) real vanilla sugar, see below
2 cups (200 g) powdered sugar
½ tbsp (10 g) Kirschwasser or rum

1. Place everything in a food processor and purée for about 5 minutes. Pass through a strainer.
2. Scoop into sterilized jars and screw on the lids.
3. Set the oven to 175°F (80°C).
4. Place the jars in a hot water bath in the oven for about 20 minutes. Store in the fridge once cool.

Real Vanilla Sugar

2 vanilla beans
½ lb (250 g) regular white sugar

1. Slice the vanilla bean down the middle with a knife and scrape out the seeds.
2. Mix the sugar and the seeds in a food processor/mixer until it looks like powdered sugar with black dots in it. Sift through a strainer and keep in a closed container.

Tip!
If you commonly use vanilla beans when you boil jam or make desserts and ice cream, you can do the following: Clean and dry the used vanilla beans. When you have about 1 ¾ oz (50 g) dried beans, add 16 oz (450 g) white sugar and do as described above. This cheaper vanilla sugar is good for pastries, soft cakes, and so on.

Chestnut Purée for Game

5 oz (150 g) peeled celeriac
1 ¾ lbs (850 g) peeled chestnuts
2 cups (500 g/5 dl) chicken stock

1. Dice the celeriac and roughly chop the chestnuts. Boil them in the stock until they are falling apart.
2. Drain in a strainer.
3. Purée in a food processor and pass through a strainer.
4. Scoop into sterilized jars and screw on the lids.
5. Set the oven to 175°F (80°C).
6. Place the jars in a hot water bath in the oven for about 20 minutes. Once cooled, store in the fridge.

When warming for serving, add some whipping cream, salt, and pepper. Serve the purée with game.

Preserved Chestnuts in Rum or Whiskey

Store in the fridge and let sit for 6 weeks. Serve with whipped cream and vanilla ice cream.

2 lbs (1,000 g) peeled chestnuts
4 cups (1,000 g/1 liter) water
2 lbs (1,000 g) sugar
1 vanilla bean, preferably Tahiti
3 ¼ cups (75 cl) dark rum or whiskey

DAY 1

1. Bring the water and ½ lb (250 g) sugar to a boil. Add the chestnuts. Let simmer for 15 minutes.
2. Add another ½ lb (250 g) of sugar and let it simmer for 15 more minutes.
3. Repeat the procedure two more times. Pour into sterilized glasses and let them sit overnight.

DAY 2

1. Drain the chestnuts in a strainer and place them in sterilized jars.
2. Cover with your alcohol of choice and screw the lids on. Store in the fridge.

Taste after 6 weeks.

Chestnut Jam with Rum

4 ½ lbs (2,000 g) chestnuts
(1 ⅔ lbs [750 g] net weight)
1 ⅔ lbs (750 g) muscovado sugar per 2 lbs (1 kg) of chestnut purée
2 vanilla beans
½ cup (100 g/1 dl) dark rum

1. Boil the peeled chestnuts in 2 cups (500 g) water until they are falling apart.
2. Drain in a strainer and purée in a food processor.
3. Mix the sugar and vanilla seeds into a powder.
4. Measure the amount of purée and add 1 ⅔ lbs (750 g) sugar per 2 lbs (1 kg).
5. Empty everything in a pot and boil while constantly stirring with a long ladle (chestnut jam splashes a lot).
6. Boil for about 5 minutes, when the jam should no longer stick to the walls of the pot.
7. Add the liquor.
8. Pour the jam into sterilized jars and screw on the lids right away. Turn the jars upside down a couple of times.

Makes about 3 lbs (1,400 g) jam.

Varieties:

- Mix the finished jam with 1 lb (500 g) of drained preserved chestnuts and scoop into the jars, see picture on p. 197.
- Add 12 oz (350 g) chopped chocolate, Valrhona Grand Cru Pur Caraïbe, to the finished jam.
- Add about ½ lb (300 g) sun-dried cherries or cranberries to the finished jam.

Walnuts

Juglans regia

The walnut originated in South East Europe and Asia. From there it has spread all over the world. Today, China, the United States, and Turkey are the largest manufacturers. The tree can grow up to 98 feet (30 meters) high and has a wide crown. The fruits are green. A fleshy layer surrounds the nut. The layer cracks and loosens when the nut ripens.

Preserved Green Walnuts

Young walnuts should be harvested at the end of June and beginning of July. They should still be green and their skin should be soft. Preserved green walnuts taste magnificent with cheese, or with pears boiled in red wine and cinnamon ice cream.

2 lbs (1,000 g) ripe young walnuts with soft skin
⅓ oz (10 g) alum
2 ¾ lbs (1,250 g) sugar
4 cups (1,000 g) water
2 cloves
¾ inch (2 cm) real cinnamon stick
⅓ cup (120 g) honey
1 jalapeño chili pepper, preferably red

DAY 1

1. Clean and rinse the nuts carefully. Poke them all over with a small fork.
2. Cover the nuts with cold water and ⅓ oz (10 g) alum and let them soak overnight. Change the water and let them soak for 4 more days. Change the water twice each day.

DAY 5

1. Boil the walnuts until completely soft in a generous amount of water. Let them drain and dry in a strainer.
2. Pour 2 lbs (1,000 g) sugar and ½ cup (100 g) water into a pot. Bring to a boil and add the nuts and spices. Bring it to a boil and empty into a bowl. Cover with plastic wrap and let it sit at room temperature overnight.

DAY 6

1. Pour everything back into the pot with the remaining sugar and honey, plus the rinsed and finely chopped chili.
2. Bring to a boil and remove all foam. Brush the inside of the pot with a brush dipped in cold water to prevent sugar crystals in the preserve.
3. Fill the jars with walnuts and syrup and screw on the lids right away. Turn the jars upside down a couple of times.

Let the preserved walnuts sit for 6 weeks so that they ripen before you stir them.

Cinnamon Ice Cream

6 servings

¼ tbsp gelatin (1 sheet)
1 ¼ cup (250 g/2 ½ dl) whipping cream
1 ¼ cup (250 g/2 ½ dl) whole milk
2 tbsp (25 g) Swedish honey
2 tsp (10 g) freshly ground cinnamon
About 6 egg yolks (120 g)
½ cup (100 g) light muscovado sugar
1 ½ tbsp (2 cl) dark rum

DAY 1

1. Dissolve the gelatin according to the package directions (or soak the gelatin sheet in cold water for at least 10 minutes).
2. Pour whipping cream, milk, honey, and cinnamon into a saucepan. Bring it to a boil and set aside.
3. Whisk the yolks and sugar for 5 minutes. Pour half of the egg mixture in with the yolks and mix well.
4. Pour everything into the saucepan and warm to 185°F (85°C) while stirring.
5. Remove the saucepan from the stove. Add the dissolved gelatin (or drain the gelatin sheet) and stir it in with the ice cream mixture. Stir until the gelatin has completely melted.
6. Pour into a bowl and cool it quickly in cold water while stirring.
7. Cover with plastic wrap and set in the fridge overnight.

DAY 2

If you have an ice-cream maker, you may freeze the ice cream in that. If not, place the bowl in the fridge and stir now and then until it feels firm.

Crystallized Cognac Walnuts

This is also great with cheese, especially blue cheeses.

1 lb (500 g) fresh walnuts, preferably French from Grenoble
½ lb (250 g) sugar
⅔ cup (150 g) water
Juice of 1 lemon
2 ½ tbsp (50 g) honey
⅔ cup (150 g/15 cl) cognac

1. Set the oven to 300°F (150°C), and place the walnuts on a baking sheet. Roast the nuts for 5 minutes.
2. Boil sugar, lemon juice, and honey to 240°F (115°C).
3. Add the warm walnuts and let it all boil until the sugar has melted while stirring rapidly.
4. Add the liquor.
5. Pour directly into sterilized jars and screw on the lids right away.

1 Praline Paste with Almonds. 2 Praline Paste with Hazelnuts. 3 Preserved Green Walnuts. 4 Crystallized Cognac Walnuts. 5 Chestnut Jam.

Praline Paste with Hazelnuts or Almonds

This wonderful nut or almond cream is perfect on toast or as a base for desserts or pralines. Try to get Spanish Marcona almonds or Italian almonds from Bari. If you use hazelnuts, try to find a Spanish variety, or hazelnuts from Piedmont in Italy, which are the very best.

1 lb (500 g) hazelnuts or almonds
½ cup (100 g) water
Just under 1 lb (400 g) sugar
1 vanilla bean, preferably Bourbon
1 lb (500 g) dark chocolate, preferably Valrhona Grand Cru Guanaja 70.5% or Marabou dark, or 1 ½ lbs (750 g) milk chocolate, Valrhona Jivara Lactee

1. If you wish to make this with hazelnuts, then roast the nuts for 5 minutes in a 390°F (200°C) oven until the shells start coming off and they are golden brown. Rub the shells off with the help of a kitchen towel and remove.

The almonds should be in the shell if you choose dark chocolate and shelled if you choose milk chocolate. Roast the almonds, if shelled, until they are golden brown.

2. Boil water and sugar in a pot with the scraped vanilla bean.
3. Brush the inside of the pot with a brush dipped in cold water to prevent sugar crystals. Boil to 234–240°F (112–114°C), or perform sugar or hand test, see p. 14.
4. Add the hazelnuts or almonds and keep stirring while the mass is boiling.
5. When the sugar has whitened and is starting to crystallize, the next step will begin—the sugar will start melting.
6. Caramelize the entire mass until it is golden brown. Remember to keep stirring.
7. Pour the mass onto a piece of parchment paper to cool.
8. Pour the mass into the food processor and mix until it is fluid and has a temperature of 160°F (70°C).
9. Add the chopped chocolate and keep mixing until the chocolate has melted.
10. Pour the mass out on a plate to cool. Next, place in a bowl and carefully warm in a microwave oven to 80°F (28°C). Stir now and then.
11. Pour into jars and shake them to remove any air pockets. Keep in the fridge or pantry.

Makes about 3 lbs (1,400 g) praline paste. *Photo on p. 197.*

Preserved Green Almonds

Green almonds can be preserved the same way as citrus peels.

They make an amazingly pretty preserve. You can use green walnuts as well.

2 ¼ lbs (1 kg) fresh green almonds are rinsed and soaked in water with a pinch of salt and a pinch of alum per 4 cups (1 liter) of water. They are blanched completely soft. Cool them in cold water afterwards and make sure that all the salt is removed.

Then preserve by following the recipe for Preserved Citrus Peels, see p. 107.

Coconut

The coconut is the fruit of the coconut palm, Cocos nucifera. Coconuts can be 8–12 inches (20–30 cm) long and usually weigh 4 ½–6 ½ lbs (2–3 kg). Within the hard shell is the endosperm, which consists of white fruit meat rich in oil and coconut water or coconut milk. The hardened endosperm can be eaten as is, but it is also used as the raw material for coconut flakes and coconut butter. The fruits are harvested year-round. The coconut can be used for a number of things—cakes, desserts, pralines, and dinner foods, etc.

Added Flavor
Dried Spices: e.g., cinnamon, star anise, licorice root, tonka bean, and vanilla bean.
Herbs: lemongrass, lime leaves, basil, and holy basil.
White sugar.
Fruit combinations: limes, lemons, pineapples, papayas, passion fruit, and more.

Coconut Marmalade and Coconut Marmalade with Chocolate.

Coconut Marmalade

You may make two varieties of this. It is as sweet as candy and is great with tropical fruits like pineapple. The variety with chocolate can be eaten with ice cream and tropical fruits. In Asian grocery stores, you will most often find frozen coconut meat, grated or diced. Otherwise, cut open a coconut and scoop the meat out.

2 lbs (1,000 g) freshly grated coconut
1 lb (500 g) sugar
10 lime leaves
Juice of 2 limes
1 ¼ cups (250 g/2 ½ dl) coconut milk
1 ¼ cups (250 g/2 ½ dl) condensed milk
½ cup (100 g/1 dl) Bacardi white rum

1. Place the grated coconut in a saucepan with sugar, lime leaves, and lime juice.
2. Add milk and cook, stirring, until the preserve thickens, which takes about 10–15 minutes. Brush the inside of the pot with a brush dipped in cold water to prevent sugar crystals.
3. Add the eggs and remove the lime leaves.
4. Pour into sterilized jars. Screw on the lids and turn the jars upside down a couple of times.

Makes about 3 1/3 lbs (1,500 g) marmalade. See photo on p. 199.

Coconut Marmalade with Chocolate

Add 12 oz (350 g) dark chocolate, Valrhona Grand Cru Guanaja 70.5% or Marabou dark, at the end of the boiling time.

Makes about 3 ⅓ lbs (1,500 g) marmalade. *See photo on p. 199.*

Pâté à Tartiner Caramel

This caramel cream is delicious on warm pancakes, as a filling for crêpes with ripe pears, or as a sauce with ice cream. Salt is a great contrast for caramel.

2 vanilla beans, preferably Tahiti
2 ½ cups (500 g/5 dl) whipping cream
¾ cup (300 g) glucose
2 tsp (10 g) fleur de sel (French extra-fine salt)
½ lb (300 g) sugar
½ cup (100 g) butter

1. Cut the vanilla beans down the middle and scrape the seeds out. Boil the seeds and beans with the whipping cream and salt in a saucepan. Set aside.
2. Pour the glucose into a pot and boil on high heat until it browns. Add a third of the sugar and melt into caramel while stirring.
3. Repeat this procedure twice more with the remaining sugar.
4. Add the vanilla cream and remove the beans. Bring it all to a boil and remove from the stove.
5. When the temperature has gone down to 120°F (50°C), mix in the butter with a hand mixer or a whisk.
6. Pour into sterilized jars and screw on the lids right away. Turn the jars upside down a couple of times. Keep in the fridge.

Makes about 1 ¾ lbs (800 g).

Milk Marmalade—with chocolate and vanilla.

Milk Marmalade

Milk marmalade in Spanish is *Dulce de leche*, or as the French say, *Confiture de lait*. This Argentinean specialty has a wonderful texture and is great as a filling in pastries such as Swiss roll cakes and desserts.

Sometimes caramelized almonds or nuts are added as well. There are also variations with chestnuts and walnuts. Adding lemon or orange zest can also make for delicious varieties. All suitable spices and herbs may be added, and also saffron and orange with dates for a Christmassy feel. However, this vanilla variety is unbeatably tasty.

1 vanilla bean, preferably Bourbon
2 lbs (1,000 g) sugar
17 cups (4,000 g/4 liters) whole milk
Pinch of sea salt

1. Cut the vanilla bean down the middle and scrape the seeds out with a knife.
2. Combine everything in a pot and boil for 2 hours until the mass is reduced and is starting to thicken and brown. Brush the inside of the pot with a brush dipped in cold water to prevent sugar crystals.
3. Pour into sterilized jars and screw on the lids right away. Turn the jars upside down a couple of times.

Makes about 3 ⅓ lbs (1,500 g) marmalade.

Good to know

Caramelizing is a thermal decomposition of sugar that happens when sugar is heated above 210°F (100°C). The caramelizing process speeds up as the temperature increases and especially with low pH values. At the end of the process, you will have sweet brown sugar molecules.

Variation with Chocolate

12 oz (350 g) chocolate, Valrhona Grand Cru Guanaja 70.5% or Marabou dark

Finely chop the chocolate and stir it in with the boiled cream until completely melted. Scoop into jars as you did with the milk marmalade.

Photo to the right.

FLOWERS

Roses, Violets, and Other Flowers

Rose petals can be used for marmalades. Other flowers that can also be used are violets, sunflowers, dandelions, acacia flowers, and lilacs.

Flowers can also be candied, which is a specialty in Toulouse, France. The most commonly candied flowers are violets, rose petals, and lilacs, mimosa flowers, and peppermint. These will keep for years.

Rose Marmalade

This classic, oriental marmalade is almost seductive in its beauty.

2 ¾ lbs (1,250 g) green apples
4 cups (1,000 g) water
Juice of 2 lemons
1 lb (500 g) red currants
½ lb (250 g) red rose petals from unsprayed roses
Amount of sugar equal to the weight of the juice

1. Wash and cut the apples and place them in a pot with the water, lemon juice, and currants.
2. Bring everything to a boil and let it simmer under a lid until the apples are soft.
3. Pour everything into cheesecloth and let it drain for 60 minutes.
4. Weigh the juice and add an equal weight of sugar. Pour into the pot and add the rose petals.
5. Boil while stirring to 220°F (105°C), when the rose petals are transparent. Perform a jelly test on a cold plate.
6. Pour the marmalade into sterilized jars. Screw the lids on right away and turn the jars upside down a couple of times.

Makes about 2 ¾ lbs (1,300 g) marmalade. *Photo on p. 207.*

Violet Marmalade

4 ½ lbs (2,000 g) apple jelly
½ lb (250 g) violet petals

1. Make a batch of apple jelly, see p. 16.
2. Add ½ lb (250 g) of fresh violet petals.
3. Boil the jelly with violet petals.
4. Fill sterilized jars in batches and allow to solidify between so that not all the petals float to the top but are spread evenly in the marmalade.
5. Screw on the lids immediately and turn the jars upside down a couple of times.

Makes about 4 ½ lbs (2,000 g) marmalade.

Crystallized Violets

When I worked in Switzerland, we made Violettes succrées, or crystallized violets.

3 oz (80 g) freshly picked violets
½ lb (200 g) sugar
5 tbsp (80 g) water

DAY 1
Let freshly picked violets dry on a cooling rack overnight.

DAY 2
1. Boil sugar and water to 245°F (118°C), or a light marble test, see Boiling Sugar, p. 14.
2. Add the flowers and remove the pot from the stove. Stir until the flowers crystallize.
3. Scoop them out of the pot to cool and keep them in airtight jars.

We used to sprinkle these on, for instance, an ice cream bomb with violet ice cream and apricot ice cream.

For Pralines
The crystallized violets can be laid in candying syrup, see p. 208, to make classically candied flowers.

Rose Marmalade.

Candied Flowers

This traditional process for conserving confectioneries and flowers was performed in Sweden for candied marzipan, which was a Swedish specialty. It is still practiced by certain confectioners today.

The pastry chef Carl J. Grafström first introduced the technique in Sweden during the 1800s, after his internship in Paris.

Toulouse in France is the home of candied flowers, where it is considered an art form.

Crystallization is a process where a chemical compound moves from a liquid to a solid, crystalline form. The crystals in the syrup grow on the flowers and accelerate the formation of new crystals. Use fresh, unsprayed flowers.

½ lb (250 g) fresh, edible petals (e.g., roses, lilacs, violets, peppermint, marigolds)
1 egg white
Granulated sugar

Candying Syrup
2 ½ lbs (1,200 g) sugar
2 ½ cups (600 g/6 dl) water

1. Lightly whisk the egg white and carefully fold in the petals.
2. Carefully coat the petals in sugar so that each petal is covered.
3. Let them dry on cooling racks for 24 hours.
4. Boil a candying syrup out of water and sugar in a saucepan. Constantly brush the inside of the pot with a brush dipped in cold water.
5. Pour into a measuring cup and measure the syrup with a hydrometer. It should be at 33–34° Baumé, see p. 29. (It usually works out fine even without an aerometer because the proportions of sugar and water are usually precise. After boiling, the syrup will usually be at 32–33° Baumé or 60–62° Brix, which represents 220°F (105°C).
6. Let the syrup cool completely.
7. Normally you will now place the flowers in a candying pan with a rack at the bottom, a so-called *candissoire*. You then place racks on top and pour the cold syrup over the petals.
8. Cover the whole surface with plastic wrap and check the candying process after 12 hours by taking one petal and looking at the size of the sugar crystals. If it feels like the whole petal is covered in crystals, you may let the syrup drain off by uncorking the side of the pan. (If you do not have one of these pans for candying, you place the petals in a deep glass bowl, cover them with the syrup, and cover with racks and plastic wrap. When they feel ready, you simply pour the syrup off.)
9. Place the petals on a rack to dry.

May later be stored dry and will keep for years.

SLICED MARMALADES

What pastry chefs used to call fruit paste or Russian marmalade is now usually referred to as marmalade or sliced marmalade. This kind of candy is most likely one of the oldest kinds there is. In Europe, all patisseries prepare generous quantities of these. In France they are called *pâté de fruit*. When I worked in Switzerland, we would prepare heaps of these in summertime, when we had access to fresh berries.

Black Currant Paste with Rum

Read about boiling fruit paste on p. 22. Red currant paste is made the exact same way as black currant paste, but use cognac instead of rum. If you prefer not to add any alcohol at all, you can do that as well.

2 lbs (1,000 g) black currants
1 ½ cups (350 g/3 ½ dl) apple juice per 2 ¼ lbs (1 kg) of fruit
¼ cup (40 g) dark rum
Amount of sugar equal to the weight of the fruit purée and apple juice

1. Rinse the berries by running them under water.
2. Boil the berries in ¾ cups (200 g/2 dl) water for about 5 minutes, until they feel soft. Pour them into a food mill. Add the apple juice and pass through the strainer.
3. Weigh everything and add as much sugar as the combined weight of the entire fruit mass.
4. Pour the fruit mass and the liquor in a pot. Bring it to a boil while stirring with a long ladle. Boil until the mass is starting to hold together and no longer sticks to the walls of the pot. Occasionally brush the inside of the pot with a brush dipped in cold water to prevent sugar crystals in the finished paste. Remove foam if needed.
5. Pour into a baking pan and let it stiffen for 24 hours. Cut into small squares and roll them in sugar.

Strawberry Paste

Read about boiling fruit paste on p. 22.

2 ½ lbs (1,200 g) ripe strawberries
1 ½ cups (350 g/3 ½ dl) apple juice
Juice of 1 lemon
1 ½ cups (40 cl) Kirschwasser
Amount of sugar equal to the weight of the fruit purée and apple juice

1. Rinse the berries and remove the calyxes.
2. Boil the berries in 2 cups (500 g/5 dl) water until they have fallen apart.
3. Pass through a food mill and weigh the fruit purée and apple juice.
4. Add as much sugar as the combined weight of the purée and juice.
5. Pour the mixture into a pot with lemon juice and liquor. Boil while stirring with a long ladle. Boil until the mass holds together and no longer sticks to the walls of the pot. Occasionally brush the inside of the pot with a brush dipped in cold water to prevent sugar crystals in the finished paste.
6. Pour directly into a baking pan and let it stiffen for 24 hours. Cut into bite-size pieces and roll them in sugar.

Kiwi Paste

Read about boiling fruit paste on p. 22.

2 lbs (1,000 g) kiwis, ripe
1 cup (25 cl) white wine
Juice of 1 lemon
1 ½ cups (350 g/3 ½ dl) apple juice
Amount of sugar equal to the weight of the fruit purée and apple juice

1. Peel the fruit and dice.
2. Boil the fruit in the wine and lemon juice until soft.
3. Pass through a food mill.
4. Weigh the purée and apple juice and add the equal weight of sugar.
5. Boil and follow the recipe for Black Currant Paste, see above.

Mango Paste

Read about boiling fruit paste on p. 22.

2 ½ lbs (1,200 g) ripe mangos
(about 2 lbs [1,000 g] net weight)
4 cups (1000 g/1 liter) water
Juice of 1 lemon
1 ½ cups (350 g/3 ½ dl) apple juice
Amount of sugar equal to the weight of the fruit purée and apple juice

1. Peel the mango and carve the flesh away from the pit. Dice.
2. Boil the fruit in 4 cups (1000 g/1 liter) water and the lemon juice until soft, about 10 minutes.
3. Pass through the food mill.
4. Add the equal weight of sugar as the combined weight of the fruit purée and apple juice.
5. Boil and follow the recipe for Black Currant Paste, p. 210.

Apple Paste with Calvados and Cinnamon

Read about boiling fruit paste on p. 22.

3 ⅓ lbs (1,500 g) green apples
(2 lbs [1,000 g] net weight)
1 ¼ cups (300 g/3 dl) apple cider
Juice of 1 lemon
Pinch of freshly ground cinnamon
1 ½ oz (40 g) calvados
Amount of sugar equal to the weight of the fruit purée and apple cider

1. Wash the apples, remove the cores, and cut into wedges.
2. Boil the apple soft in cider and lemon juice, about 30 minutes.
3. Pass through a food mill.
4. Weigh as much sugar as the combined weight of the fruit mass and apple cider.
5. Pour everything into the pot with cinnamon and calvados.
6. Boil it and follow the recipe for Black Currant Paste, p. 210.

Raspberry Paste

See Fruit Paste with Pectin, p. 23.

½ oz (12 g) liquid citric acid (¼ tsp [6 g] water and ¼ oz [6 g] citric acid)
1 ⅓ lbs (600 g) raspberries
(1 lb [500 g] raspberry purée net weight)
7 oz (200 g) whole raspberries
5 oz (150 g) glucose
½ oz (15 g) pectin
1 ¾ lbs (825 g) sugar
2 tbsp (25 g) Eau de vie aux framboise (raspberry liquor)

1. First blend the citric acid. Take ¼ tsp (6 g) warm water and ¼ oz (6 g) citric acid and stir until it has dissolved.
2. Mix and pass 1 ½ lbs (600 g) of raspberries through a strainer.
3. Pour purée, raspberries, glucose, and 1 ⅔ lbs (750 g) sugar in a pot.
4. Bring it to a boil. Blend the remaining sugar with the pectin and add that to the pot as well.
5. Boil to 220°F (105°C) or 75° Brix. Remove all foam. Brush the inside of the pot with a brush dipped in cold water to prevent sugar crystals in the finished paste.
6. Remove the pot from the stove and stir in the citric acid liquid and liquor. Pour into the pan right away and let it stiffen for 24 hours. Cut into squares and roll them in granulated sugar.

Passion Fruit and Apricot Paste

See Fruit Paste with Pectin, p. 23.

½ oz (12 g) liquid citric acid (¼ tsp [6 g] water and ¼ oz [6 g] citric acid)
12 oz (350 g) passion fruit purée or frozen passion fruit purée
12 oz (350 g) apricot purée or frozen apricot purée
1 ¾ lbs (825 g) sugar
5 oz (150 g) glucose
¾ oz (18 g) pectin
1 tbsp (10 g) cognac or Kirschwasser

1. First blend the citric acid. Take ¼ tsp (6 g) warm water and ¼ oz (6 g) citric acid and stir until it has dissolved.
2. Slice open the passion fruits and scoop out the flesh. Pass through a strainer.
3. Scald the apricots and cool them under cold running water. Peel the skins off and remove the pits.
4. Pour the apricots into a food processor and purée. Weigh the right amount of fruit purée.
5. Pour the fruit into a pot with 1 ⅔ lbs (750 g) of the sugar and the glucose. Bring it to a boil while stirring.
6. Carefully blend the pectin with the remaining sugar and whisk it in with the fruit mass. Boil while stirring. Brush the inside of the pot with a brush dipped in cold water to prevent sugar crystals in the finished paste. Remove foam during boiling.
7. At 226°F (108°C), remove the pot from the stove and add the citric acid and the liquor. Immediately pour into a pan and let it stiffen for 24 hours. Cut into squares and roll them in granulated sugar.

Sliced Pear Marmalade with Preserved Ginger

See Fruit Paste with Pectin, p. 23.

1 ¾ oz (50 g) finely chopped, drained ginger, see Preserved Ginger on p. 164
⅔ oz (18 g) liquid citric acid (⅓ oz [9 g] citric acid and 1 ¾ tsp [9 g] oz water)
2 lbs (1,000 g) ripe Williams pears (or 1 ½ lbs [700 g] frozen pear purée)
(1 ½ lbs [700 g] purée net weight)
1 ¾ lbs (825 g) sugar
5 oz (150 g) glucose
1 vanilla bean, preferably Bourbon
½ oz (15 g) pectin
1 tbsp (10 g) Eau de vie aux Poire Williams

1. Finely chop the drained ginger and let it drain in a strainer.
2. Blend the citric acid. Take 1 ¾ tsp (9 g) warm water and ⅓ oz (9 g) citric acid and stir until it dissolves.
3. Clean, peel, and core the pears. Boil them in ¾ cup (200 g/2 dl) water for about 20 minutes until they have fallen apart.
4. Purée the pears in a mixer and weigh the right amount.
5. Pour into a pot with 1 ⅔ lbs (750 g) sugar and the glucose as well as the sliced and scraped vanilla bean.
6. Bring everything to a boil. Mix the remaining sugar with the pectin and whisk it in with the contents in the pot. Brush the inside of the pot with a brush dipped in cold water to prevent sugar crystals in the finished paste.
7. Boil to 224°F (107°C) or 75° Brix.
8. Remove the pot from the stove and stir in the liquor, ginger, and liquid citric acid. Immediately pour into a pan and let it stiffen for 24 hours. Cut into squares and roll them in granulated sugar.

Rhubarb Paste

See Fruit Paste with Pectin p. 23. In addition to rhubarb, you can vary this with fruits and berries.

⅔ oz (18 g) liquid citric acid (⅓ oz [9 g] citric acid and 1 ¾ tsp [9 g] oz water)
2 lbs (1,000 g) tender, pink rhubarb (or 1 ½ lbs [700 g] frozen rhubarb purée)
1 ¾ lbs (850 g) sugar
5 oz (150 g) glucose
½ oz (15 g) pectin
1 tbsp (10 g) cognac

1. Blend the citric acid. Take 1 ¾ tsp (9 g) warm water and ⅓ oz (9 g) citric acid and stir until it dissolves.
2. Rinse the rhubarb. Cut it into smaller pieces. Boil them for about 10 minutes in ½ cup (100 g/1 dl) water until soft.
3. Mix and pass the fruit mix through a strainer. Weigh the right amount.

Follow the recipe for Passion Fruit and Apricot Paste from step 5 onwards, see p. 213.

Jelly Raspberries

Jelly raspberries were among the first sweets I learned to make within the pastry chef profession. I introduced this Swedish specialty at the patisserie Vete-Katten in Stockholm. Unfortunately, most jelly raspberries you find today are flavored with raspberry extract instead of raspberry purée. These are easy to make and taste great.

I still remember how the powder from the powder crates would smoke up the entire room when we sifted the dry starch in the crates and spread them out with a ruler. After that we would dip the ruler with plaster stamps in the shape of raspberries in the powder. This way we would get impressions we could make the jelly in.
If you don't have powder crates and plaster stamps, you can use a baking pan and bought raspberries, which you rinse, dry, and stick on a ruler with ¼ inch (5 mm) spaces in between. If you want to look like a real professional, you can buy a couple of raspberries in plaster and fasten them on a ruler, which is somewhat wider than the pan. (Chromkoll in Stockholm carries these, as well as powder crates). You may use the powder, or cornstarch, multiple times as long as you warm and sift it before use.

2 lbs (1,000 g) cornstarch
6 tbsp (23 sheets) gelatin
½ lb (300 g) raspberries
(½ lb [250 g] raspberry purée net weight)
1 ¼ lbs (560 g) sugar
1 ¼ cups (300 g/3 dl) water
6 ½ oz (185 g) glucose
⅓ oz (9 g) citric acid
1 tsp (3 g) crème of tartar

1. Dry the starch for 24 hours in a 175°F (80°C) oven.
2. Sift the starch in a clean baking pan (or powder crate) and whisk. Spread it out evenly with a ruler and create small indents in the powder.
3. Dissolve the gelatin in water according to the package directions, or soak the gelatin sheets in a generous amount of cold water for at least 10 minutes. Feel free to keep the water running for a cleaner taste.
4. Purée the raspberries in a food processor. Pass through a strainer.
5. Blend the sugar and water in a saucepan and bring to a boil. Brush the inside of the pot with a brush dipped in cold water to prevent sugar crystals. Make sure to remove all foam. Add the glucose and boil to 285°F (140°C).
6. Warm the raspberry purée and add to the water and glucose. Bring to a boil and remove all foam. Brush the inside of the pot. Boil to 260°F (125°C).
7. Remove the pot from the stove and add the dissolved gelatin or drained gelatin sheets, citric acid, and crème of tartar. Stir carefully till everything is melted. Pour the mass into a ketchup bottle or similar. Squeeze generous amounts of the mass into the indents. (Or do as the pros do and use a casting funnel.)
8. Let it stiffen overnight. Sift all of the powder off the raspberries and cool them in cold water in a strainer. Let them drain and dry for a couple of hours.
9. Roll the jelly raspberries in sugar and try to store them without eating them all right away.

Photo on p. 215.

CHRISTMAS MARMALADE AND MORE

Christmas Marmalade

I sometimes call this marmalade Limited Edition. At Olof Viktors in Glemminge, Sweden, the recipe varies from one year to the next. The marmalade is great with ice cream, whipped cream, and some tasty ginger snaps. It is even terrific for duck or goose liver terrine. A nice present for your friend at Christmas.

3 ½ oz (100 g) dried apricots
3 ½ oz (100 g) dried figs
3 ½ oz (100 g) dried prunes
2 cups (500 g/5 dl) dark rum
1 lb (500 g) green apples (½ lb [300 g] net weight)
1 lb [500 g] pears (½ lb [300 g] net weight)
2 oranges
2 lemons
2 lbs (1,000 g) dark muscovado sugar
1 lb (500 g) frozen raspberries
1 vanilla bean, preferably Bourbon
2 tsp (10 g) freshly ground cinnamon
Pinch of freshly ground ginger
Pinch of freshly ground cloves
3 ½ oz (100 g) sweet almonds, preferably Spanish Marcona almonds
3 ½ oz (100 g) walnuts, preferably French from Grenoble
3 ½ oz (100 g) pistachios, preferably from Sicily
3 ½ oz (100 g) macadamia nuts
7 oz (200 g) pitted dates
7 oz (200 g) dark chocolate, Valrhona Grand Cru Guanaja 70.5% or Marabou dark

DAY 1
1. Finely chop apricots, figs, and prunes.
2. Pour the liquor on top and cover with plastic wrap. Let it rest at room temperature for 24 hours.

DAY 2
1. Peel and dice the apples and pears.
2. Quick-preserve the lemon and orange peels. See Quick-Preserving p. 107.
3. Squeeze the oranges and lemons and pour the juice into a pot with the sugar, raspberries, pears, and apples.
4. Slice the vanilla bean down the middle.
5. Add the vanilla bean with the freshly ground spices. (Use a spice grinder.)
6. Boil the blend in the pot while stirring. Boil to 220°F (105°C). Continuously brush the inside of the pot with a brush dipped in cold water to prevent sugar crystals.
7. Finely chop the drained orange and lemon peels. Add the rest of the ingredients, except the chocolate, and bring to a boil once more.
8. Lastly, add the chocolate.
9. Pour the marmalade into sterilized jars right away. Screw the lids on and turn the jars upside down a couple of times.

Makes about 6 ½ lbs (3,000 g) finished marmalade.

Photo on p. 217.

Rumtopf

A wonderful berry and fruit preserve with an adult taste to it. The name is German and means rum pot. The French call it *Confiture des vieux garçons*, preserve for grown boys, while the British say *Old Bachelor's Bottled Fruit*. This is fantastic for the Christmas dinner table or in beautiful jars as a Christmas present.

The fruit needs to sit for 4 months before you eat it. So be patient; it is worth the wait. Every year we make a "Limited Edition," based on the variety of fruits and berries we use. The most important thing to remember is to use berries that maintain their shape and look beautiful. Many choose to use apricots and peaches as well, but personally I really like this blend. Serve with whipped cream and a really good freshly made vanilla ice cream or a classic rice pudding with little almond tarts.

I mostly use frozen berries when I prepare this preserve. This way I have access to all of the berries at the same time. You can freeze berries over the seasons and then use all of them at the end of July.

4 ½ lbs (2,000 g) berries
1 lbs (500 g) raspberries
½ lb (250 g) blackberries
½ lb (250 g) blueberries
½ lb (250 g) black currants
½ lb (250 g) red currants
1 lb (500 g) dark-red pitted cherries, either morellos or sour cherries

2 vanilla beans, preferably Tahiti
3 ¾ lbs (1,750 g) light muscovado sugar
⅓ inch (1 cm) real cinnamon stick
1 ¾ oz (50 g) raw ginger root
Pinch of grated nutmeg
Pinch of grated tonka bean, if desired
8 ½ cups (2,000 g/2 liters) dark rum

1. Place the berries in a jar, preferably one large jar that can hold all of the berries.
2. Place the vanilla beans, sugar, and spices in a food processor and mix into powder. Add the liquor and mix until the sugar has melted completely.
3. Pour the syrup over the berries and blend carefully with a ladle.
4. Cover with the lid and stir once a week.
5. Scoop into beautiful jars and store in the fridge.

Tip!
Rumtopf *keeps for years and, like English plum pudding, it only gets better with age.*

Photo on p. 219.

Fruit Vinegar like Olof Viktors's

Raspberry vinegar and black currant vinegar are my two favorites. Both of them have a strong and characteristic aroma. You can use the leftover berries to boil a preserve the way you would boil jam by adding the equal amount of sugar as the weight of the berries. You can use the preserve to flavor sauces.

4 ½ lbs (2,000 g) berries, for instance, raspberries, strawberries, blueberries, black currants
6 ½ cups (1 ½ liters) white wine vinegar
1 cup (250 g/2 ½ dl) cognac
About ⅔ cups (150 g) sugar, depending on how ripe the fruits are

DAY 1
1. Empty all of the ripe berries into a large glass bowl and cover them with vinegar.
2. Cover with plastic wrap and let it sit at room temperature for 72 hours.

DAY 4
1. Pour all of the berries into cheesecloth and let them drain for 3 hours or overnight.
2. Blend the drained vinegar with the cognac and sugar. Stir until the sugar has dissolved.
3. Place the bowl in a boiling water bath and let it stew for 60 minutes, while never allowing the vinegar to boil.
4. Remove any foam and other impurities with a spoon so that the vinegar remains completely clear.
5. It is very important that the vinegar does not boil. Let it cool and drain through cheesecloth.
6. Pour directly into sterilized bottles.

SOME PASTRIES THAT GO WELL WITH PRESERVES

Pain de Gêne

We used to bake this fabulous-tasting and soft cake daily at the Confiserie Honold in Switzerland. In the bottom we would place a paper with the words Pain de Gêne. This wonderful almond cake, served with a good, fresh jam and whipped cream or ice cream, is great with an afternoon cup of coffee or tea, or as a dessert.

1 round baking pan, 8 ½ inch (22 cm) diameter and 4 inch (10 cm) high

For the Pan
2 tbsp (25 g) butter
4 tbsp (25 g) all-purpose flour

Almond Cake

4 ½ oz (125 g) sweet almonds
½ cup (125 g) granulated sugar
½ cup (125 g) butter
About 3 eggs (150 g)
About 2 egg yolks (40 g)
¼ cup (50 g/5 cl) dark rum
¼ cup (50 g/5 cl) triple sec or Cointreau

⅓ cup (40 g) potato flour
Pinch of baking powder
About 2 ½ egg whites (75 g)
1 tsp lemon juice
2 tbsp (25 g) sugar
¼ cup (35 g) potato flour

Almond Flour
1. Set the oven to 210°F (100°C).
2. Scald the almonds in boiling water and remove the shells.
3. Spread the almonds out on a baking sheet and let them dry in the oven for 2 hours until completely dry.
4. Pour the almonds and sugar into a food processor and mix it into a so-called tpt (tant pour tant), meaning equal amount of each.

The Cake
1. Melt the butter in a small saucepan and set aside. Butter the pan with a brush. Pour the flour into the pan and shake it so that it spreads. Remove any extra flour.
2. Set the oven to 340°F (170°C).
3. Pour the almond flour into a bowl that holds 8 ½ cups (2 liters) and add the eggs, yolks, and liquor. Whisk into a stiff foam, about 10 minutes.
4. Sift potato flour and baking powder into the bowl. Mix it with a silicone spatula till you have an even mass.
5. Whip a stiff meringue out of egg whites, lemon juice, and sugar.
6. Sift the ⅓ cup (35 g) of potato flour into the meringue and keep whipping into a stiff foam.

7. Fold the egg mass into the meringue with a silicone spatula. Use a ladle to stir in the butter. Lastly, fold the cream into the mass and mix it until smooth and airy.
8. Pour the batter into the pan. Push the batter up along the edges of the pan so that the cake ends up even after baking.
9. Bake for 45–50 minutes. The cake should be dry all the way through: test with a toothpick. Remove the cake from the oven and let it sit for 5 minutes before you turn it out onto a cooling rack.

Waffles

If you choose to make many waffles at once, warm them in the oven afterwards before serving with delicious jam and whipped cream.

1 ½ cups (165 g) all-purpose flour
½ tbsp (10 g) real vanilla sugar
Pinch of fleur de sel, sea salt
⅓ cup (85 g/85 cl) whole milk
1 cup (250 g/2 ½ dl) whipping cream
About 3 egg yolks (60 g)
½ cup (85 g) salted butter
About 3 egg whites (90 g)
1 tsp lemon juice
2 tbsp (20 g) granulated sugar

¼ cup (40 g) melted butter for baking the waffles

1. Sift the flour into a bowl. Add the vanilla sugar and salt.
2. Pour in milk, whipping cream, and yolks. Stir until smooth.
3. Melt the butter and add that to the batter as well.
4. Pour the egg whites and lemon juice into a clean copper bowl or stainless steel bowl and whip into foam. Use a hand whisk or an electric beater.
5. Add the sugar and whisk into a stiff meringue.
6. Fold the meringue into the batter with a silicone spatula. see 7. at top of col.
7. Bake the waffles in a very hot waffle iron and brush with the melted butter between each waffle.

Tip!
Sometimes I sprinkle powdered sugar over the waffles and caramelize them in a hot oven on a baking sheet. This makes them even more delicious!

Pancakes

Start with a traditional pea soup with thyme, sausage, and cured pork with mustard, served with hot punch. The warm pancakes should then be served with cloudberry jam (or raspberry jam or queen jam) and lightly whipped cream. Warm them in the oven right before serving, so you won't have to worry about baking them at the last minute.

6–8 servings

1 ¾ cups (180 g) all-purpose flour
Pinch of fleur de sel, sea salt
2 tbsp (20 g) sugar
Pinch of real vanilla sugar
About 4 eggs (200 g)
1 ¾ cups (450 g/4 ½ dl) whole milk
½ cup (100 g/1 dl) Vichy water (carbonated mineral water)
1 ¼ cups (300 g/3 dl) whipping cream
¼ cup (50 g) butter
¼ cup (80 g) melted butter for baking

1. Combine flour, salt, and sugar in a bowl. Add the eggs one at a time and mix well with a ladle.
2. Stir in the milk, Vichy water, and cream one at a time. Stir smooth.
3. Pass though a chinoise.
4. Boil the butter in a saucepan and whisk in with the batter.
5. Let it rest for at least 1 hour before you bake them golden brown in melted butter.

Almond Tarts

It is almost impossible to only eat one of these amazingly delicious almond tarts.

Makes about 60

2 cups (425 g) salted butter
Just under 1 lb (410 g) sugar
2 eggs (100 g) eggs
5 oz (150 g) finely ground almonds
1 ¾ oz (50 g) finely ground shelled bitter almonds
Pinch of salt
4 cups (425 g) all-purpose flour

DAY 1
1. Warm the butter to room temperature. Mix all of the ingredients into dough. (Do not overwork the dough. It should only be blended together; it is a type of shortcrust.)
2. Leave in the fridge overnight.

DAY 2
1. Set the oven to 340°F (170°C).
2. Roll the dough out, 1 ¼ inches (33 mm) thick, and line the cookie pans with the dough.
3. Place on a baking sheet and bake golden brown for about 12–15 minutes. Empty the cookie pans and repeat until you are out of dough.

Klenäter (Swedish Bow Knots)

These tasty, airy, and light pastries with a strong taste of lemon are a Christmas favorite. You can serve them with lingonberry pears on the side.

Makes about 90 klenäter

1 lemon
⅔ cup (150 g) salted butter
¼ cup (50 g/½ dl) whipping cream
1 ¾ tbsp (25 g/25 ml) cognac
1 egg (50 g)
4 egg yolks (80 g)
1 ⅓ cups (150 g) powdered sugar
Pinch of salt
4 cups (450 g) all-purpose flour
1 tbsp (15 g) baking powder
4 ¼ cups (1 liter) frying oil
Sugar

DAY 1
1. Wash the lemon and finely grate the zest.
2. Melt the butter in a saucepan and set aside. Add cream and cognac.
3. Whisk eggs, yolks, lemon zest, sugar, and salt for about 5 minutes until foamy.
4. Fold the butter mixture in with the batter and work in the dough and baking powder carefully while making sure not to overwork the dough.
5. Place the dough in a plastic bag and leave it in the fridge overnight.

DAY 2
1. Roll the dough out, ⅛ inch (3 mm) thick, and slice lengths the width of a ruler. Create a small slit in one end of each slice and slip the opposite end about halfway through the slit, creating a bow-like shape. Each should weigh about 1 ¾ oz (50 g). Place them on a lightly floured piece of parchment paper and let them harden in the fridge.
2. Warm the oil to 360°F (180°C) and fry the bows golden brown in multiple batches. Drain them on a cooling rack and roll them in granulated sugar. (Many also use cinnamon sugar.)

Swedish Cream Cake

A childhood memory that tastes great with cherry jam. Serve the cake warm with jam and whipped cream.

9 inch (22 cm) soufflé pan
2 tbsp (25 g) butter and 3 tbsp (25 g) flour for the pan

1 lemon	⅔ cup (150 g/1 ½ dl) whipping cream
½ cup (110 g) sugar	¾ cup (90 g) all-purpose flour
4 egg yolks (80 g)	4 egg whites (120 g)
½ tbsp (10 g) real vanilla sugar	1 tsp lemon juice

1. Set the oven to 340°F (170°C).
2. Butter the pan. Sprinkle flour inside and shake the pan to spread out evenly. Remove any extra flour.
3. Clean and finely grate the lemon zest.
4. Whisk half of the sugar with the yolks, vanilla sugar, and lemon zest until foamy.
5. Whip the cream into foam with the lemon juice in a clean metal or copper bowl. Whisk by hand with large strokes.
6. Add the remaining sugar and whisk into a firm meringue either by hand or with an electric beater. (The volume will be greater if you whisk by hand.)
7. Fold the meringue in with the egg mixture and stir into an airy mass.
8. Pour into the pan and bake for 20–25 minutes.

Cones

Cones filled with whipped cream and jam are an old Swedish tradition.

6 servings

2 eggs
About ½ cup (100 g) sugar
About 1 cup (100 g) all-purpose flour

1. Set the oven to 390°F (200°C).
2. Weigh the two eggs and add the same weight of sugar and flour in a bowl.
3. Add the eggs and stir into a smooth batter.
4. Cover with plastic wrap and let it rest for 30 minutes.
5. Spread a large tablespoon of the batter out on a baking sheet in the shape of a circle the size of a large plate.
6. Bake only 4 cones on each sheet. Bake them golden brown, but still light in the middle.
7. Remove the baking sheet from the oven and lift one circle at the time. (You have to be quick so that they do not stiffen.)
8. Place the cones in a glass and let them stiffen. Continue this process until you have used all of the batter. Fill them with whipped cream and jam.

The Best Baked Bread

This perfect loaf is best when eaten fresh with butter and marmalade.

When I attended the Coba School in Basel, we would pick up bread at a small bakery right next door to the inn where I stayed. They baked the best loaves I had ever tasted. Every morning they served the bread with fresh butter and tasty strawberry jam. One day I worked up the courage to ask the manager of the bakery for the recipe. He laughed and answered that if I showed them a Swedish recipe, they would show me theirs. The next morning I baked cinnamon buns, cream buns, and cardamom knots with them. I got the recipe while they were still tasting the pastries, mildly surprised that we would put cardamom in a wheat dough.

4 loaves

4 long foil pans, 4 ¼ cups (2 liters) each
2 tbsp (25 g) butter for the pans
1 egg and a pinch of salt for brushing

Ideal dough temperature is 75°F (24°C)

4 tbsp (60 g) yeast	12 egg yolks (240 g)
2 ½ cups (600 g) whole milk	¾ cup (180 g) salted butter
½ cup (120 g) sugar	1 tbsp (20 g) sea salt
2 lbs (1,000 g) all-purpose flour	

1. Dissolve the yeast in the milk. Add the sugar and half of the flour. Work into dough.
2. Empty into a plastic bowl brushed with oil and let it rise to double its size for about 35 minutes.
3. Scoop the dough up and add the remaining ingredients, except butter and salt. Work into elastic dough in the food processor, first for 5 minutes on low speed. Add the butter. Work the dough for another 10 minutes and add the salt.
4. Work the dough until even more elastic for about 5 minutes.
5. When you can pull a thin membrane out of the dough, it is done. Fold the dough together. Place it back in the plastic bowl and let it rest for 30 minutes.
6. Empty the dough out onto the kitchen table and knead out all of the air. Fold it together like a pillow and place it back into the bowl. Let it rest for another 30 minutes.
7. Butter 4 foil pans with a brush.
8. Place the dough on a flat surface with a layer of flour. Divide it into 20 pieces and roll hot-dog buns. Place the buns in the foil pans.
9. Place the bread in the closed oven and let them rise to twice their size for about 60 minutes.
10. Sprinkle some water on top occasionally so that the dough stays moist. Remove the bread from the oven.
11. Set the oven to 445°F (230°C). Brush the bread with the eggs. Bake the bread for about 35 minutes at decreased temperature: lower to 375°F (190°C) after 5 minutes.
12. Make sure that the temperature inside the bread is 208°F (98°C).
13. Remove the pans from the oven and turn out the bread.
14. Place the bread without the pans on baking sheets and let it sit in the oven for an additional 5 minutes so that it obtains a nice crust all around. Let cool on a cooling rack.

Good for freezing.

Scones

On the cruise ships Vista/Fjord and Saga/Fjord, we would always serve these enjoyable scones with jam and clotted cream for the afternoon tea. The scones are very good if kept lukewarm when serving. Remember not to overwork the dough, as the scones may turn out hard. Just press the leftover dough bits together once you finish one batch and repeat until you've finished the entire dough.

Makes about 12 scones

1 lb (500 g) bread flour
1 tbsp (10 g) baking powder
3 tsp (10 g) sea salt, preferably fleur de sel
2 lbs (1,000 g) sugar
¾ cup (160 g) unsalted butter
1 cup (250 g/2 ½ dl) whole milk
2 eggs for brushing and a pinch of salt

1. Set the oven to 430°F (220°C).
2. Sift the flour and baking powder in a bowl.
3. Add the salt and sugar, as well as the room-temperature butter. Stir into a crumbly mixture with a wooden spoon.
4. Add the milk and carefully work everything into a loose dough.
5. Roll the dough out on a surface covered with a thin layer of flour. Roll out to a thickness of ⅔ inch (2 cm). Press out round cookies with a cookie cutter with 2 inch (6 cm) diameter or a glass.
6. Place the rounds on a baking sheet lined with parchment paper.
7. Whisk the eggs with a pinch of salt. Brush the top of the rounds with the mixture. Place the sheet in the fridge for 15 minutes then brush the rounds once more. (When you brush them twice they get a nice shine, while resting for 15 minutes allows the dough to pull together.)
8. Bake for 15 minutes, until the scones are golden brown and have a beautiful color.

Let cool on a cooling rack.

The writer and his apprentice Jan-Erik Lilja selecting fruit for the day's preserving at the Möllevångsmarket in Malmö.

CHEESE
JAM

About Cheese and Jam

By Lena Brandsten

The cheese house in Malmö, which I run, works closely with Olof Viktors bakery and we sell their bread, marmalades, and jam; this is how I first met Jan Hedh. It turned out that he was the master behind all their amazing breads—and the plum tomato marmalade that half the city soon depended on. Not to mention the fact that this delicious marmalade seemingly suits almost every cheese I can think of.

A Quick History of Cheese

Cheese and bread have been the pillars of our diet since humans settled after living as nomads and hunters. Already during the Egyptian times the people knew the art of curdling with rennet; we can read about cheese in the Old Testament and it was an important food for the Romans. They would even separate between cream cheeses and hard stored cheeses. It was the custom for Roman soldiers of Rome to receive a ration of cheese, bread, wine, and salt.

Monastery monks would always be on the lookout for foodstuffs that could be stored for long periods of time. Wine, olive oil, spices, and cheese were only a few of many foodstuffs the monks prepared and stored. Many famous cheeses originated in monasteries around Europe. The Munster cheese from Alsace originally came from a Benedictine monastery. In fact, it was the monks that brought the knowledge of cheese to us in the North during the 1000s.

During the Middle Ages, cheese curdling became a relatively common practice. Most large farms and manors wanted to boast of their stored hard cheeses. In smaller farms and crofts, they worked to be self-sufficient. Larger farms would produce hard cheeses of cow milk and each region or area would have their own variety. The smaller, simpler households would often produce cream cheeses or cheese out of sour milk from goats and sheep.

Up until the 1850s, the production of cheese was mostly on a small scale. Cheese was mostly curdled for personal use and in the cities the women could meet for "curdle guilds." In the middle of the 1850s, the dairy industry underwent a small revolution when the French microbiologist Louis Pasteur invented the pasteurizing machine, which basically was a process of heating the milk so that the bacteria would die. Up until this time, no cheeses were pasteurized. The process of pasteurizing created a basis for larger-scale productions. Real cheese lovers proclaim that pasteurizing was the death of cheese. The natural enzymes in the milk die during pasteurization. When the live bacteria culture disappears, it takes a lot of the aroma, taste, and other natural ripening processes with it.

The Cheese Families and Garnishes

Nobody knows the exact number of cheese varieties in existence. In Europe alone we have more than a thousand kinds, and France is the home of at least 350 of them. The assortment varies with the seasons. In line with tradition, different cheeses are prepared during different times of the year. Many cheeses are only produced with summer milk. In the summer the animals graze outside which gives the milk a different quality. During winter other types are manufactured that might not need the high fat content that the summer milk contains. If you closely taste a well-stored Swiss Gruyere made with summer milk, you will find herbs, flowers, and alp grass hiding in the flavor.

In order to get some kind of overview over the many cheese varieties, you need some kind of classification system. Personally, I think it is easiest to divide the cheeses into different families to create an understandable picture of the variety of cheeses. This way it is slightly easier to locate one's favorites.

Soft Cheeses

These cheeses are the most sensitive and they don't keep very well. They all taste somewhat tart. Simply put, we can say that they are all made with sour cream. Many of these are great for cooking, such as cottage cheese, mascarpone, feta, and cream cheeses. None of them are prepared with rennet as part of the process.

Champagne Cheeses

This is a collection of lesser-known cheeses that taste wonderful. They have been given this name because of their compatibility with light champagne. They are from France, but not all from the same region. A few examples of these cheeses are savarin, l'explorateur, Pierre Robert, Saint-Felicien, and chaource. If you want to give a little something to someone special I highly recommend these cheeses, with some bubbly, and strawberries or strawberry jam, or alternatively a classic raspberry jam with fresh raspberries on the side.

The champagne cheeses are made with cow milk, both pasteurized and unpasteurized. They are reminiscent of the soft cheeses in that they have a short shelf life. Furthermore, they have a tart taste as well, but they are more creamy and filling than fresh cheeses. Champagne cheeses should be enjoyed without the company of other cheeses—they are too delicate in their taste to compete with other cheese varieties. Fruit and berries, on the other hand, are great with these. Somewhat unique to these cheeses is that they go perfectly with red berries.

The champagne cheeses are great as both luxurious appetizers or as desserts, dependent on what you serve them with. Why not try some of the following goodies:

- Apricot jam with almonds
- Vanilla poached peaches
- Cloudberry jam
- Stirred wild strawberry purée
- Preserved strawberries

White Mold Cheeses

Among the white mold cheeses you will find some of the most famous dessert, i.e. Brie type cheeses, and cheeses with a white mold crust. These may be divided into two subgroups, pasteurized and unpasteurized. Pasteurized white mold cheeses are very mild and bland compared to the unpasteurized cheeses. The crust or the white mold is completely edible—this only enhances the taste. This kind of cheese is made with cow, sheep, and goat milk.

There are also some blue mold cheeses that are covered with a white mold crust. These are called white and blue mold cheeses. In recent years this kind of cheese has become the most popular for desserts. The most famous is the German Cambozola and Bavarian blue. Lesser-known varieties are Domaine de Bresse and Brilliant Blue from France. The one thing all of these have in common is that they are relatively young—they have been modified to reach a larger group of people. Commonly they have a slight ammonia scent, but that's just a sign that they are ripe. It is also common for them to have a champignon scent.

Here follows a selection of white mold cheeses from France, which is the home of the Brie.

Brie—The World's Most Famous Cheese

All Brie cheeses originate from the area Île de France, which is situated in the region Brie, between the Seine and Marne. All Brie-type French cheeses get their names from the cities or towns they are from: Meaux, Melun, Coulommiers, and so on.

Brie is manufactured all over the world and may be viewed as the world's most famous and successful cheese. The cheese had its international breakthrough at the Vienna Congress in 1815, where they had a cheese competition during break time. The Brie de Meaux was a clear winner. This unpasteurized, distinctive cheese may be called the mother of all white mold cheeses. Once you've tasted one of these delicacies, there is no going back to cheap fabricated "brie" from Denmark ever again.

Brie cheese has most likely gained its popularity because of its clean taste and simplicity. Few other cheeses are as usable and easily combined with other flavors. Brie works as an ingredient in cooking, as a dessert, or in the company of other cheeses. A multitude of fruits go with Brie; most often it is the accompanying drink that may limit the fruit selection. If one has chosen wine or beer with the cheese, it might be harder to find a suitable fruit. Jams and fruit that fit particularly well with Brie are:

- Cherries, as fruit or as a jam in various shapes, are a classic with Brie.
- The soft taste of apricots, e.g. apricot chutney or apricot compote with vanilla, is great with both pasteurized and unpasteurized Brie cheeses.
- Various plums, preserved, candied, or fresh. Fantastic in the picnic basket on a warm summer day.

Camembert

Like many delicacy cheeses, Camembert is French and originated in Camembert in Normandy. In order for the cheese to bear this name, it has to be from that exact area, be unpasteurized, and lie in a traditional wooden box.

It is believed that the cheese has roots all the way back to the 1600s, but all we know with certainty is that a lady with the name Marie Harel in Camembert produced this cheese in the 1790s. It should also be mentioned that at that time the cheese was a blue mold cheese. It was not until 1910 that it received its current shape. The most revolutionizing development for this cheese was when it got its wooden box in 1890. The box made transportation a lot easier and soon the Camembert could be found all over Europe.

Today cheeses all over the world are called "camembert," or we might just call them small Brie cheeses. They vary in quality and taste and often people don't know the difference between the real Camembert and the imitations.

You may enjoy a Camembert in many ways, on a cheese plate with some wine, with a baguette, in a food dish, or as the classic fried Camembert with cloudberry jam. Cloudberries may sometimes feel too sweet, and in those cases figs are a great substitute. Since the dish then loses a lot of its sweetness, it can be served as an appetizer. Nuts and arugula salad are great with this cheese.

Sheep Cheeses

Sheep cheeses come in all different shapes and sizes: white mold cheese, fresh cheese, mold cheese, and hard cheese with a variety of crusts. They often stem from regions with a barren landscape, an environment that suits sheep farming. It is therefore not that surprising that most of the sheep cheeses come from southern Europe and the United Kingdom, which traditionally have a significant sheep farming culture.

Sheep cheeses have a unique flavor that is very different from goat cheese's tart undertones. Generally they have a balanced and round taste with a low salt content; there might be a hint of nuttiness, often with a lasting aftertaste without the wool taste of the goat cheese. The exception is the feta cheese and the Italian pecorino cheeses, especially pecorino romano from Southern Italy. The feta is salty because it is cured in brine, and the pecorino romano because of its unique preparation. These salt cheeses go great with olives and olive marmalades, which are usually not recommended with cheeses because of the salt. Try, for instance, black olive marmalade with pears and thyme and pecorino cheese, preferably from Sardinia, and a nice baked bread with olive oil.

A well-known sheep cheese is the Spanish Manchego, which stems from La Mancha. These cheeses obtain a fabulous taste when stored. Quince marmalade and Manchego has almost become a classic; walnuts and fig marmalade are also good alternatives.

One of the biggest manufacturers of sheep cheese is Corsica. If we are lucky, we sometimes get a hold of Brin d'Amour. This is a wonderful sheep milk cheese rolled in rosemary, summer savory, thyme, coriander, and juniper, and decorated with small chili fruits. This is perfect with some preserved chestnuts and rose hip marmalade.

Goat Cheese

You either love goat cheese or you hate it! No other cheese seems to stir up as many opinions. The mecca of the goat cheese is in the Loire valley. The French are masters of the goat cheese. The shapes are incredibly inventive and the taste rarely disappoints. The Loire cheeses are often powdered with ash. They have a very sensitive surface and in order to store them, they are powdered with ash. The French goat cheese tradition goes way back.

Goat cheeses are manufactured all around the world on varying scales. France is the absolute largest when it comes to both production and quality. In previous times it was common for farms around Europe to produce goat cheese; goats were called the "poor man's cow" and their milk wasn't good for much else besides cheese. Goat cheeses from France usually have lengthy names that are hard to remember: one that signifies that they are made with goat milk, one for its shape, and lastly one for the place it is from—for instance, chèvre chabichou du Poitou.

Nowadays we eat more goat cheese than ever before. The wool taste has been eliminated and goat cheeses are considered a delicacy and an appreciated addition to cooking ingredients. One of the main reasons behind this may be that those who are lactose intolerant can still consume goat cheese. This is because these cheeses have a different protein composition than the cow milk cheeses. Goat cheese is especially good for vegetarian dishes and great for small sauces and dips. It can "spice up" many dishes and be an exciting flavoring. When serving goat cheese in combination with other cheeses, one should avoid strong and salty varieties. It can also be difficult to find wines that go well with the acidity in goat cheese.

Goats are very common in Spain, where they commonly combine goat milk and sheep milk, as in the Manchego. But there are also many treasures made purely out of goat milk, such as Monte Enebro and Sant Mateu, two of my favorites.

At the top in boxes: Banon, pélardon, ca briolu. In the middle: Bleu des basques, le charolais, crottin de touraine. At the bottom: Clochette, picadon, selle sur cher, chabichou du poitou, tomme de chèvre, pelardon, valencay.

Because of its high acidity, it can be hard to combine goat cheese, not only with other cheeses but also with other foods. Below are a few recommendations for things that the taste buds will usually appreciate with goat cheese:

- Sea buckthorn, both as jam and jelly. Sea buckthorn suits the acidity in goat cheese and it is an exciting taste that may be new to many.
- Red beets and goat cheese is an undisputed combination. The fact is that red beets and goat cheese almost "marries." Red beets, warm as well as cold, as chutney or jam (except preserved), are great with goat cheese. It is the sweetness of the beets that works so well with the acidity of the goat cheese.
- Figs are seemingly a fruit that works with almost any cheese, including goat cheese. All varieties of figs as well as nuts are great with goat cheese.

Mold Cheeses

Mold cheese is one of the world's oldest delicacies. Roquefort was considered a delicacy in France as early as the 1400s. But Gorgonzola is also a historical cheese. Mold cheese may be produced with all kinds of milk, but cow milk is the most common. What many do not know is that real Roquefort cheese should be made with sheep milk. All mold cheeses have a very high salt content.

In previous times people would freely allow mold to colonize the cheeses during storing. Today most cheeses are sprayed with controlled mold at the beginning of the storing process. The flavor of mold cheeses can vary greatly; this usually depends on the storage time, the milk, the fat content, and the mold culture. The production of mold cheeses is particularly difficult. Mold cultures can be very unpredictable and if the mold starts to grow at a faster pace, it may be very hard to control. One of the commonly used mold cultures is *Penicillium roqueforti*. The world's most famous mold cheeses are Gorgonzola, Roquefort, and Stilton. A newer addition to this cheese family that also deserves a mention is Saint Agur.

Similar to many other cheeses, Gorgonzola got its name from its geographic home, Gorgonzola, a city east of Milan. The cheese used to be called Stracchino di Gorgonzola. Stracco means tired in Italian, and in this case it was referring to how the cows would be tired when they arrived in Gorgonzola, which they passed by during the fall, when it was time to leave the Alps. They would then have access to great quantities of milk. The fact that it became a mold cheese is mostly because it was stored in grottos with airborne mold.

Gorgonzola has been an internationally known product since the 1800s. Today, a multitude of manufacturers produce the cheese and it is copied in many countries. Unique to this dessert cheese is that it is sold with different levels of storing time, ranging from the almost white Gorgonzola called "dolce" to the robust and well-stored cheese with an intense scent and pink tones. Personally, I believe it is important to be careful with the use of Gorgonzola in cooking as the intense flavor may overpower other tastes.

Stilton is the most famous British cheese and the English are very proud of it. Unfortunately, all Stilton cheese is pasteurized today and is no longer produced on farms, but it is still of very high quality. The production is confined to certain regions. There are three counties that manufacture the cheese: Derby, Leicester, and Nottingham. They all proclaim that Stilton originated in their area. The cheese has been known since the 1600s and was popular among the kings and nobility right from the beginning. Stilton is produced with the summer milk that contains more fat, after which the cheese is stored for at least 3 months. It may even be stored for up to a year. It will then obtain a more robust taste and a brownish color.

In Sweden, Stilton has become something of a Christmas cheese. It has squeezed its way onto the Swedish Christmas table next to the Swedish cheddar and has become a popular addition that is often enjoyed with gingerbread and port wine. Jan Hedh's wonderful plum tomato marmalade tastes fantastic with this.

A fairly young mold cheese that has gained instant popularity is Saint Agur. This French green mold cheese from the 1980s has a milder taste and a more comfortable salt content compared to other mold cheeses. The Saint Agur is an octagon-shaped pasteurized cow-milk cheese from an area called Massif Central. This cheese is well worth knowing. In contrast to many other mold cheeses, it is great on a cheese plate. Mold cheese will often overpower other cheeses and you should therefore usually avoid placing Roquefort and other mold cheeses on a cheese plate.

The salt in mold cheeses works best with sweet marmalades. In combining mold cheeses with less salty cheeses, a preserve may work as a taste-bridge between the two—it is generally a lot more comfortable for the taste buds when there's some preserve on the cheese plate. Good preserves with mold cheeses:

- Fig marmalade and figs are great with all mold cheese.
- Cloudberry and blackberry jam works with mold cheeses; it may, however, be a bit too sweet for some.
- Cherry jam and stronger mold cheeses like Roquefort and the Spanish Queso Hoja is a nice combination.
- Preserved tomatoes and mold cheeses always go well together. Pairing them with wine, however, might be more difficult. My favorite is Jan's tomato jam with Tahiti vanilla and Marcona almonds.

Washed Rind Cheeses

Cheeses with a light red rind are usually referred to as red rind cheeses. The texture is often half-soft and the crust somewhat sticky; many of these cheeses will also have a less pleasant odor. A few of the cheeses in this family are quite intense. The most famous washed rind cheese is Port Salut. This is also one of the mildest of the washed rind cheeses. Many Danish cheeses, so-called Danbo cheeses, have a tendency to release intense odors. This is because the rinds are washed. In other words, it's not the cheese itself that smells but rather the treated surface. In Italy the washed rind cheeses are produced in Taleggio. There are many different sizes with a variety of pungency. There are a multitude of French washed rind cheeses as well. Vacherin, Chaumes, and Saint Albray are some of the more common varieties, and they are quite mild. In Northern France you may find some of the more exciting washed rind cheeses, such as Livarot, Pont l'Évêque, and Langres. The Epoisse cheeses, from Bourgogne, are a special kind of washed rind cheese, which are stored in wine. The strongest of all washed rind cheeses is the famous Munster from Alsace.

In the washed rind family you can find anything from the mildest Port Salut to Munster, which demands more accustomed taste buds. I recommend the following complements for washed rind cheeses:

- For milder washed rind cheeses, such as Port Salut, I recommend apricot jam and peach marmalade. Port Saluts cheeses are fine breakfast cheeses and as such, citrus fruits are also great.
- Plums, pears, and quince are great fruits for washed rind cheeses. A strong washed rind cheese should be enjoyed alone, maybe with a sweet beverage.

On top: Appenzeller extra, affidelice, gruyère reserva, plaisir chablis.
In the middle: Clochette, selle sur cher, tomme de savoie, crottin de touraine, brebille, banon (cavet fermier), bollnäs grevé.
At the bottom: Brebiou, pont l´éveque, ca briolu, alkmaars roem, soumaintrain, parmigiano reggiano, tartufo pecorino, rochebaron, saint agur, bleu de gex, roquefort Papillion.

Hard Cheeses

The family of hard cheeses is exceptionally large. In Sweden we often think of hard cheeses and breakfast cheeses. Swedish manor house cheese, Swedish priest cheese, and grevé are common breakfast cheeses. Classic complements for breakfast cheeses are orange jam, apricot jam, and peach jam. We Swedes are especially fond of raspberry and strawberry jam. Internationally it is most common with toast and orange marmalade for breakfast. It is not uncommon for people to wrinkle their noses a bit when they hear about the very Swedish combination of cheeses and jam.

In Sweden we produce a variety of hard cheeses. Sweden and Switzerland are the best manufacturers of hard cheeses. Both of these countries have a long tradition of producing cheese. Switzerland is famous as a "cheese country," and the mention of names such as Emmental, Appenzeller, and Gruyere makes mouths water all over the world.

The French later copied many of the Swiss cheeses: Cantal, Beaufort, Comte, and plenty more are usually called French Gruyere. These cheeses are in no way less flavorful than the Swiss cheeses. Some of them are called alp cheeses because the milk comes from cows that have been grazing the green grass of the Alps during the summer months.

The Dutch produce a multitude of hard cheeses and are very good with exports. No matter where in the world you go, you can find Gouda. Maasdammer and Leerdammer are two other Dutch cheeses that are heavily exported. The long-stored Gouda is a Dutch delicacy; this cheese is simply wrapped carefully and then stored for three years.

Italy doesn't produce many hard cheese varieties; however, they do manufacture one of the world's absolute best—the Parmesan. Grana Padano is related to Parmesan, but it is far from the same cheese. A real Parmesan bears the name Parmigiano-Reggiano and is produced in the province Emilia-Romagna. It is only produced with unpasteurized summer milk and may be stored up to four years. The shortest storing time for the Parmigiano-Reggiano is one year. The cheeses weigh about 88 lbs (40 kg) and about 210 gallons (800 liters) of milk go into making it. This magnificent cheese has roots all the way back to the 1200s.

Cheddar is produced in many countries. It originated in Britain and it got its name from the city Cheddar in Somerset. The flavor of the cheese may vary greatly depending on where it is from. The cheddar cheeses most worthy of any attention are the Swedish and the British varieties. Cheddar doesn't have larger holes like the Emmental, but nor is it as tight as the Swedish Manor house cheese. Cheddar is made with pasteurized cow milk. The size may vary from 7 oz (200 g) to about 11 lbs (5 kg). Most often the larger cheeses are wrapped in a woven fabric to allow a longer storage time. A young cheese will be very mild, but if the same cheese were to be stored for 24 months, it would become very pungent. In Sweden, all cheddar is produced in Kvibille.

My favorites among hard cheeses are many: Appenzeller and Gruyere from Switzerland, extra old Gouda from Holland, stored dry Manchego from Spain, preferably with salt corns so that they crunch when you chew, Parmesan stored for three years, long-stored Swedish cheeses, for instance, manor house from Umeå and Grevé from Bollnäs. Personally I think that all of these cheeses deserve to be the main attraction and be consumed alone, or on a cheese plate.

There is nothing better than eating hard cheeses with a glass of good wine and some carefully chosen sides. Figs, prepared in any way, are always a safe choice for both cheese and wine. Rose hip marmalade can work well with Swedish rag-barreled cheeses, for instance, well-stored Swedish Priest cheese. Olives may be very good with salty cheeses—why not try an olive marmalade? Plum marmalade is also a great alternative for younger hard cheeses. A marmalade that is absolutely amazing with hard cheeses is Jan's Christmas Marmalade. It is fantastic with Swedish manor house cheese, stored for two years.

Some Tasty Cheese Plates

FOR THE GOURMET
Black appenzeller
Rouquefort
Brie de Meaux
Munster
Complements: fig marmalade with bay leaf

FOR THE GOAT LOVER
Chistera, Basque goat and sheep cheese
Chevre fermier cendre
Banon
Crottin de Chevre
Complements: A type of sea buckthorn marmalade or pear jam with figs, cardamom, and Armagnac—or physalis jam.

THE FRIDAY NIGHT FAVORITE
Saint Agur
Brie Rustique
Prima Donna
Complements: Tomato jam with Tahiti vanilla and Marcona almonds.

THE CHEESE HOUSE FAVORITES
Gruyere, grotto-stored
Roche Baron
Altesse
Brebille
Affidelice
Complements: cherry jam with almonds and rum or a milder quince marmalade.

Additional sides, which will work whenever you want to enjoy some flavorful cheeses:

Unsweetened, preferably oven-baked bread, various nuts, not salted but roasted is fine, grapes, but without wine, fresh figs, pears, red bell pepper.

My advice for anyone who wants to serve cheese or cheese plate: Do not mix too many cheeses with distinct flavors. Do not overdo the sides; find your favorite and let the tastes evolve naturally. Enjoy the cheese just like you would a glass of wine!

At the top: Grand pont l'éveque.
At the bottom: Altesse, and above from the left: Soumaintrain, pont l'éveque, livarot.

INDEX